*Donated
to the students
of Ohio –
our environmental
leaders
of the future –
by BP America*

**The Environmental
Careers Organization**
formerly The CEIP Fund, Inc.
286 Congress Street
Boston, MA 02210

About Island Press

ISLAND PRESS, a nonprofit organization, publishes, markets, and distributes the most advanced thinking on the conservation of our natural resources—books about soil, land, water, forests, wildlife, and hazardous and toxic wastes. These books are practical tools used by public officials, business and industry leaders, natural resource managers, and concerned citizens working to solve both local and global resource problems.

Founded in 1978, Island Press reorganized in 1984 to meet the increasing demand for substantive books on all resource-related issues. Island Press publishes and distributes under its own imprint and offers these services to other nonprofit organizations.

Support for Island Press is provided by Apple Computers Inc., The Mary Reynolds Babcock Foundation, The Educational Foundation of America, The Charles Engelhard Foundation, The Ford Foundation, The George Gund Foundation, The William and Flora Hewlett Foundation, The Joyce Foundation, The J. M. Kaplan Fund, The John D. and Catherine T. MacArthur Foundation, The Andrew W. Mellon Foundation, The Joyce Mertz-Gilmore Foundation, The New-Land Foundation, Northwest Area Foundation, The Jessie Smith Noyes Foundation, The J. N. Pew, Jr. Charitable Trust, The Rockefeller Brothers Fund, The Florence and John Schumann Foundation, and The Tides Foundation, and individual donors.

THE
COMPLETE
GUIDE
TO
ENVIRONMENTAL
CAREERS

THE COMPLETE GUIDE TO ENVIRONMENTAL CAREERS

The CEIP Fund

Lee P. DeAngelis
Project Director

Stephen C. Basler
Staff Writer

Loren E. Yeager
Researcher

ISLAND PRESS

Washington, D.C. ☐ *Covelo, California*

All photos courtesy of The CEIP Fund / Heidi Brett.

Cover design by Ben Santora
Text design by Irving Perkins Associates, Inc.

Library of Congress Cataloging-in-Publication Data
A Complete guide to environmental careers / the CEIP Fund, Inc.
    p.   cm.
   Includes index.
   ISBN 0-933280-85-8 — ISBN 0-933280-84-X (pbk.)
   1. Environmental protection—Vocational guidance.   2. Natural resources—Management—Vocational guidance.   3. Environmental protection—United States—Vocational guidance.   4. Natural resources—United States—Management—Vocational guidance.   I. CEIP Fund
TD170.2.C66   1989   89-1947
363.7′0023′73—dc19   CIP

Printed on recycled, acid-free paper
Manufactured in the United States of America
10 9 8 7 6 5

Contents

PART IV
NATURAL RESOURCE MANAGEMENT 221

Preface

Congratulations! By picking up this book you have shown interest in what promises to be one of the most dynamic and diverse fields of the 1990s. We are in the midst of a resurgence of concern for the environment. Americans are grappling with how to manage increasingly scarce land, water, and wildlife, how to provide for increased demands for outdoor recreation, and how to balance growth while preserving open space. Adequately cleaning up our air and water still eludes the nation, while a whole host of relatively new issues demand attention: hazardous and solid waste, toxic air and water pollution.

A large part of our success in addressing these issues will depend on the next generation of environmental professionals. Given the diversity of tasks, there is something for everyone, whether a person's interests lie in developing new pollution control technologies, studying the habitat of endangered species, teaching ecology to school children, or one of hundreds of other opportunities.

This book provides the two essential elements of environmental careers and job hunting: the nuts and bolts information (job outlook, salary level, entry requirements, and so forth) and the nature of careers in the field. There are chapters on career decision making and job search strategies, obtaining an education for an environmental career, and volunteering in the field. In addition, there are ten subject chapters, covering such topics as hazardous waste management, environmental education and outdoor recreation. Drawing on the collective experience of environmental professionals, each chapter includes information on getting started in a field. In addition, each chapter has a section on key issues, trends, developments, and their relationship to future careers. Finally, each chapter has a description of organizations, publications, and job listing services that will allow the reader to utilize the information presented.

What sets this book apart and makes the careers come alive, however, are the people featured in these chapters. Each subject chapter contains a Case Study of an agency, business, or organization, and profiles of active professionals. All told, this book contains the backgrounds, advice, and job descriptions of numerous active environmental professionals.

This book has grown naturally out of the work of The CEIP Fund. Established in 1972 and currently operating out of regional offices in Cleveland, Boston, Seattle and San Francisco, CEIP (formerly, The Center for Environmental Intern Programs) has become the largest on-the-job trainer for environmental careers in the country, placing college students and recent graduates (called CEIP associates) in short-term, paid professional level positions with corporations, consultants, government agencies and nonprofit organizations.

If the people in this book communicate one theme, it is this: The scope of your vision is the only limitation to the opportunities in the environmental field and your chance to have a real impact on environmental management. Welcome aboard and good luck!

ABOUT THE CEIP FUND

CEIP's primary program is Environmental Associate Services. Since 1972, we have placed over 3,400 college students and recent graduates in short-term, professional level positions with corporations, consultants, government agencies and nonprofit organizations. In a given year, over 300 young people will be employed by CEIP working an average of 20 weeks or more at median salaries of over $360 per week. This makes CEIP the largest on-the-job trainer for environmental careers in the country.

CEIP staff work with managers of a wide variety of organizations to develop projects. Once contracts for projects are signed, the regional staff coordinates the recruiting, evaluation, referral, and placement of students and graduates as CEIP associates to work with the organizations on the projects.

After their projects are completed, CEIP associates return to college to finish their undergraduate or graduate degrees, or they may take permanent positions in the organization where they were an associate. CEIP stays in contact with the alumni, many of whom become sponsors, volunteers for CEIP programs, and financial supporters of CEIP's work.

What kinds of projects do CEIP associates accomplish? This book describes all types of projects in the Profiles which highlight associates, alumni, and sponsoring organizations. Here is a further sampling of CEIP's work:

- Water quality is an important issue in the four regions CEIP serves. In 1987, 46 associates worked on water quality projects, which included assisting with large scale efforts to clean up San Diego Bay, San Francisco Bay, Puget Sound, the Great Lakes, and Narragansett Bay. Other Associates worked on projects addressing groundwater protection, wastewater treatment, limnology research, and drinking water standards.
- Environmental health and safety in the workplace and in the community is a growing focus for CEIP. Over 40 associates in 1987 worked with industries, consultants, and government agencies in this high priority area. Projects included assisting with toxicological risk assessments, compliance with community "right-to-know" legislation, and industrial hygiene monitoring and management of data bases.
- Species protection and the management and protection of wetlands and open space were the subject of over 30 projects in 1987. An associate in California prepared a report on the present status of marine resources and wildlife in Monterey Bay for review as a possible national marine sanctuary. Five associates in Washington, Massachusetts, and Rhode Island conducted wetlands inventories and updated maps to permanently protect threatened natural areas.

The second major program offered by CEIP—and an important growth area for the organization—is Environmental Career Services. Through this program, CEIP provides publications, conferences, seminars, and other services designed to help students, recent graduates, career changers, and current professionals with their environmental career planning.

As part of its Career Services program, CEIP sponsors a national environmental careers conference that focuses on career development and job search strategies. Environmental professionals offer the participants a wealth of timely information and advice on education, job search techniques, and current trends in their fields of expertise. The conference is held in a different region of the country each year. To extend the impact of the conference nationwide, CEIP produces a conference summary that contains all the highlights, insights, and important advice of the speakers and discussion leaders. CEIP also sponsors environmental career seminars to complement the conference. These are usually half-day programs held on the weekends. Each CEIP regional office offers up to four of these every year.

CEIP is also a significant funder of environmental projects for public and nonprofit organizations through Environmental Grants, a small grants program. In 1987, $257,000 granted by CEIP was matched by recipient organizations to provide more than half a million dollars' worth of positive environmental results. This program was funded by foundations, corporations, and individuals.

Above all, CEIP works through people to improve the environment. Although laws, regulations, funding and public support are crucial to environmental quality, it takes people—individuals such as those featured in this book—to implement the solutions, create the innovations, enforce the laws, and wisely manage funding. CEIP is making sure there will continue to be talented and motivated people working for the environment.

John R. Cook, Jr.
President
The CEIP Fund, Inc.

For more information on CEIP's programs and publications, contact any one of the following CEIP offices:

Headquarters

The CEIP Fund, Inc.
68 Harrison Ave.
Boston, Mass. 02111
Phone: 617-426-4375

Northeast Regional Office

The CEIP Fund, Inc.
68 Harrison Ave.
Boston, Mass. 02111
Phone: 617-426-4783

Serving the states of Massachusetts, Maine, Vermont, New Hampshire, Rhode Island, Connecticut, New York, and northern New Jersey.

Great Lakes Regional Office

The CEIP Fund, Inc.
332 The Arcade
Cleveland, Ohio 44114
Phone: 216-861-4545

Serving the states of Ohio, Michigan, Illinois, Indiana, and western Pennsylvania.

Pacific Northwest Regional Office

The CEIP Fund, Inc.
731 Securities Building
Seattle, Wash. 98101
Phone: 206-625-1750

Serving the states of Washington, Oregon, and Alaska.

California Regional Office

The CEIP Fund, Inc.
512 Second St.
San Francisco, Calif. 94107
Phone: 415-543-4400

Serving the state of California.

Acknowledgments

It is hard to imagine writing a book that involved the help and cooperation of more people than assisted in this publication. Giving adequate recognition to these people is impossible.

This book is a project of The CEIP Fund, Inc., and is a collective, dynamic effort of the entire staff in the Central and four Regional offices who spent countless hours helping outline chapters and digging up contacts.

Special thanks go to the Board of Trustees, Kevin Doyle, Marla Meyer, Elizabeth Eckl, and Heidi Hopkins. The collective knowledge of The CEIP Fund in environmental career development is staggering. This publication passes this wisdom on to the reader. It is also interesting to note that the organization practices what it preaches in that the book was researched and written by CEIP Associates—young people just out of college and in graduate school.

Lee DeAngelis, the Director of Environmental Career Services, oversaw the planning and completion of this project. His insight and knowledge of the environmental field and his enthusiasm provided key energy to the overall project. Loren Yeager, the Research Associate, conducted many of the interviews, wrote most of the profiles, and was a partner in the planning of the book—while attending school full-time. Thanks also go to Carol Shaw, Helen Fuertes, and John DeCore of the CEIP Great Lakes office in Cleveland, Ohio, where the book project was based.

The main dynamo of the project was Stephen C. Basler—a CEIP alumnus who agreed to "come out of retirement" to drive the 12-month project. While the book was the idea of CEIP as a creative way to use its resources, it was Steve who brought the work together. This included the 2,950-person survey, the background research and interviews, and finally, the drafting of the manuscript. Steve is an individual of talent, energy, and drive, as reflected by the fruits of his labors in this book. He is also representative of the people who have dedicated themselves to pursuing environmental solutions now and in the future.

Our gratitude is extended to The Pew Charitable Trusts, which funded the research behind the book, as well as contributed creativity and enthusiasm through their Project Director, Jon Jensen. This also evolved out of a grant from The George Gund Foundation, which launched the Environmental Career Service in 1986.

This book is about people. More than 300 people active in their fields were interviewed for this book. Some are profiled or mentioned in the book; many more provided essential background material. The time, energy, and patience these environmental professionals gave made this book possible. Thank you for your service to the next generation.

All the persons mentioned left their mark on this book. We thank them for their contributions. I dedicate this book to the environmental professionals who daily complete the good work of protecting the environment—often in a low profile, yet creative manner. Their dedication and intelligence in finding the solutions to these complex problems inspire us all in our own efforts—present and future.

John R. Cook, Jr.
President, The CEIP Fund

THE
COMPLETE
GUIDE
TO
ENVIRONMENTAL
CAREERS

Introduction to Environmental Careers

Lynn Bakker *is a forester with the Michigan Department of Natural Resources. She handles the surveying, sales, planting, and overall administration of 100,000 acres of Michigan forest near Kalkaska, Michigan.*

Richard DiSanza *is a waterfront planner with Emanuel Associates, a consulting firm in Nyack, New York. He is updating a master plan for the city of Stony Point, on the Hudson River. This includes an inventory of the city's natural resources, integration of residents' priorities, and development of policy recommendations.*

Carol Olsen *is involved in the promotion of recycling for the city of Seattle, which is working toward a 40 percent participation rate in their citywide recycling program. She develops public service announcements for the media and coordinates production of promotional materials and activities.*

Elaine Price *is the manager of environment, health, and safety for American Steel and Wire Corporation in Cuyahoga Heights, Ohio. One day she may meet with a representative of the U.S. Environmental Protection Agency, and the next will see her in a hard hat and steel-toed boots helping to design and install a company's new wastewater treatment system.*

Sam Mehta *is an engineer with the Illinois Hazardous Waste Research and Information Center. He assists small manufacturers with environmental regulatory compliance through on-site visits and technical assistance.*

THE CAREERS of these professionals differ greatly from one another, yet all of them are concerned with some aspect of the environment. Environmental professionals are found in all sectors of the economy, all over the globe, using every skill found in the work world.

By choosing to enter the environmental field, you embark upon a cutting-edge career, one that is young and evolving every year as new technologies and policies come into play. Perhaps the most exciting element about environmental careers is the people themselves. While environmental professionals come from all backgrounds and walks of life, most bring a love or passion for the environment to their work and careers. Environmental careers have unlimited potential to be deeply satisfying and creative.

To better understand the nature of environmental careers now, it is useful to know where we have been, both as a nation and as a profession. There are two sides to our nation's relationship to the environment. In our quest for progress, and in the name of free enterprise, we have often violated and abused the environment. After 100 years of building an industrial powerhouse and overlooking or ignoring our environment, we began to reap what we had sown: Our lakes and rivers were dying, our skies had a layer of haze, cities were becoming concrete monstrosities, and wildlife was fading from the picture.

Fortunately, we have another side, one that has been too quiet for too long. Americans do love the land, and the waters, and the skies, and they place a high priority on their preservation. This is borne out by poll after poll and is clearly revealed in the fabric of our nation's life-styles and heritage. When we can get away from the office we go outdoors: to play, to exercise, to reflect, to worship. No other park system rivals that of the United States in its scope and diversity.

In the 1960s this side of the United States sat up and took action. We stood on the brink of ecological disaster, looked down at the future, and made a collective decision to move away from the edge. Citizens' activities culminated with Earth Day in 1970, an event whose popularity, among a broad range of participants, took even its organizers off guard. The National Environmental Policy Act of 1970 set the tone of new environmental policy by requiring the federal government to *first* consider the environmental consequences of a proposed action. This instituted what has proved to be a fundamental shift in the priorities of doing business in the United States.

Dozens of landmark legislative packages have followed: major amendments to the Clean Air Act (1970) and the Clean Water Act (1972); the Comprehensive Environmental Response, Compensation, and Liability Act of 1980, or Superfund; the Resource Conservation and Recovery Act

(1976); and the Forest and Rangeland Renewable Resources Planning Act of 1974, to name a few. To implement these acts, the President's Council on Environmental Quality and, later, the Environmental Protection Agency (EPA) were created. State governments quickly followed with the creation of their own environmental protection agencies.

Many are not satisfied with the actual results of this legislation, and additional complicated environmental problems have arisen. One thing is certain: The work of the past 25 years has begun a process of institutionalizing the strong but sometimes overshadowed environmental ethic of the United States.

A vital part of this institutionalization has been the creation of a broad-based profession for those who wish to make their livelihood by protecting the environment. Before 1960 the environmental field consisted primarily of rangers and foresters and a handful of public health officials and advocates. Today, there are environmental professionals working for every municipal government in the nation. Each state has an environmental protection agency, and one would be hard pressed to find a federal agency without a variety of professionals working on environmental issues. The great number and variety of environmental consulting firms that have sprung up offer services ranging from hazardous waste management to the development of interpretive programs for nature centers.

Even small companies are likely to have environmental health and safety staffs; large firms may have environmental personnel at every level from headquarters to plant, including engineers, public relations staff, and lab technicians. Nonprofit organizations exist not only in Washington, D.C., but in communities around the country; they are engaged in public education, research, advocacy, and natural resource stewardship. Universities and technical schools have expanded or created departments to educate these professionals and are engaged in solving a multitude of environmental problems. Finally, the design and production of pollution control equipment is a multibillion-dollar-per-year industry.

Many environmental professionals have scientific and technical backgrounds. One of the strongest messages of this book, however, is that the environmental field also has a critical need for liberal arts graduates, especially for those with both scientific and liberal arts training. A few of the professions mentioned in this book are not often considered part of the environmental field; accountants, computer specialists, journalists, educators, real estate professionals, lawyers, financiers, entrepreneurs, managers (and more managers), political scientists, and librarians all can contribute to the work of improving the environment.

A remarkable aspect of the environmental field is the pace at which change occurs. While some subfields remain stable, many aspects of the profession today would have been unrecognizable even five years ago. If the past 25 years are any indication, the pace can only increase. This prompts Sylvia Taylor, a wildlife biologist with the state of Michigan, to say, "I believe that 80 to 90 percent of the jobs that will exist in the environmental field five years from now haven't been created yet."

John R. Cook, Jr., founder and president of The CEIP Fund, offers an explanation for this rapid evolution: "The development of the environmental profession can be compared with the historical development of other professions. Right now, I believe the field is going through a maturing phase, just as medicine or law did hundreds of years ago. First, everyone is off doing what works best for them. Gradually, knowledge and experience grow and are shared; there is specialization and standardization, accreditation and development of professional ethics and codes of conduct. It is very exciting to be in a profession during this formative period, and it gives individuals the opportunity to have a profound effect on the field for generations to come."

The modern environmental movement is a quarter century old. Much has been accomplished; enormous challenges lie ahead. Can we continue on the course set by our predecessors? Can we do better? In this increasingly global community, the course we chart, the tone we set, will have a dramatic direct and indirect impact on the environment of the entire world. Charles Odegaard, Pacific Northwest regional director of the National Park Service, while speaking before The CEIP Fund's annual national environmental career conference in Seattle, stated, "The field in which you are presently engaged is the most important field. For what you and I do is going to make a difference as to whether this world exists or does not exist. Whether you're in private enterprise, government, or a private citizen, the challenge you have is to make sure this world goes on, and that it should remain a great place in which to live rather than just exist." Environmental professionals have found that challenge also means opportunity.

HOW THIS BOOK CAN HELP YOU

This book has ten chapters on specific fields in the areas of environmental protection (solid waste and hazardous waste management, air and water quality), natural resource management (land and water conservation, fishery and wildlife management, parks and outdoor recreation and forestry), environmental planning, and environmental education and communications. As background to the chapters on particular careers, the book begins with four chapters that provide an overview of current and emerging issues in the environmental field, discuss how to obtain the necessary education and training for an environmental career, describe the importance of being a volunteer or intern, and outline the methods for landing your first environmental job.

Many career publications do not give the reader a sense of what a job actually entails—what do you do? Nor do they discuss the issues and challenges that drive the field. The reader is often faced with a collection of job descriptions woven together with some text but little context. Why do these jobs exist? Where are they going? What are they like?

This book adds issues and people to the menu. The chapter on hazardous waste management is not merely a list of job descriptions—toxicologist, chemical engineer, and so on. You'll read about some of the issues that affect professionals in the field: the rewrite of the Resource Conservation and Recovery Act, concern over the scope of Superfund, state and local initiatives in hazardous waste management, exploration of new disposal and waste reduction technologies. Besides learning about issues and trends, you'll come to understand what kinds of jobs are available or will be available *because of* developments in the field. This information allows you to develop a skill that is useful not only while you are looking for your first job, but also during later career moves: how to make employment projec-

Cuyahoga Department of Health, Cuyahoga, Ohio. Terry Allen collects water samples from used tire lots to track the disease-carrying Asian tiger mosquito.

tions and decisions based on legislation and other events that affect and rapidly change the various environmental fields.

The people element is introduced by giving descriptions of the actual work of professionals in the field. In the chapter on hazardous waste management, the Case Study focuses on the work of the staff at EPA's Region 10 Superfund Branch and also on Environmental Toxicology International, Inc., a Seattle-based consulting firm working on toxic and hazardous waste issues. Next come the Profiles of three professionals: an environmental coordinator for a mid-sized manufacturer in Michigan, an entry-level environmental compliance officer with Chemical Waste Management, Inc., in St. Louis, and the deputy commissioner for environmental protection for the city of Chicago. These people discuss their overall job goals, day-to-day activities, career paths, and educational backgrounds, and give advice to job seekers.

An important part of many chapters is the Getting Started section, which gives the reader advice on how to prepare for the various careers in the field, what the entry-level jobs are like, how to get them, and what range of entry-level salaries to expect (in 1988 dollars). This section is a collection of the best advice from the more than 30 professionals interviewed for each chapter. Each chapter ends with a Resources section, which arms you with the information needed to dig further into your field of interest.

This book is written for undergraduate or graduate students and recent graduates who are interested in the environmental field. Those who have not decided on an environmental career will gain insight into the nature of specific jobs and how they fit into the larger scheme. Career changers (from within or outside the environmental field) will find the entire book, but especially the Resources sections, useful. Finally, the environmental field depends heavily on the involvement of an informed public, whether or not they are environmental professionals. This book provides an overview of the issues and challenges in the environmental field, which should be helpful to those who would like to volunteer their time.

Part I

JOB HUNTING
IN THE
ENVIRONMENTAL
FIELD

1 Careers and Issues

TRENDS IN THE ENVIRONMENTAL FIELD

In his 1982 best-seller *Megatrends*, John Naisbitt detailed ten trends that are fundamentally changing society. His book has proved to be a useful tool for organizations and individuals as they plan for the future and try to see the forest through the trees. In the same vein, several overriding trends affect employment in the environmental field, and it is wise to keep them in mind as you prepare for your career. Some of these trends affect specific sectors of the field, whereas others apply to environmental careers in general.

MATURATION OF THE PROFESSION

The past 20 to 25 years have witnessed tremendous growth in the environmental profession as we know it today. The term *upheaval* is still accurate in describing change in most environmental fields. Change has been going on long enough, however, that the field is now maturing: Disciplines are sorting themselves out, professional societies exist, and educational programs and career tracks are evolving.

PUBLIC SUPPORT FOR ENVIRONMENTAL PROTECTION

Public support for environmental protection has never been stronger in the United States. The desire to protect the environment and preserve natural resources is no longer considered a fad but an enduring characteristic. The challenge of the environmental professions is to translate this support into action. The goal of keeping people at the forefront of determining environmental policy has been resisted by many policy makers in the 1980s.

SPECIALIZATION AND INTEGRATION

An often confusing dual shift is occurring in the environmental field. On the one hand, professionals increasingly specialize as problems become more technical and the bank of knowledge grows. At the same time, however, most agree that professionals need to have a more broad-based, integrated knowledge of environmental issues. For example, the environmental protection field needs hazardous waste specialists who understand air and water quality issues; the natural resource field is calling for wildlife biologists who understand forestry, ecology, and, ideally, environmental protection issues. Environmental professionals working in the isolation of their own specialization are ignoring the fundamental tenet of the inter-relatedness of the environment—at the ultimate expense of the environment these professionals are seeking to protect.

FOCUS ON POSTGRADUATE AND LIBERAL ARTS EDUCATION

Many professionals are finding it necessary to obtain a graduate degree to have the specialization *and* diversity of skills necessary to grow with their chosen field. This often works best when professionals have some work experience between undergraduate and graduate school. Graduate degrees are often used to develop a specialization, but they are also used to diversify one's skill base as when, for example, a chemical engineer obtains an M.A. in planning or a forester returns to school for a master's in business administration.

Liberal arts skills are increasingly important in a complex work environment, where professionals must be able to communicate effectively. They must also be able to work with a wide variety of persons. Professionals must be flexible and able to change and grow as their field changes. A majority of professionals interviewed for this book state that when push comes to shove, liberal arts skills are more important than technical knowledge.

LESS FEDERAL INVOLVEMENT

Much of the impetus for environmental protection efforts came from sweeping national legislation and creation of new federal agencies such as the U.S. Environmental Protection Agency. There has been a shift, however, toward more local initiatives and implementation. This is a trend that goes beyond the new federalism of the 1980s. Perhaps the most compelling explanation for this phenomenon is that environmental challenges like toxic waste dumps and proposed new development occur at the local level. Citizens and units of government are responding to local problems with local solutions. This is possible because of the steadily increasing technical competence of state and local governments, many of which are acting because they don't want to wait for national legislation, which might be ten years down the road. In addition, reauthorization of major national environmental legislation, such as the Resource Conservation and Recovery Act (RCRA) and the Clean Air and Clean Water acts, is structured so that state and local governments are the implementers, enforcers, and often designers of the legislated remedies.

There are many who feel this decentralization can be, and in some cases has been, taken too far. They argue that only the federal government is adequately equipped to research, develop, and enforce many of the environmental regulations. An equally persuasive argument is that consistent, strong national legislation protects areas with weak environmental records and prevents corporations from pitting states against each other. This structural issue is far from resolved.

MORE CONSULTING FIRMS

Mirroring a trend found throughout business and government, the environmental profession is steadily increasing its use of consultants in all sectors. As part of an effort to be lean, mean, and competitive, companies are reducing in-house environmental staff and relying on specialists—consultants—to develop and implement environmental programs to keep them in compliance with regulations. Environmental professionals at the plant level, therefore, are now more likely to manage projects carried out by consultants. The government is also hiring consultants for work ranging from testing and planning to training and research.

DEVELOPMENT OF THE NONPROFIT SECTOR

When people think of the nonprofit environmental sector they often think exclusively of advocacy. Advocacy has been, and continues to be, a critical part of the nonprofit organization's agenda. However, this sector has expanded and diversified its role tremendously. Environmental nonprofits teach about the environment in schools, conduct research and planning, own and manage natural areas through land trusts, develop community gardens, and operate publishing houses. With the maturation of this sector, salaries, while still below the private sector, have improved considerably. Much of the cutting-edge work still begins with and is carried out by the nonprofit sector.

ENVIRONMENTAL CAREERS IN THE 1990s

THE PLANNING PROFESSION

Planning encompasses many different disciplines, and there are many types of planners. Thus, the issues and job markets for planners differ greatly depending on the region and the type of planner. For example, urban planners in northern cities are feeling budget crunches, while they are flourishing in the Southwest. Environmental planning is making a comeback of sorts as policy makers begin to appreciate the integrated nature of environmental issues and the recurring reality that development often has unanticipated environmental consequences. Professionals in this area include land-use planners on the East and West coasts, water quality planners everywhere, and, in more and more state governments, planners working on such issues as solid waste management. Planning is a process and, as such, there are many process skills that must be mastered: analytical thinking, communications, negotiation, goal setting, implementation, and the ability to take the long-term view. The technical skills that are required, such as design, drafting, and the use of computers, depend on the type of planner you wish to become. A liberal arts or planning degree with a master's in planning or landscape architecture are among the more common methods of entering the field. Aspiring environmental planners are often advised to obtain an undergraduate degree in a hard science or natural resource area, work awhile, and go back to earn a master's in planning.

ENVIRONMENTAL EDUCATION AND COMMUNICATIONS

As the environmental field continues to diversify and become ever more technical, educators and communicators are needed to help the experts communicate with the public and one another. This does not, unfortunately, mean that there exists or will exist a multitude of jobs in this area. Environmental education and communications jobs are often one-of-a-kind positions: writing for a trade publication, working for a nonprofit and visiting classrooms to lead environmental projects, interpreting at a state park, or consulting with firms on the proper disposal of hazardous wastes. Plotting a career requires creativity; the jobs are definitely there and can often be created. A useful preparation includes developing inter-personal skills and studying a hard science. Those who wish to enter journalism or public relations need a combination of skills in writing and hard science.

SOLID WASTE MANAGEMENT

Virtually all larger cities in the United States, as well as many small towns, are facing the problem of dwindling landfill space for their munici-pal solid waste. Given environmental concerns, prospects for opening new landfills are slim. Consequently, municipalities are scrambling to develop recycling programs and environmentally safe incineration systems. This is a wide-open field and one that can be entered from almost any discipline—whether you are an engineer, a journalist, an accountant, or anything in between. The majority of jobs are at the local level, with county or munici-pal governments or with consulting firms doing solid waste planning or developing and implementing solid waste treatment strategies. Service-oriented companies are developing recycling programs and incineration systems; nonprofit organizations are establishing recycling programs, as well as monitoring the environmental impact of landfills and proposed incineration projects. State government is increasingly overseeing the regulation and planning of solid waste management. The federal govern-ment focuses on research and, to a much lesser extent, regulation. A few particularly useful disciplines for aspirants in this field are engineering, environmental science, urban studies and planning, and a combination of business, management, and finance. Given the boom times in this field and the fact that there are few formal educational programs, hands-on experi-ence through work or internships plays a major role in landing a job.

HAZARDOUS WASTE MANAGEMENT

The leaking of hazardous waste from landfills into water and air has become the most visible environmental issue in the United States. Since 1980 federal estimates of seriously leaking sites have climbed dramati-cally. While officials are trying to deal with the immediate crisis of leaking dumps, many are calling for hazardous waste generators to pay more attention to long-term issues: developing safer disposal methods, recycling hazardous waste, and, ideally, changing processes so the waste is not generated in the first place. The federal government has taken the lead in regulation with two major legislative acts: the RCRA, which classifies hazardous waste and regulates its disposal, and the Superfund Amend-ments and Reauthorization Act (SARA), which deals with cleanup of existing contaminated sites. States are charged with enforcing RCRA, and many have their own Superfund-style programs to determine siting of hazardous waste facilities. Consultants are working for everybody, whether it is helping generators comply with regulations or overseeing remediation at a hazardous waste site in the Superfund program. Opportunities exist for those with expertise in many disciplines, but the necessary background is generally more technical in nature than that required in the solid waste field. Liberal arts graduates can enter this field but should take a strong core of hard science courses. Engineers and chemists as well as those with strong lab and field skills are in particularly high demand.

AIR QUALITY

Many goals set by the first generation of air quality regulations remain unmet, even as a whole new set of pollution issues demands attention. Most major urban areas are still out of compliance with carbon monoxide and ozone regulations—some dramatically so. Now concern has been raised over airborne toxins—cadmium, polychlorinated biphenyls (PCBs), dioxins—and indoor air pollution. Further, acid rain, carbon dioxide buildup (the greenhouse effect), and depletion of the protective ozone layer have become issues of international concern. Despite this widening array of issues, the job market in air pollution control is tight relative to other environmental protection fields. Local governments and consultants provide the greatest opportunities. Air pollution control is a technical field in which sophisticated monitoring, analysis of many chemicals, computer modeling, and statistical analysis are the tools of the trade. Technically oriented managers are in high demand. As in all environmental protection fields, generalists who are skilled communicators and possess some technical background will do well.

WATER QUALITY

The first generation of water quality legislation focused on visible, conventional pollutants in open bodies of water—trying to save our nation's dying rivers and lakes. Although these programs were moderately successful, much is left to be done and significant new problems are being discovered. The biggest of these is toxic pollutants contaminating open bodies of water and groundwater. Other focuses are nonpoint-source pollution from runoff and erosion and the degradation of coastal waters, wetlands, and estuaries. The major federal legislation is the Clean Water Act, which was significantly amended in 1987, with major new responsibilities given to state and local governments. Consultants are helping private industry to design, construct, and maintain new wastewater treatment systems as well as providing technical expertise to local governments. Demand remains steady for the traditional disciplines of civil, environmental, and mechanical engineering. New fields in demand include chemical engineering, hydrology, and water quality planning. As in many other environmental fields, water quality officials are seeking those with good project management skills who have knowledge across disciplines. The nonprofit sector is very much involved in water quality efforts ranging from advocacy to research.

LAND AND WATER CONSERVATION

The field of land and water conservation is in need of professionals from numerous disciplines, since it involves both environmental protection and natural resource management. Land and water conservation issues include such diverse topics as development pressures in New England, water shortages on the West Coast, or preserving open spaces for an urban park. Besides natural resource managers and specialists, the field employs environmental planners, lawyers, land acquisition experts, and advocates. Much of the activity occurs at the state and local levels, using such tools as legislation of development and subdivisions, natural resource inventory programs, and geographical information systems. The flourishing nonprofit sector includes 740 local land trusts and numerous national, state, and local organizations. The job market is tough, with the edge going to professionals with a broad base of skills and a variety of hands-on experience. As in the field of environmental education, jobs are often one of a kind and must be actively sought and sometimes created.

FISHERY AND WILDLIFE MANAGEMENT

Fishery and wildlife professionals work to maintain or manage various fish and wildlife populations. This involves study of habitat, food supply, habits, and distribution of populations. Increasingly, the work of fish and wildlife professionals is being integrated into broader natural resource management and planning efforts. As a result, these professionals are required to develop an ecological perspective so they can understand and work with other natural resource managers. There is also a shift toward programs that focus on nongame species. In the fisheries area, aquaculture, or fish farming, is a growing field.

Fisheries and wildlife are two of the toughest environmental fields to break into. Most in this area work for federal, state, and local governments, where employment levels have been stagnant. Yet, as always, jobs exist for those who are the most determined and resourceful. Development of sound ecological skills, possibly through an accompanying major such as forestry, will aid in seeking employment, as will possession of work experience and relevant technical skills. Graduates are urged not to neglect unique jobs with utility companies, nonprofits, game preserves, and universities.

PARKS AND OUTDOOR RECREATION

This is one of the more popular of the environmental fields; many of us have wanted to become a ranger at some point. In addition to traditional rangers, this field includes recreation planners, interpreters, administrators, natural resource managers, and research and maintenance staff. Only a small percentage of employment is with the National Park Service. Other federal agencies, state and local park systems, and private nature centers provide the majority of jobs. Demand for outdoor recreation continues to climb, in part because more and more people live in urban areas and want recreation closer to home. Also, an aging population with more free time wants to use recreational areas year round, not just for hiking, but for many other activities, such as exercising and learning. Consequently, park professionals have to deal with a variety of complicated multiple-use issues. Balancing recreation and preservation tops the list. The field can be tough to break into, and seasonal and volunteer work is an absolute necessity. Beyond experience, interpersonal skills combined with some background in hard sciences are the next most important prerequisites. Be prepared to relocate often in your career.

FORESTRY

The days of foresters who spent most of their time in the field are over. The field now employs professionals with diverse backgrounds and a variety of forestry-related specialties. The Society of American Foresters lists over 700 types of jobs in forestry, many of them for specialists such as forest economists or forest hydrologists. Increasingly, foresters are moving out of the forest and into the office.

There is an emphasis on multiple uses of the forest: as recreational area, watershed, fish and wildlife habitat, and source of timber. The fastest-growing demand is for foresters to stem the decline of U.S. urban forests. Finally, foresters are working on issues related to the health of forests (acid rain, smog) and global deforestation. About a third of foresters work for the federal government, a third for state and local government, and the remainder, a growing percentage of the work force, for private timber companies or as forestry consultants. Employment of foresters is rather cyclical; it is currently somewhat below average. Declining admissions to forestry schools and an aging work force are expected to boost employment prospects over the next five years. Today's forester should have good communication skills in addition to technical experience. Because of specialization, many more foresters are obtaining graduate degrees than ten years ago.

HOW TO TRACK OPPORTUNITIES IN THE ENVIRONMENTAL FIELD

This book's ten chapters on fields of employment describe the present conditions in those areas and outline where they are likely to be headed. However, the environmental field is changing and evolving dramatically. Career planners and futurists project that the vast majority of those entering the work force now can expect to change *careers*, not just jobs, several times over the course of their working years. There will be at least as much, if not more, change in the environmental field.

Therefore, this book is designed to teach you how to analyze trends as they develop. In this way, you can learn what opportunities there are; the perfect job for you might be out there without your knowing it. Understanding how to spot trends will also help you prepare for a given field and know when and how to make your move.

The key word is *focus*. There are literally mountains of material on the environmental field and careers. A scattershot approach is going to wear you out before you make a decision on a first job, let alone start one. But to begin, let's assume you are at the starting point and haven't yet focused: You think you want to pursue an environmental career, but you aren't sure in what field.

Don't start by asking, "Where are the jobs?" There are already too many unhappy employees in the work force who selected a career path based solely on a forecast of job prospects. Take a look at the subject chapters in this book, talk to people in the field, do some volunteer work and some career planning and assessment exercises to help you identify likes and dislikes. *What Color Is Your Parachute?*, by Nelson Bolles (Ten Speed Press, annual), is a classic among career planning books and also lists numerous other resources. Talk to professors and college career counselors. Other useful tools for getting an overview of the environmental field are multi-issue environmental books available in libraries and bookstores. The annual *State of the World*, by Lester R. Brown and others (Worldwatch Institute), and *An Environmental Agenda for the Future*, edited by Robert Cahn (Island Press, 1985), are two places to start.

Give yourself some time to reflect on and mull over various choices and ideas. Look at the process from the perspective of a Great Opportunity, not the Dreaded Decision; your career will be the result of many decisions, and the bad decisions sometimes prove to be as useful as the good ones. Don't let events make your decisions for you; make a decision, move on, and if it is not right, change it. Your conversations with environmental professionals should focus on the varied roads they have taken in their careers.

REFERENCE MATERIALS

Once you have narrowed your focus to one or several areas of the environmental field—maybe hazardous and solid waste, or fisheries and wildlife, or forestry—you are ready to get a pulse on these particular fields: what are the growth areas, what is on the way in or out, what are some of the unique opportunities that might be perfect given your skills and avocations?

There are a couple of elements to this strategy. First, know the legislation and regulations that govern the field. Many jobs in the environmental field are created as a direct result of legislation and the regulations that are promulgated as a result of the legislation. This fact is often overlooked. A graduate of a four-year water quality program recently inquired about job opportunities in her field. As the conversation progressed she acknowledged she was not aware that the Clean Water Act had been reauthorized that fall, bringing about major changes and new programs in the field.

To research regulations, start with the major federal legislation in a given field. In hazardous waste, for example, it would be RCRA and Superfund. The subject chapters of this book discuss major legislation in the various fields. To dig deeper, consult trade association publications or *Environment Reporter,* published by the Bureau of National Affairs, Inc. (BNA), and available in most college libraries. See what level of government is implementing the regulations, what type of programs will be created, what kinds of expertise or professionals will be required. If you really want to dig, find the economic impact analysis, which must accompany most federal regulations; it specifies the cost to businesses and the government of implementing regulations. The *Federal Register,* which is available in most major libraries or through the implementing agencies, details expenditures and personnel needs. Congressional Quarterly's *CQ Weekly Reports* provides analysis of upcoming legislative packages.

Don't neglect state and local legislation, which give rise to a growing proportion of environmental regulations. This information is often available from professional associations and state and municipal environmental protection agencies. For state regulations, also see BNA's *Environment Reporter*. You may be zeroing in on a state or municipality where you want to work, but more than likely what you are looking for are trends: Are states regulating groundwater in the absence of federal standards? Are state hazardous waste regulations tougher than RCRA? What environmental issues are large cities focusing on? One clue that a major federal legislative package might be on the way is the passage of similar environmental legislation in a number of states.

General environmental publications, which cover the bigger picture, should also be on your reading list. These include *Sierra, Audubon, Amicus Journal, Environmental Action,* and *Environment.* After you have narrowed your search for a field, you can also begin to tap into reams of specialized information. The publications of trade and professional organizations, such as *JAPCA* (published by the Air and Waste Management Association), are often very useful sources of information. Another source of information are specialized newsletters, often weekly and always expensive, which have sprung up in recent years; examples of these are *Air/ Water Pollution Report, Hazardous Waste News,* and *Toxic Materials News.* Some of these might be available at college libraries.

Budget a small amount of time each week to stay on top of trends in environmental careers. You will spend years and thousands of dollars getting an environmental education; by comparison, an hour or two a week and $100 for subscriptions is a small investment.

PROFESSIONAL AND TRADE ASSOCIATIONS

Some of the best sources of environmental information are professional and trade associations, which are made up of people working in the field. They sponsor events and conferences, publish magazines and special reports, and often have job listing services. It is a good idea to join one or several organizations of interest and get involved in the local chapter; student membership and participation is welcomed and usually sought. Many of these professional associations are listed under Resources at the end of the subject chapters. The *Encyclopedia of Associations* (Gale Research Company), at libraries, provides an exhaustive listing.

ENVIRONMENTAL PROFESSIONALS

Talking to people actually involved in a field is the source of probably the best and most current information. This includes the often misunderstood process of informational interviewing (see chapter 4, or consult *What*

Color Is Your Parachute? for a thorough discussion of informational inter- viewing). No doubt, it can be more than a little intimidating to call on professionals for information, but if you do it in the right way, the friendli- ness of their responses might surprise you. After all, most people like to talk about themselves and their life's work as well as help those who show an interest in a similar profession. Have questions prepared ahead of time; suggest setting a phone or personal interview time convenient for their schedule; and take less than 20 minutes of their time. This is a particularly good method for those looking at the job market and developments in a geographical area or in a particular company. Your first contacts could come from trade associations, authors of articles, or even the phone book. Ask those you call for more contacts and your list will quickly expand.

To emphasize a point made earlier: Do not make career decisions based on which fields offer the most jobs. This strategy tips the odds heavily in favor of an unsatisfying career. Those who are the most motivated get jobs in every field, and you are going to be the most motivated in the field where your passion lies. Pick the field that most interests you. If you want to be a wildlife biologist, go for it. We talk about job prospects for each field *only* so that you know what to expect and can assess your motivation and prepare accordingly. Follow your heart. It will get you a job.

WHERE ENVIRONMENTAL PROFESSIONALS WORK

When students make decisions on the course of study they wish to pursue, it is usually based on interest in a particular issue or subject, whether it is water quality, wildlife biology, politics, or accounting. That is how the educational system is structured in the United States. However, selection of a compatible work environment or series of work environments is going to be at least as important in determining whether your career is ultimately satisfying. Here are just some of the variables in your work environment:

- Do you have contact with large numbers of new people every day or are your dealings restricted to several coworkers?
- Do you deal with people in a cooperative way or sometimes in an inherently adversarial manner (for example, with regulators, journal- ists, lawyers)?
- What is the pace of the office—do you work on long-term projects or many day-to-day tasks; are there seasonal 65-hour weeks with lulls in the winter (or 65-hour weeks year round)?

- How pervasive is the bureaucracy and paper chase?
- Is it an urban or rural environment, office or field?
- How much traveling will you do?

Different people thrive and wilt in different environments—and your work environment is what you must face every morning.

The good news is that, even though there are characteristic work environments for particular careers, you can usually find almost any work environment in any career, provided you are resourceful and creative. There are foresters who sit behind computers, who interact with dozens of people daily, who work for fast-paced consultants, and who do research for universities and foundations.

PRIVATE SECTOR

Environmental employment in the private sector is of almost infinite variety. Environmental professionals work at the corporate or headquarters level in areas ranging from policy to public relations to overall management functions of environmental programs. At the plant level, where entry-level positions tend to be located, professionals develop, install, and maintain pollution control systems, work with consultants and regulators, and do sampling, lab work, and research. The difference between a large and small company can be dramatic. A small operation might have one staff person doing everything from sampling and lab work to employee training and designing pollution control systems.

The bureaucratic roadblocks to getting things done and getting promoted are generally not as pervasive as in the government. Usually, the bigger companies are, the more bureaucratic they become. The pace is often quicker and the hours longer than in the public sector, slower and shorter than in consulting firms. Pay, on the whole, is higher than in the public sector, but job security should not be assumed. In corporations where environmental staff are primarily involved in regulatory compliance, professionals complain that sometimes production-oriented staff see them as a necessary evil. Environmental compliance, even in the most enlightened companies, is a cost of doing business that does not generate revenue or product. Therefore, companies do their best to keep staffing low and costs down. Environmental staff sometimes may feel like outsiders who must work hard for cooperation from other departments. This is not the case when environmental professionals work for companies formed for the purpose of protecting the environment or managing natural resources, such as waste management firms or timber companies.

BP American Laboratories, Cleveland, Ohio. John Cuzowski (right) and Mike Markelov use laboratory robotics to analyze environmental samples.

CONSULTING FIRMS

As the economy, industrial processes, and regulations become more complicated and continue to change rapidly, the demand for consultants skyrockets. Consultants are involved in all aspects of the environmental field: They are the specialists companies and agencies can't afford to keep in house; they also serve as the point people, who, because of experience, can pull together the pieces of a large project, whether it is a study, a business plan, or a wastewater treatment facility. As a consultant, your meal ticket is your ability to have the answers (or know where to find them), to get things done, and to find people who will pay you for this service. This field is for those who like the fast lane, and all that goes with it. Hours tend to be long and the pace is often hectic, although there may be extended lulls (which means you don't have enough business). As one consultant half complains, "I am either starving or I have three clients each of whom feels the other two don't rate any of my time." You will meet many new people, and while the size of firms varies, the chances are that your company will have fewer than 15 employees.

A very important feature of consulting, sometimes overlooked, is the sales aspect. You are expected to bring in clients, and your salary and survival is often based on the volume of work that you bring to the firm. Professionals generally have strong reactions to work in the consulting field; they either love it or dislike it intensely.

NONPROFIT SECTOR

Environmentally oriented nonprofit organizations have rebounded from cuts in public support in the late seventies and are flourishing in an era of rapid change. Nonprofits are involved in a range of activities that is wide and getting wider. Offices tend to be small, and the pace, though usually on the fast side, varies. A number of factors—the time it takes to achieve goals, chronic understaffing and overwork, the high level of personal involvement, and frequent encounters with people whose degree of personal involvement can wear you down—easily lead to burnout if you can't develop patience and take the long view. There is always too much to do in a nonprofit organization, and for survival one must learn to leave the work at the office. On the positive side, nonprofit organizations encourage, even demand, that staff stretch their creative potential to the fullest. Usually, you work on a number of projects and it is up to you to guide them to completion. Nonprofit organizations are also known for flexibility, fair treatment of employees, and promulgating democratic principles in the workplace. If you like to take occasional sabbaticals, this is the sector where that is most often possible.

If you progress far enough in the nonprofit sector, you are likely to become involved in fund-raising. To survive, nonprofits must pay expenses. In a sense, they are like consulting firms, soliciting grants or donations to perform services or engaging in fee-for-service activities such as conducting energy audits of housing or helping a public agency establish a recycling operation.

PUBLIC SECTOR

FEDERAL GOVERNMENT

As in the private sector, virtually any imaginable environmental career exists at the federal level, in dozens of departments, agencies, commissions, and bureaus. The federal government has been slowly recasting its environmental role in the direction of developing broad regulatory guidelines, conducting research, providing technical assistance and training to state and local governments, and overseeing their environmental enforcement. Increasingly, federal employees have become managers of consultants who carry out much of the government's research and studies. Some of the stereotypes of working for the federal government have merit, in particular the image of a great bureaucracy. However, there is leeway for creativity. You do not have to search far to find a federal environmental professional with a very dynamic career; a number are profiled in this book.

Those looking to start a federal career would do well to research not only where the jobs are and how to get them but also the various career tracks and how to take advantage of professional development opportunities within the federal government. The danger in working for a large bureaucracy is getting lost in the shuffle and pigeonholed in a dead-end job. There are opportunities to transfer within the government, but mobility can be constrained and subject to politics. In many areas an old-boy network still persists. Job benefits are excellent at the federal level, as is job security. Salaries, while generally not at the level of the private sector, are the highest of any in the public sector.

STATE GOVERNMENT

One of the themes of this book is the increasing involvement and expertise of state governments in environmental matters. Most federal environmental regulations are passed on to state governments, which become responsible for implementation and enforcement. In addition, states are going beyond federal regulations and taking initiative in matters not covered by federal statutes, such as land-use and growth planning or groundwater protection. States offer much of the diversity of the federal government, from parks to research laboratories. In general, however, the emphasis is less on research and more on carrying out specific programs, distributing state funds to municipalities, and conducting statewide planning projects. Programs vary widely depending on finances, environmental circumstances, and the history of environmental involvement in a given state. Salaries are generally lower than at the federal level and vary significantly by state. The work environment can be fraught with politics, but less so than in the past.

LOCAL GOVERNMENT

The capacity and initiative to deal with environmental issues are also increasing at the local level, partly as a result of federal and state regulations, but more because of the demands of local residents who want responses to environmental problems in their communities. Environmental professionals work in municipal and county government, for regional commissions, at wastewater treatment plants, and with local park systems. The extent of environmental employment in a locality can range from one person who does environmental inspections among many other things to departments that rival or even surpass those of state governments in size and complexity.

Local-level environmental work is characterized by its hands-on emphasis, whether it is inspecting corporate wastewater treatment systems, developing recycling programs, or mediating between developers and residents. There is a lot of lab work and fieldwork, program development, management, and inspections and enforcement. In general, pay is lower than for state and federal employees. The work environment is also more political than at any other level of government, but as the need for technical capacity increases and urban political reform movements spread, competence rather than connections is becoming the norm. Local government is often an excellent place for professionals to start their environmental careers. Turnover is high and, given the hands-on focus, entry-level professionals are quickly given responsibility and the opportunity to learn skills that are useful throughout their careers.

TYPES OF WORK ACTIVITIES

What type of work do you want to be doing at this point in your career? In your first job do you want to do fieldwork, lab work, sales, production-oriented work, education and training, policy work, planning, or something else entirely? Combined with consideration of the environmental issues and work environments that most appeal to you, an understanding of the type of work you are most drawn to can lead to an idea of your ideal job.

You may decide that you want to work for a small consulting firm that trains companies in how to comply with hazardous waste regulations. Although it is useful to have such a specific image of your ideal first job, you should be flexible and think about your priorities. You might be most interested in working for a consulting firm and be willing to compromise on the size of the firm (your work environment). You might be interested in working on air and water quality issues in addition to hazardous waste. The third important element here is the type of work you want to do. If you can't find a position as a trainer, what would be your second choice? Could it be that it would be a wiser career move to acquire another skill before becoming a trainer?

Remember that you are forming a picture of what you want to do right now, in your first (or next) job. Then paint a larger picture of the general direction of your career. Your interests and priorities will most likely change over the course of your career; the environmental profession will also change. If you pay attention to the possession of diverse and transferable skills, then you have the flexibility to alter course in line with the changes around you.

What follows is a list of some of the major types of work activities, and the fields and sectors in which they commonly come into play. Keep this list in mind as you read the subject chapters in this book, and think about what types of work you would add to it.

- *Lab work.* Those working in the environmental protection fields in the private and public sectors as well as in consulting firms have the chance to do a lot of lab work.
- *Fieldwork.* Entry-level jobs in many environmental protection and natural resource professions entail fieldwork. If fieldwork is all you want to do, consider becoming a technician.
- *Planning and design.* Some of the hot planning areas include water quality and watershed planning, solid waste planning, land-use planning, and integrated natural resource planning, which includes forestry, fishery, wildlife, water issues, and recreation.
- *Policy making.* Nonprofit organizations may be the quickest way to get into policy work, albeit from the outside. Entry-level public sector jobs for those with bachelor's degrees are unlikely to include policy-making responsibility. You are even further away from a policy-making role in your first job in the private sector.
- *Regulatory compliance, enforcement, and investigation.* State and local governments are the front-line agencies in the enforcement and implementation of environmental regulations. Plant-level private sector employment and many consulting positions will also get you involved in regulatory issues.
- *Public information and education.* Almost all jobs in the nonprofit sector involve a substantial public information and education component. Interpreters for park systems are a large segment of employees in this category, followed by public information and relations staff in public agencies and, to a lesser extent, in corporations.
- *Research.* Academia is probably your best bet. Besides hiring professors, universities hire many types of environmental researchers. Running a close second is the federal government, followed by the private sector and state governments. Many research outfits are set up as nonprofit organizations by trade associations, foundations, and conservation groups.
- *Teaching.* Again, academia is your best bet, even though demand for

professors is somewhat stagnant, depending on the field. There are very few environmental educators at the primary and secondary school levels; you usually have to integrate environmental education into another discipline, such as biology or chemistry. Much environmental education is conducted by nonprofit organizations and by consulting firms that conduct employee training programs.

- *Data, information, and computers.* Public agencies that are trying to implement increasingly technical regulations need information specialists to design and operate systems for monitoring airborne trace toxins, for example. At the other end of the regulatory pipeline, companies must be able to process and store the data necessary to comply with environmental regulations. Data processing and information management are skills in demand in all sectors, whether for establishing the effectiveness of a regulation for the federal government, developing a program to operate an industrial wastewater treatment system, or putting together a data base for a nonprofit organization.
- *Working with people.* Working with people is a component of many environmental careers. Some of the jobs in which you are sure to get your fill: interpreter, recreation specialist, consultant, public information officer, lobbyist, environmental manager, and almost any position in the nonprofit sector.

VALUES, ETHICS, AND YOUR ENVIRONMENTAL CAREER

An issue that professionals and career counselors too often avoid is that of personal values in one's environmental career. Yet these questions are raised repeatedly by students and job seekers. Many people decide to pursue environmental careers out of a desire to be stewards of the environment.

Is the integration of your values and ethics into your career an area of concern to you? If so you have already begun to formulate a personal code of professional ethics. Environmental professionals repeatedly stated in interviews that much of the satisfaction in environmental careers comes from feeling you have in some way improved the quality of the environment. It is difficult to gain this satisfaction unless there are certain values and ethics that serve as benchmarks for your professional conduct and objectives.

Be careful in making blanket assumptions about certain careers or fields, especially in the private sector. Stereotypes and generalizations have a way of taking on a life of their own, often quite separate from reality. Get your own information. Don't assume you will have no trouble being a purist if you have avoided the private sector. Harriet Saperstein, recreation facilities coordinator for the Detroit Recreation Department, observes, "In the public sector there is a lot of politics and a lot of compromise. Long-term goals often require short-term compromise. The hardliners rarely get much accomplished, even toward their personal goals." She adds, "It is precisely this constant need for compromise which makes it necessary to start from an advocacy perspective." The nonprofit sector, despite its reputation for promoting advocacy and strict ethics—a reputation that has been earned—has its own ethical challenges: Funders often have notions of what they want you to pursue and ignore, as do board members and influential policy makers who could make life so much easier for you if you would only "go along with them on this one."

There are companies and agencies in which you might have to significantly compromise your personal values. The point is to evaluate these situations one by one rather than make unproductive generalizations. How do you go about this evaluation? Much information can be gained from the research you should do as a matter of course when considering working for a company: Read their annual report, do a literature search on the company. For larger companies, you can call or write some of the national environmental organizations—such as the Citizen's Clearinghouse for Hazardous Waste, Natural Resources Defense Council, Environmental Action, and the Wilderness Society—for information on a company's reputation. Greenpeace keeps a detailed record of flagrant corporate polluters. Land trusts may be able to tell you about developers with unsavory environmental reputations. Find local environmental activists and organizations to talk to. Consult with public regulatory agencies. Is the company in line with their permits? Don't hesitate to check references and call individuals and companies the firm has worked with, realizing you are going to have to do a lot of reading between the lines.

Finally, when you are being interviewed, remember you should also be interviewing. Employers respect this; it is actually a plus to ask questions at an interview. Ask for a tour of the plant. Bill Walters, president of the National Association of State Park Directors, advises, "Don't just look for particulars, but try to understand the overall philosophy of any agency, company, or organization. You might dislike working somewhere because of their attitude and what they *don't do*." Ultimately, it will boil down to a judgment call on your part. Armed with as much information as you can find about the company or the agency, ask yourself if you can picture yourself working there, given your values. Focus on the tasks and objectives you would face day to day.

Adherence to personal ethics will not always be easy, regardless of which sector you choose to work in. Charles Odegaard, Pacific Northwest regional director of the National Park Service, puts it this way: "Being and remaining a professional is very difficult. Not to keep your job, but to keep being a professional—those are two entirely different things. For example, once a decision has been made with everyone's input you have two choices: Either you give it 100 percent of your loyalty or you quit. Either way you remain a professional. It takes guts, honesty, and integrity."

2 Education for Your Environmental Career

IF YOU want to be a lawyer, go to law school; a doctor, go to medical school; an accountant, major in accounting; an environmental professional . . . well, take your pick from any number of educational opportunities. The environmental field is diverse, interdisciplinary, and ever changing, encompassing many types of professions and activities. Since the environmental field has evolved rapidly there are dozens of new disciplines being formed, often as combinations of more traditional fields. Often, the same job can be approached from numerous directions, since educational preparation is not as formalized as in some other fields.

Your strategy for structuring your education and training for an environmental career should have several stages. For your formal education, you need to choose a field of study and at least one educational institution. But your informal education is equally important and continues long after your formal education is complete. Career changers may need some educational retooling, and everyone needs to know how to find the educational resources most helpful to them.

It is easy to see the diversity of educational backgrounds of environmental professionals: English majors are working at state parks, botanists are working in wildlife management, business majors are running waste disposal facilities. Some jobs, of course, have more formalized requirements; for your chosen career you might be required to have an engineering degree, plain and simple. However, you might have a degree in civil or mechanical engineering, and your experience in communications or another area might give you the edge over other applicants who have only engineering degrees. This does not mean that any education will do for an environmental career. But we can broaden the way we view education to include not only degrees but also the relevant skills needed for your first job and to meet long-term career goals. A focus on acquiring skills is critical for tomorrow's job market. Those who survive and flourish will be individuals who develop and can market transferable skills that will allow them to be flexible and fill many different roles.

In the environmental field, new disciplines are constantly being created in response to demand. There is not a formal training program for every job, so employers focus on applicants' relevant skills, experience, and education. For example, there are few, if any, formal recycling education programs. Consequently, recycling employers look for various combinations of skills and experience in business, engineering, communications, and management.

There are two kinds of transferable skills relevant to environmental careers. The first are skills in areas closely related to the particular field you are pursuing: Hazardous waste managers should know about water quality issues, and natural resource managers should understand planning issues. A frustrated supervisor for a state department of natural resources comments on the practice of "boxing in" environmental disciplines: "Our wildlife biologists know wildlife, but they can't talk to our foresters. How, then, can they possibly perform the integrated natural resource management that is being called for?" They could if they had taken some forestry courses or had seasonal positions in forestry.

A second type of transferable skills are broader in scope: These are the liberal arts skills, which include interpersonal skills. Writing, speaking, management, problem solving, computers, and analytical thinking are a few of these process skills. Professionals in all disciplines stress the importance of these abilities. A vice president of a large timber company, for example, says, "What separates the forest managers from the technicians is not their knowledge of forestry but the liberal arts skills: Can they work with people, can they communicate, can they see and solve problems?"

Along with the question of what to study comes the query "How long?" Some fieldwork positions require a high school education and hands-on training; most technicians have two-year associate's degrees. Professional positions may require applicants to have a B.A. or B.S., a master's, or a Ph.D. As in many other fields, however, there has been some "educational bracket creep," so that jobs that once called for a high school education often require a two-year technician's degree, many technician's jobs are going to college graduates, and so forth.

Environmental professionals hold a wide range of degrees. At one end are broad, interdisciplinary degrees such as environmental studies (hard sciences and liberal arts or social science course work) and environmental sciences (a variety of hard sciences and environmental science course work). The structure of these degrees is as varied as the number of institutions offering them. Other professionals studied the basic sciences, such as biology, chemistry, or physics, or obtained more specialized degrees, such as in chemical engineering. Finally, many have focused on the liberal arts. But whatever the degree, remember that the diploma is designed to be a key, not a lock. Acquire the skills and then market them and retool as necessary. And keep in mind all of the other factors in an employer's decision whether to hire you.

It is beyond the scope of this book to list specific schools or programs to look to for your education for an environmental career. Over the past 20 years, there has been a tremendous increase in the diversity of programs and the number of colleges offering them at all degree levels. Where to start? Check your public or college library for *Peterson's Guide to Four-Year Colleges* (published annually) or *Peterson's Annual Guides to Graduate Study*.

The 1989 edition of the undergraduate guide includes lists of colleges under 40 academic majors related to environmental fields. Miniprofiles are given for all colleges; two-page descriptions are given for most. You will have to write to the colleges to obtain program information.

The *Guides to Graduate Study* come in five volumes. Volume 1 provides an overview. The publication lists colleges under 31 academic majors related to environmental fields. Miniprofiles are given for all colleges; two-page descriptions are given for most. A real value of these guides is that they present miniprofiles and often two-page descriptions of environmental programs, departments, and schools. Included in the descriptions are listings of faculty along with their research interests. This is helpful information in considering graduate programs.

Using these guides and other Resources, listed at the end of this chapter, you can find the program that's right for you.

CHOOSING YOUR EDUCATION

You will get the most out of this section if you have already read chapter 1 and, possibly, some of the subject chapters and have some idea of your career goals. Ideally, you would decide on what type of career you want and then select the education that will best prepare you for that career. More often, however, a career decision is made during, and as a result of, your education, and it may be far from solidified when you graduate. This is a bit of a Catch-22: You make an education decision based on a career decision, but your career decision evolves from your education decision.

The best way to resolve this stressful contradiction is to do your homework. Career decisions are easiest when you have as much information and experience as possible. Presumably, you have decided you have some interest in an environmental career. Through reading, experiencing, reflection, and talking to professionals, you should be able to come up with a general direction for your career. Then you move forward to your education and adjust or alter your course as you learn more and refine your priorities.

UNDERGRADUATE PROGRAMS

Maybe you are in high school looking at colleges, a freshman thinking about transferring, a sophomore agonizing over declaring a major, or a professional thinking about going back to school. In any event, remember that the particular undergraduate degree you obtain is not as important to your career as many would have you think. Most employers consider your degree as one of a number of hiring criteria, and many professionals have careers that are only tangentially related to their undergraduate degrees. Part of the reason for this is that you generally can't do very specialized work in college, unless you are working toward a narrowly focused degree in, say, wildlife management. For the most part, undergraduate education is intended to develop a broad base of skills and to learn how to learn. After graduation you build on this foundation through formal and informal education to determine your career. In other words, five years out of school your view of your career will be related less to your degree than to what you have done in the work force over those five years.

Ideally, the college you select should have a diversity of environmental majors. This gives you the flexibility to try different types of courses and switch majors if necessary. If you are interested in environmental protection and have a science and engineering orientation, you might want to attend a college that has undergraduate majors in environmental engineering or environmental health or both. If your interests lie in environmental protection with a communication, education, or policy orientation, you could consider a college that, besides an environmental engineering or health major, also offers a communications, education, or public administration major.

If you are interested in natural resource management with a science orientation, you might want to attend a school with a strong selection of natural resource options. For example, the Ohio State University School of Natural Resources offers 34 options in seven major environmental fields. Those with a natural resource management focus and an interest in policy should go to a similar school and take communications, public administration, management, and other social science courses.

Such advice would appear to lead you toward a larger university, and, indeed, this is where you are likely to find the largest variety of degrees. However, you can obtain an excellent general undergraduate preparation for an environmental career at a smaller college. One noteworthy benefit at smaller institutions is closer contact between students and professors, which can be critical to giving direction to your career. In a smaller school, however, you must take the initiative to get a more diverse education through innovative scheduling, independent studies, and internships. Another alternative is to take some of your prerequisites at a smaller school and transfer to a larger one for specialization during the later years of your education.

If you have the motivation, double majors or a major and a minor are an excellent way to build a strong foundation of liberal arts and analytical skills. Employers love combinations such as chemistry and political science, or environmental science and business. Be prepared, however, for resistance from professors and advisers if you express interest in double majors that include hard sciences and the liberal arts—employers tend to like them more than academics do.

Whatever orientation or major you are considering, you should take a very close look at the programs or departments that interest you. Visit the college and talk with faculty, staff, and students. Ask about the graduates of the program: How many go on to jobs or graduate school? What type of jobs and graduate programs? What are typical first positions for graduates?

You should look closely at a program's or department's career counseling and job placement activity, especially in the area of the environment. Cornell University's Department of City and Regional Planning and the University of Michigan School of Natural Resources in Ann Arbor are two examples of programs with environmental career placement offices. Some programs or departments have advisers who can guide students in environmental career planning and help with job searches and internship placement. See if there is an environmental career resource center, equipped with directories, newsletters, and books related to environmental career planning and job searching. This not only helps you with your career planning, but it says a lot about the program's orientation and commitment to students after they leave their lectures.

Finally, write to relevant professional associations (see Resources sections in the appropriate chapters) to see if the schools you are considering are accredited by these organizations. Many fields, such as fisheries, wildlife, forestry, and planning, have a comprehensive accreditation process established by professional societies.

GRADUATE SCHOOLS

Graduate school is *not* two more years of college before getting a job. There are key differences in how graduate school is structured and the purpose it serves. Graduate school teaches you a specific discipline and set of skills that allow you to enter a particular profession or job.

Your preparation and motivations for entering graduate school should be quite different from those that went into deciding on your undergraduate education. Unfortunately, many—especially those in academia—do not see it this way. You may experience significant pressure from college faculty, fellow students, and the marketplace to go directly to graduate school. However, although getting a master's degree is almost a prerequisite to being a professional in certain fields, many professionals have

A graduate seminar in forestry at Utah State University, taught by Professor Glen Edwards.

established successful careers by the right combination of work experience and undergraduate degrees.

Graduate school requires a lot of work, time, and money. Spend some energy on your decisions involving this investment. The first step is to ask the question What do I want to do—what type of professional do I want to become? You should be able to cite the types of work you could do after you receive the degree, including examples of positions. This should be fairly specific, not "I'll work in hazardous waste" or "I can work for a state department of natural resources or a consulting firm" but, for example, "I am getting a master's in environmental engineering with a focus on hazardous waste management because I want to work for an environmental consultant assessing hazardous waste sites and developing remedial action plans. I am looking for hands-on work, and consultants are the ones who go to sites and do the fieldwork and develop site plans. With a master's I will probably start out in the field as part of a site team and gradually progress to managing a team. Eventually I could head a consulting firm's hazardous waste division or at least a regional office of a national firm involved in this work." This is a very well thought out plan leading to a decision to attend graduate school. What follows is an overdramatized example of a disaster in the making. "I'm going on to get a master's in fishery biology because I majored in fishery biology. I would look for a job now, but my friend said you need a master's to get a job in this field. I am not sure what the program will be like, but I figure I'll decide what to focus on after I start. This way when I hit the job market I'll have all my education behind me and I'll be ready to go." Big surprises and frustrations may await this student.

If you are fresh out of college, don't know what to do, and are dreading the thought of looking for a job, the answer is not to go immediately to graduate school, but to clarify your interests and strengths through some work experience. This way you can learn about yourself, work environments, and your field before you specialize. You are not setting your career back by postponing graduate school—despite what classmates, parents, and even professors might tell you. Sylvia Taylor of the Michigan Department of Natural Resources asserts, "Employers like to see candidates who approached their graduate degree with some sense of purpose and direction, rather than just going immediately on to graduate school after obtaining their undergraduate degree. What did you set out to learn? What skills did you pick up? Get some work experience, find out what you like and don't like. *Then*, armed with this information, head off to graduate school."

Assuming you have done all your homework and have decided to go to graduate school, the first step is to obtain catalogs and additional information from the schools that interest you. Thoroughly research the full range of available programs by looking at the various directories of graduate

Those interested in the environment can choose from diverse educational opportunities in undergraduate and graduate study as well as in continuing education.

programs. Ask professionals in your field where they did their graduate work.

A potential graduate student should not only look at the program but at the department, school, or university that houses the program. Is this a program that is strong compared to the other programs in the department or school? Is it growing or decreasing in importance? Are there other environmental graduate programs at the university besides the one that interests you? A university that has other such programs will present additional opportunities and resources. Another key area to consider is the faculty and their research and professional interests. Do they fit your goals?

Using this process, you should be able to select about five to ten programs that deserve closer scrutiny. If possible, visit these schools to talk with faculty and students before applying. Also, talk with graduates, especially those who have jobs that interest you. Did their degree help them obtain their position? Ask questions about the placement of graduates: How many graduate? Where do they work? What is the range of starting salaries? Be wary of any program that is hazy on this information or will not refer you to graduates.

COMMUNITY COLLEGES AND TECHNICAL SCHOOLS

Some people enter the environmental field primarily because they want to spend a lot of time outdoors. So they get a B.S. and maybe an M.A. to ensure getting a good job. Much to their chagrin, they find that they are spending a lot of time *indoors*, doing paperwork, managing staff, overseeing projects, talking on the telephone, and developing budgets. And it gets worse with every promotion. These people may have been happier obtaining a two-year associate's degree or a technician's certificate, both of which might have taught them skills that would have allowed them to stay in the field and outdoors. If you think you might be such a person, or if a four-year degree is not currently in your plans, read on.

Community colleges offer two-year associate's degrees in a range of environmental subjects: conservation, ecology, environmental studies, environmental engineering technologies, environmental health sciences, forestry, fisheries, wildlife management, landscape architecture, natural resource management, parks management, and pollution control technologies.

You *can* get a job in the environmental field with a two-year degree. Most of these jobs are for technicians. They are heavily oriented toward fieldwork or lab work and hands-on skills. For example, Hocking Technical College in Nelsonville, Ohio, profiled graduates of their two-year programs in recreation and wildlife technology and also forestry technology. Graduates' job titles included state game protector, park maintenance supervisor, environmental education director, forestry technician, environmental specialist, and land management technician.

On the environmental protection side, two-year degrees can prepare you to work as an air pollution control technician, wastewater treatment plant operator, and hazardous waste remediation worker. You would also be qualified for a wide variety of field and laboratory positions in the area of environmental health. As these fields become more technical, an increasing number of technicians' jobs will become available.

Do some research on the reputation of the school. Is it accredited? What is the placement record of its graduates? Where are they working? Are they really getting the jobs that the school claims to train its graduates for? If, for example, you are told that a two-year degree in fisheries will get you a job doing original research, watch out. Another word of caution: Check with employers beforehand on the employability of those with technicians' degrees in that particular field. In some of the more competitive fields, such as fisheries and wildlife, you might be competing during dry spells with graduates of four-year colleges for technicians' jobs. Finally, the job placement services of technical schools are very important.

Many environmental programs at community colleges prepare their students for transfer to a four-year program. Often there are arrangements with four-year colleges whereby the community college serves as a feeder; that is, acceptance to the four-year college is practically guaranteed and all credits earned at the community college are transferred if certain standards are met. Because community colleges are close to home and have lower tuitions, they serve as a low-risk testing ground for your interests and abilities.

LOCATIONS OF SCHOOLS

It is often to your advantage to attend school in the region where you would like to work after graduation. This way you can begin to seek out potential employers while in school. It will be easy to search for internships and permanent positions, and the chances are good that your school has alumni working for firms in the region. College faculty may be doing research on issues in the region; part-time faculty may even have full-time jobs in firms or agencies that are potential or current employers of the program's graduates.

EDUCATIONAL OPTIONS FOR CAREER CHANGERS

Not so long ago, changing a career after about the age of 25 was considered a mistake or, at best, a setback. This attitude is changing, albeit slower than the reality of the work world. A worker spending a lifetime with one corporation is less and less common: Whole new industries are being created, and others are becoming obsolete. From one angle this is terrifying, but the flip side is that the opportunity to have a diversified and exciting career has never been greater.

The key to successful career changing is the strategy of focusing on the acquisition, packaging, and marketing of skills. You may desire to change fields within the environmental world or to enter the environmental profession from an entirely separate area. In either case you should not automatically assume that you need to go back to school. Look first at the tools that you already possess and see if they can be used to build your new career.

Take Michael Zamm, for example. An elementary school teacher for seven years, he began volunteering at the Council on the Environment of New York City and is now their director of environmental education. Lys McLaughlin worked five years for a public relations firm. Using these skills, she became communications director for the Council on the Environment. She is now the executive director. These are people who have transferred into the environmental field using skills developed in other professions. If you are already an environmental professional, it is even easier to find transferable skills. Environmental employers like to hire professionals with broad experiences and capabilities.

The first step in this process is to decide what it is you want to do in the environmental field. Read through the introductory chapters of this book for the bigger picture and hints on making decisions about environmental careers. Read the chapters on specific fields that interest you. Then do your own research: Talk to environmental professionals, read, do some volunteer work.

Next, you must assess your skills, talents, and interests in the context of the job market. Are there positions that you are qualified for right now? Don't assume that you aren't qualified for a job. Ask potential employers and read the job descriptions. For many positions, you may not need to obtain additional education. For some, you may need some additional education to round out your credentials, such as a series of courses on landscape architecture, or a two-month urban tree care program, or a one-week course sponsored by a trade association on current regulatory developments in the waste management field. Career changers in particular should look to nonformal educational opportunities.

For some, the need for further formal education will depend on how dramatic the career change. For example, if you are a business manager, you can use your skills and experience in an environmental agency, consulting firm, or nonprofit without additional schooling, if you want to manage contracts or budgets (some demonstrated interest and knowledge of environmental issues will also help you get a job; volunteer work would be useful). If, however, you want to get involved in designing remedial action plans for hazardous waste sites, then you may have to go back to school to study engineering and science.

If you need to go back to school, choose your program carefully. If you already have a bachelor's degree, you should seriously consider obtaining a master's degree rather than a second undergraduate degree; to employers an undergraduate degree is educational foundation while a graduate degree translates to job-related skills. You may need to take a few prerequisites and an entrance exam before being accepted into graduate school, although these are sometimes waived if an older student shows a capacity to succeed in formal education.

THE OTHER HALF OF YOUR EDUCATION

A degree from an educational institution provides a useful foundation and, as one professional says, "proves you are trainable." As far as the success of your career is concerned, however, your informal education is at least as important as your degree.

John R. Cook, Jr., president of The CEIP Fund points out that "employers are desperate for employees with a wide range of skills. Often these are skills you just can't develop in the classroom. This brings up the important distinction between education, which occurs at an institution, and learning or training, which is a very personal process and occurs everywhere throughout your career. The key is linking learning with acting. People have gone far in the environmental profession by acting, by going out and doing something—and not always doing it right. This is how learning becomes real."

Every chapter of this book profiles people who took the initiative and responsibility for their informal learning. Consider the following professionals:

- After studying biology for several semesters at the University of Oregon, Al Solonsky moved to Israel and eventually found a position at an aquaculture research station in the Sinai desert. Armed with his experience, he returned to the United States to obtain a B.S. and M.S. in fisheries biology, conducting research with professors during the summer. He is now an aquatic biologist with a consulting firm in Seattle.

- Jane Armstrong has a B.A. in literature and a master's in library science. She started as a librarian at the U.S. Environmental Protection Agency (EPA) Motor Vehicle Emission Lab in Ann Arbor, Michigan. Dissatisfied with this position, she transferred to a technical position with the lab. Having learned largely on the job, she is now senior project manager and oversees technical investigations and studies related to compliance with the motor vehicle emission component of the Clean Air Act.

- When David Miller couldn't get a job with a nonprofit organization after graduating with a B.A. in environmental science and economics, he moved to Washington, D.C., and volunteered full time with the National Audubon Society. During the day he delivered information to legislators' offices and wrote action updates. At night he waited tables. A question he asked at a conference so impressed an employer that he was hired by Scenic Hudson, Inc., a nonprofit agency in New York. Four years later he became the executive director of Great Lakes United in Buffalo, New York.

While you are still in school there are many ways to begin to obtain informal education. There are a multitude of internship possibilities, some associated with colleges, some not. College credit can be obtained for many of these positions. Summers between school years provide great opportunities to gain volunteer experience, even if only part time. Another option is to design an independent project to do during the school year. See chapter 3, Volunteer Programs and Internships, and the Resources sections of the subject chapters for information on organizations you might work for. Chapter 3 also shows you how to find and structure an internship that is rewarding for both you and the organization. Although this process best occurs while you are attending school, so that there is a constant interplay of theory and practice, it doesn't stop upon graduation. Every job is part of your informal education, part of the ongoing process of building and honing skills. In other words, the education never stops.

For professionals who want to grow, or even keep up, continuing education and training programs are ideal ways to expand their base of knowledge and to retool for quickly changing work conditions. Professional associations, consultants, government agencies, nonprofits, colleges, and industries all sponsor short courses, seminars, conferences, and workshops. (Many offer scholarships for students; some will waive tuition altogether. If you can demonstrate that you wish to attend to gain information for a paper or, better yet, an article for a newsletter, you can almost always at least stand in the back. Ask if you can help out in exchange for attending the sessions for free.)

The professional associations listed as Resources at the end of each subject chapter offer a range of national, state, and regional conferences and seminars. Consultants sponsor seminars, especially for those in business and industry, on environmental compliance and management. Government agencies like the EPA sponsor short courses for professionals to keep them trained on EPA-approved environmental testing methods. Colleges also have short courses for environmental professionals. Some of the best sources of information on these various programs are trade association publications. If you start sending for information on a particular field you will soon find yourself on numerous mailing lists and learn of many such events.

Conferences and workshops on environmental policy and technical issues are constantly offered all over the country. For example, one month's *EPA Environmental Events Calendar* from Region 5 (subscription free) included information on such programs as "Pond Stabilization Seminar," "National Conference on Enhancing State Lake Management," "Portable Gas Chromatography," "Annual Conference on Great Lakes Research," "Waterworks Operators' School," and "Hazardous Materials Managers' Review Course." These programs were sponsored by public, private, and nonprofit organizations.

Lee DeAngelis, director of environmental career services for The CEIP Fund, says of the importance of ongoing, informal education, "A college degree will provide you with general and some specific skills, but the real education comes from on-the-job experience supplemented by short courses, conferences, seminars, and workshops aimed at your particular profession. The real value of college thus may be whether or not it taught you how to learn. In the environmental field the learning never stops."

RESOURCES

Where do you start all of the necessary research on the education for your environmental career? The first stop should be a public, college, or even high school library. There you will find directories and guides to help you identify the colleges with majors that interest you.

Next, write for college catalogs and ask for any information beyond a description of courses and requirements. College environmental programs and departments often have booklets and brochures that explain their programs in more detail and give you examples of the types of careers their graduates have pursued.

Write to the professional associations in the field that interests you, and ask for a list of colleges that offer majors related to the field. State, regional, or local chapters of associations may provide useful information on nearby schools. Faculty of those schools are probably members of the association.

In your research, watch for college programs that are starting, restructuring, or being phased out. More often than not, there is a lag between when a field demands certain types of graduates and when the universities begin to prepare students to meet that demand.

Be sure to check the journals, magazines, or newsletters in the environmental fields that interest you. Sometimes colleges advertise their programs, especially the new ones, in these publications. This is also a good source of information on seminars and other informal educational opportunities in your field.

Meeting Environmental Workforce Needs: Education and Training to Assure a Qualified Workforce. Proceedings of the conference of the same name, April 1985. Cosponsored by the EPA, Tennessee Valley Authority, and *Pollution Engineering* magazine. Information Dynamics, Inc., 111 Claybrook Dr., Silver Spring, Md. 20902.

Educational Resources Information Center (ERIC). Sponsored by the U.S. Department of Education, ERIC provides access to literature dealing with education. This includes about 10,000 documents related to environmental education. Computer searches can be done on such topics as careers in environmental education. ERIC also develops special publications. Two examples are *Using Computers for Environmental Education* and *Strategies and Activities for Using Local Communities as Environmental Education Sites.* For more information: Dr. John Disinger, Associate Director, ERIC/SMEAC (Science, Mathematics, and Environmental Education),

Ohio State University, 1200 Chambers Rd., Room 310, Columbus, Ohio 43212.

Conservation Directory (annual). Contains information on education programs in the natural resource management field. National Wildlife Federation, 1412 16th St., N.W., Washington, D.C. 20036.

The Solar Jobs Book, by Katharine Ericson (1980). Covers educational programs. Brick House Publishing Co., 3 Main St., Andover, Mass. 01810.

Environmental Protection Careers Guidebook, by EPA and U.S. Department of Labor (1980). Includes information on education. U.S. Government Printing Office.

Exploring Environmental Careers, by Stanley Jay Shapiro (1982). Has information on two-year technician's degrees. Richard Rosen Press, 29 E. 21st St., New York, N.Y. 10010.

Opportunities in Environmental Careers, by Odom Fanning (1986). Includes chapter on education for environmental careers. VGM Career Horizons, National Textbook Co., 4255 W. Touhy Ave., Lincolnwood, Ill. 60646.

Peterson's Guide to Two-Year Colleges (1989). Includes lists of colleges under 32 academic majors related to environmental fields. Miniprofiles given for all colleges; two-page descriptions given for most colleges.

3 Volunteer Programs and Internships

Anne Blackburn, *a free-lance writer and editor, started Friends of the United Nations Environment Program, a nonprofit organization to support the U.N. Environment Program; edited* The Environmentalist, *an international journal covering technical environmental issues for the general public; and became a youth consultant for a soil and water conservation district. All of these were volunteer positions.*

Joe Hart, *an elementary school teacher, organizes 50 volunteers who hike to remote ponds every year to monitor loon nesting sites in the Adirondack region of New York for the Audubon Society.*

Using his 38 years of expertise in tax law, **Kingsbury Browne** *volunteers 200 to 300 hours per year for the Land Trust Exchange and the Trust for Public Land. He also helped found the Land Trust Exchange and established land preservation law seminars at Harvard Law School, where he is a visiting professor.*

In 1987 volunteers in the U.S. Forest Service logged more hours than full-time staff did.

Esther Feldman *worked as a CEIP research associate for the Planning and Conservation League, an environmental organization in California that works on legislative issues. Feldman researched the feasibility of a statewide bond act to protect or acquire open space for urban greenbelts. When the bond act failed in the legislature, Feldman, by then a permanent employee, spearheaded an initiative effort, which led to a $750 million bond act that passed overwhelmingly.*

47

*For nine months, **Laurel Collins** worked with small businesses in the Seattle/King County region of Washington state on hazardous waste disposal issues. She identified existing programs for small-quantity hazardous waste dischargers; visited businesses to study the generation, disposal, and recycling of waste; and produced a booklet for small businesses on hazardous waste disposal issues and options.*

***John Bozick** worked as an intern with North Coast Brass and Copper Company in Euclid, Ohio. The company smelts scrap into copper and brass and casts and rolls it into sheets for various uses. John monitored the company's compliance with environmental regulations and was subsequently hired as permanent staff. He also conducts education programs on hazardous materials for nearly 500 employees.*

***Vicky Gobetz,** an art student, took an internship with the Metropolitan District Commission in Boston in which she designed interpretive materials for Boston-area parks. Her tasks included painting educational signs and creating pictures for use with park brochures.*

ONE OF the elements that sets the environmental field off from many other sectors is the amount and diversity of work done by interns and volunteers. In fact, many, if not most, environmental careers exist today because of volunteers who gave of their time to make environmental protection and resource management high national priorities. Only a few other fields share this high degree of intermingling of professionals and volunteers: social service, health care, politics, education. The genuine interest of professionals and laypersons in protection of the environment is what makes this field special.

Volunteerism and the energies of interns increase the collective capacity of the field to deal with the multitude of environmental challenges; volunteerism spreads the word on environmental issues beyond professional circles. This helps avert what prevails in so many professions: narrow and constrained discussion, an internal language, and circular reasoning. Volunteers and interns provide a continual infusion of new blood and new ideas. Volunteerism makes protection of the environment what it should be first and foremost: an activity of the citizenry.

Volunteering and interning carry personal and professional benefits, especially if you know how to find the activity and organization that are right for you. There is a tremendous range of challenges and opportunities in your own backyard. Although we will look at volunteering and internships separately, remember that much of the advice given to aspiring volunteers applies to those looking for internships, and vice versa.

VOLUNTEERING TO IMPROVE THE ENVIRONMENT

WHY PEOPLE VOLUNTEER

There are as many reasons for volunteering as there are individuals: community service, personal interest, an extension of a career, social interaction, desire to make a difference, and professional development are a few. Three major categories of reasons, and corresponding volunteer strategies, are worth noting.

1. *Those who volunteer because of a personal interest in an area unrelated to their existing career.* A prime example is Lois Marie Gibbs, who was a homemaker before leading her community in a battle against hazardous waste at Love Canal in New York. She later formed the Citizen's Clearinghouse for Hazardous Wastes, Inc., which has five regional offices and is considered in the forefront of organizations fighting toxic contaminants at the grass roots level. Volunteers often contribute their professional skills, such as a banker who serves on a commission exploring ways to finance solid waste disposal options in her community.
2. *Environmental professionals who volunteer as an extension of their career and interests.* Many environmental professionals in the public and private sector sit on the boards of local environmental organizations, professional societies, or commissions. Tom Stanley, natural resource manager for the Cleveland MetroParks, for example, is founder and president of a land trust in his community. One could argue that such after-five participation by environmental professionals is the norm rather than the exception. These professionals usually assert that volunteering is a part of their professional as well as personal development.
3. *Those who volunteer to gain work experience, develop skills, explore career options, or find a job.* These volunteers are the lifeblood of many environmental organizations and agencies. One example is Ron Dodson, executive director of the Audubon Society of New York state, who recalls, "I spent several years in a capacity that can only be described as professional volunteer before landing my first job with the Audubon Society."

There are several aspects of volunteering to get a job. While in high school or college you might volunteer to get a hands-on perspective or education in a field you are considering as a career choice. Another type of volunteering is when you are looking for a job and trying to get a foot in the door, make contacts, and build up a professional reputation.

Fifteen or twenty years ago such volunteering might have been a nice way to give a job seeker an edge. Today, however, some form of volunteer work or internship is often a prerequisite for obtaining a full-time job in the environmental field. As Jill Riddell of the Nature Conservancy in Chicago puts it, "There is no excuse for not having work experience as long as there is such a high demand for volunteers in this field." This is especially true in those areas of the environmental field where the job market is competitive.

SELECTING VOLUNTEER WORK

You think you might like to volunteer but aren't quite sure what that means or where to begin. This chapter is meant to be a resource guide and also to stimulate your imagination through example. Take some time to think about your orientation: What do you want to do? Where do you want to do it? With what types of people and in what environment?

As you conduct your search, keep in mind the specific issue you would like to address. Is it advocating the removal of hazardous waste from a local dump? Lobbying for legislation that would reduce acid rain? Improving water quality? Starting a recycling center in your community? Preserving land or restoring a certain wildlife species? Improving communication in your trade association?

Then ask where that opportunity would exist. In advocacy groups such as the Sierra Club, the Nature Conservancy, and the National Audubon Society; government agencies; public commissions; boards; legislative bodies; nonprofits; professional associations; universities (assisting professors with research); parks or nature centers; arboretums; botanical gardens; or forest service districts?

Finally, ask what skills you can bring to this effort or organization. What skills can you pick up from this activity? Are you a good coordinator, manager, PR person, director, accountant, writer, research biologist, bird bander, fund-raiser? Or do you want to learn some of these skills for personal or professional reasons?

GETTING INVOLVED

How do you get started in your community—with the issues, activities, organizations, and people of your choice? Approach this task in the same manner as if you were looking for a job or researching a term paper. This includes a lot of networking, phone calling, attending meetings, research

. . . and dead ends. Take the time you need to find the position you want. The great thing about volunteering is that, even more so than in your career, if you can't find it, you can in all likelihood create it. If you are not sure what you want to do or who you want to do it with, all the more reason for some thorough research.

The Resources section at the end of this chapter will help you get started. To find out what is happening locally, start with the telephone directory. Try "Associations" and "Environmental" in the Yellow Pages. Then start calling people and organizations to talk about issues and ask for other people to call. This will quickly branch out until you have more contacts than you can handle. Try to get some literature from organizations to see what they are about and to get leads on other organizations. Call people who are quoted in the media, and check for meetings listed in local newspapers and magazines. Other resources include the electronic, computer-accessed "bulletin boards" announcing organizations and activities in a particular area or field. Check with local universities and computer societies for this resource and other information—professors often are involved in "extracurricular" activities. University bulletin boards and campus newspapers are good sources of information. Make use of your local reference librarians.

If you are interested in a particular issue, see the Resources listed at the ends of chapters 5–14. Many national associations and environmental organizations have regional, state, and local chapters whose functions you can attend. Environmental agencies and advocacy groups also band together to form cooperative organizations or coalitions; this is true in government, academia, and industry, too. For example, the New England Interstate Water Pollution Control Commission is a clearinghouse for groundwater projects in seven states; Great Lakes United is a coalition of environmental, recreational, union, community, government, and small business organizations which coordinates and unifies efforts to develop environmentally sound policies and programs. The Northeast Association of Fish and Wildlife Resource Agencies and Save San Francisco Bay Association are two more example of such conglomerates.

Be persistent. Finding the right volunteer position, like finding the right job or educational program, usually includes some wild goose chases. It takes awhile to get into the network, but once you, your work, and your interests become known, things start to fall into place. Work at the grass roots level may lead to your participation in regional, state, or national organizations or efforts. As one volunteer says, "At first *I* was approaching organizations; now *they* call and ask me to sit on a board or to help draft a policy statement. I can be much more selective now that I have laid the groundwork."

Friends of the Earth, Seattle, Washington. Kathy Blume volunteered for the Friends of the Earth campaign for increased media coverage of environmental issues in the Seattle metropolitan area.

Career-Oriented Volunteering

If your primary reason for volunteering is to get a job or gain work experience, approach your search in a somewhat different manner. Think carefully about what you want to gain from this work. Is it skills and work experience? What skills would be useful to the field you intend to enter? Put yourself in the shoes of a future employer who might be interviewing you. If you were hiring environmental educators who are to work with the public, wouldn't it be a plus if an applicant had teaching experience? If you were the head of a corporate public relations department, wouldn't you be intrigued by an applicant who had some experience working for community organizations or who had edited a newsletter?

If you are not sure of the particular environmental field you would like to enter, or have a general idea of the issue you'd like to work on or the sector you prefer, volunteering is a good way to test the waters and focus your search. You want to find a volunteer position that is diverse, one where you would meet many people and interact with numerous organizations on a variety of issues. It might be better to steer clear of positions where you would spend most of your time doing library research or working on a computer. You might not mind an internship that is a mile wide and an inch deep: You are exploring more than trying to build skills. These types of volunteer positions include writing for a newsletter, summarizing public meetings for an organization, or working with a coalition of agencies.

What if you are volunteering to get a job, period? Your volunteer position should allow you to gain and demonstrate some skills and experience, but you also want to make contacts and get yourself known by as many individuals and agencies as possible. If you have identified the employer you want to work for, try to volunteer there. If this is not possible, find out what organizations they deal with and volunteer with one of them. All of this information is only a phone call away.

Finally, make sure you will get a strong letter of recommendation from your supervisor. You want your supervisor to be able to say, at the least, "This person can produce on schedule, is competent, and gets along well with others." Conduct yourself accordingly.

Keep in Mind . . .

Here is a checklist to assist you in structuring your volunteer position to ensure it will be a rewarding experience:

- Ask yourself what type of skills or knowledge you wish to gain in your volunteer position.
- When approaching a volunteer activity, work with a supervisor to develop an assignment and goal.
- Schedule a regular period of interaction with your supervisor and others so that they may review and respond to your work.
- Set a work plan and timeline for yourself and others whose work must interact with yours. Volunteer projects that go on forever and eventually fade out occur far too frequently and are a bad experience for all concerned.
- Assume you have to manage yourself and take initiative on your project.
- Expect that the organization will make some effort to give you exposure to the broader scope of work in the field. But don't assume they will do so without your asking—maybe more than once.
- Have confidence that what you are doing is significant and worthy of the same respect accorded those in paid positions.
- If you are working for the organization's cause, find out what they need rather than imposing your wants.
- Keep a record of your accomplishments and copies of any work. This will help your supervisor in writing any letters of recommendation, and it helps you package and market your experience to future employers and schools.

- If you make a volunteer commitment, recognize it as such—just as you would at work. People and efforts are counting on you. There is nothing worse than trying to coordinate people who are unreliable and apathetic. Have some empathy for the staff person who must manage

PROFILES

Jerry Tinianow, Sierra Club Volunteer and Partner with Hahn Loeser & Parks, Cleveland

The Sierra Club is a nonprofit environmental organization with local, state, and national offices. While the Sierra Club has full-time staff in a number of cities, the bulk of the work and all of the leadership comes from volunteers. Staff structure their activities based on the mandates of elected volunteer leadership.

"I initially became involved in public affairs volunteer work as an undergraduate in Washington, D.C., where I worked in a congressional office and also worked for the congressman in his home state of Montana in the summer. My volunteering in the environmental field started in 1978, while I was a student at the National Law Center of George Washington University.

"During the summer of 1978, when I returned to Cleveland to work between terms, I felt the need to get away from purely academic pursuits, which limited my involvement in outside issues. I contacted a friend of mine, who was a volunteer with the Northeast Ohio Group of the Sierra Club, and started to get involved. At that time the Sierra Club was opposing the construction of a steel mill in Conneaut, Ohio. I spent most of my time that summer working on the Conneaut issue, which included testimony at public hearings on environmental issues related to the construction of this mill.

"The following fall, when I returned to school, I applied for a program in which one could receive academic credit for legal work for public interest organizations or government bodies. I chose to work for the Sierra Club Legal Defense Fund in Washington, and was involved in a variety of projects.

"After graduating from law school, passing the bar, and moving to Cleveland to work for a private firm, I became reinvolved in the Sierra Club chapter. I was living downtown in an apartment with a view of Lake Erie, so when the group began organizing a citizens' group to promote waterfront development, it was an issue in which I had some personal interest. Our group helped to organize a separate nonprofit, the Cleveland Waterfront Coalition, of which I was a founding member, incorporator, and legal adviser.

"I have held a variety of local and statewide offices with the club. I was a member of the local executive committee and head of the local branch of the Sierra Club Committee on Politi-

volunteers. Show your excitement, enthusiasm, energy, and responsibility—it is the best foundation for a good working relationship.

• Have some fun. You aren't going to get rid of all the toxic waste today or finance the recycling center at just one meeting. Enjoy the process.

---

cal Education. I later served as chairman of the Ohio chapter. I moved into national participation when the president of the Sierra Club asked me to become a member of the Clean Air Campaign steering committee, which I served on for four years, including the last two as chairman.

"Each level of participation within the organization—national, state, and local—has its advantages and disadvantages. The results of your work are more tangible and visible at the local level; the national level tends to consist a lot more of pushing buttons and pulling strings from afar, but at the same time the effects are more far reaching, and there is, of course, the element of prestige. The local level tends to be more time consuming because everything must be run like clockwork—meetings are held weekly, fund-raisers and activities are more frequent, as are everyday crises. At the national level, efforts are more cyclical—meetings and other events come in spurts. The tradeoff of working as a volunteer administrator at the national level of an organization is that in using your talents in managing, budgeting, and mediating disputes, you must accept the organization's philosophy and expound its views rather than pursue your own priorities.

"There are no shortcuts to the learning process of getting to know an organization. It is best to cut your teeth at the local level. I began to get involved because I had a general interest in public policy. Like most people, I operated under the belief that if you wanted to make an impact on public policy, you had to work for the public sector; that is why I began working on Capitol Hill. Since that time I have come to believe that it is really the private sector that makes the difference. If people only realized how attuned their representatives are to their opinions, I think a lot more people would become involved in private sector activism."

Jim Rogers, Corporate Manager of Energy and Environmental Affairs, Digital Equipment Corporation, Maynard, Massachusetts

Many environmental professionals volunteer their time and expertise to environmentally related activities. For most, volunteering is both an extension of their job and a source of personal satisfaction.

"My work at Digital includes responsibility for air and water quality, hazardous waste, and energy management issues. My group's job is to coordinate the activities of our 50 or so plants, making sure they are aware of the environmental laws they are responsible for and are in compliance.

"Employees at Digital are encouraged to get involved in outside organizations dealing with issues directly and indirectly related to our industry. I and others are active in groups like the Merrimack River Watershed Association, the Audubon Society, the CEIP Fund, and a number of state and federal advisory boards that coordinate activities such as minimization of waste and air toxics and groundwater quality management at a regional level.

"I volunteer a lot of my time not only during work hours but also at night and on weekends for two good reasons: first, I believe I can lend some value to these organizations in offering our company's perspective, and second, it gives me an opportunity to communicate with others and gain a better perspective on our role as private industry.

"Currently, I'm vice chairman of the Massachusetts Hazardous Waste Facility Siting Council, a commissioner of the New England Interstate Water Pollution Control Commission, and a member of the Merrimack River Watershed Association, of which I was a director for eight years. I also belong to the Massachusetts Audubon Society, the National Wildlife Federation, the Wilderness Society, and professional associations such as those concerned with water and air pollution control and energy conservation.

"Finally, I serve on various advisory boards at the state and national level. Sitting on boards and councils involves handling what I call action items, which can be anything from monitoring regulations and pro-cedures to be followed by builders of hazardous waste sites, to discussing appropriation and approval of grant money, developing scoping criteria for environmental impact statements, and participating in discussions. Environmentalists and businesses often have similar goals; where they differ is in how they believe the goals ought to be achieved. Consequently, boards often serve as mediators of conflicts between, say, developers and communities, and act as leaders in finding the middle ground.

"I've been working in the environmental area for about 18 years. When I first got started no one had environmental degrees—there were no such programs. I received a B.S. in chemical engineering from the University of Massachusetts at Amherst and later earned an MBA from Northeastern University. I started my career as a chemical engineer for du Pont and later went into process engineering at Raytheon before becoming corporate environmental manager there for ten years. I joined Digital in 1980 and am basically doing the same thing for a larger, more global company.

"I suppose I have been an environmentalist from the start. I was an Eagle Scout, nature camp counselor, and Scout leader for merit badges in wildlife management, forestry, and other nature activities. When I got into business I was looking for a way to apply these skills to better the environment. I came to the conclusion that you can do a lot from within corporations to change things and don't necessarily have to pursue a career with an advocacy or environmental organization to make a difference."

David Miller, Executive Director, Great Lakes United, Buffalo, New York, and Former National Audubon Society Volunteer

This profile presents a good example of an individual who resourcefully used a volunteer position to start a career in the environmental field.

"I wasn't long out of college when I realized the traditional method of searching for a job—sending out hundreds of résumés and letters—wasn't going to work for finding a job in the environmental field. The response was typical: 'You have a good background but you need work experience.' So I decided to pack up my things and move to Washington, D.C. I started working as a waiter three nights a week and volunteered full time with the National Audubon Society, where I was a lobbying intern. My first assignment was to collect background information on the Garrison Diversion project, a water project that would have ruined migratory bird habitats in the Dakotas. Later I delivered information on issues to congressional offices and made calls to solicit support for upcoming legislation, wrote action updates and articles, worked in the library, and put together briefing material for Audubon staff and congressional offices. I guess you could have called me a jack-of-all-trades. As the confidence in my abilities grew within the organization, so did my responsibilities as a volunteer intern.

"I was determined to stay on until I found a full-time position in the environmental field. The volunteering put me in touch with a lot of people who called me about job openings. Ironically, it was during a brief visit at home that I received a job lead. I had gone home to attend a conference where Toby Moffett, a member of the House leadership from Connecticut, was speaking. During the discussion session following his speech I asked him a question that impressed a member of the audience from Scenic Hudson, Inc. Later, she approached me and inquired whether I would like to apply for a position with the organization.

"Before I knew it I was their environmental program coordinator. This put me in charge of monitoring, studying, and finding solutions to air quality and hazardous waste issues in the Hudson Valley; developing case studies to promote and administer public policy; preparing testimony on legislation and regulations; organizing, designing, and presenting educational forums on pollution-related issues; consolidating and coordinating the work of area public interest groups; and developing appropriate media campaigns. I stayed with Scenic Hudson for almost three years, until just before the 1984 presidential election. I felt myself drawn to the environmental issues of the election and left my job to become the director of voter education programs and a political consultant for the New Jersey Difference in '84.

"During September and October of that year I directed my energies toward the environmental education program, in which we presented both the Democratic and Republican public policy platforms to citizens through organized debates, forums, and other nonpartisan educational events and materials. In November I supervised Sierra Club volunteers for a congressional campaign in New Rochelle, New York, and organized literature distribution, mailings, poll watching, and phone banks. Toward the end of the campaign I started distributing my résumé and in December I found out about Great Lakes United, an international organization dedicated to conserving and protecting the Great Lakes and St. Lawrence River. I became their executive director and have been responsible to the board of directors for publications, membership recruitment, fund-raising, public policy development, and administration of a staff that has grown to four full-time program employees and three part-time clerical employees.

"To make volunteering work for you, the first step is common sense: Present yourself well, be orderly and businesslike, and know what you want to do. Try to develop a rapport with those you are working with; as you slowly gain their confidence, you will get more in-depth projects. Be diligent and don't give up easily. The more feelers you have out, the better chance you have of being in the right place at the right time."

INTERNSHIPS: YOUR FIRST JOB

The first work experience of most environmental professionals is an internship, seasonal, or volunteer position. It is now almost a prerequisite for environmental employment, to demonstrate your abilities and, more important, show employers that you are committed to the field. One employer pointedly asks, "If they haven't been able to do some hands-on work in all their years of education, why would they even think I might pick them over the 95 percent who have one and usually several such experiences?"

FINDING AND DEVELOPING YOUR INTERNSHIP

Kevin Doyle, national general manager of The CEIP Fund, outlines a strategy for pursuing an internship where a formal program doesn't exist: "Step one is to identify where you want to work. Working from this narrowed list, identify individuals within the target organizations to talk with. Step two is to meet with the individual who is in a position to hire an intern and can identify and discuss the organization's needs. Finally, step three is to write a proposal, offering your services to meet the needs you identified. This proposal should clearly define the project, the skills you have to implement the project, and a time frame in which the project would be accomplished."

For example, in researching a local planning agency, you may read a news story about how the county it serves is running out of landfill space and the agency has been designated to develop a solid waste management plan. You might contact the manager of the planning agency and say something like, "I read in the *Gotham City Globe* that your agency will be developing a solid waste plan. I would think that one of your initial steps would be to research current solid waste management practices in the country. I have research experience, gained when I collected information on solid waste management for a case study in an environmental science class." This manager may not ultimately go for the project you have outlined, but it gets a discussion going and may lead the two of you to develop another mutually beneficial project.

What follows are some ideas for obtaining internships and part-time work in the various employment sectors.

FEDERAL AND STATE GOVERNMENT

Federal and state environmental agencies often have established intern, summer, and part-time programs. Contact these agencies during the *fall* for summer programs—at least three to six months in advance of when you are available. Think federal or state, but look on the local level for internships. If you want to work for the Environmental Protection Agency (EPA), for example, by all means contact its offices in Washington, but it is at least as important to seek out EPA regional offices, research labs, and other facilities where you would like to work. Seek out professionals, and ask them whether they have internship positions and, if so, the application procedure. Try to find out who will make the hiring decision.

The same advice holds true with agencies such as the National Park Service or U.S. Forest Service and state departments of natural resources or EPAs. College faculty and placement offices should also know about such opportunities and may have cooperative arrangements with these agencies (see chapter 13, Parks and Outdoor Recreation, for information on seasonal positions in natural resource management). The Student Conservation Association, discussed later, also helps set up internships with federal, state, and private natural resource agencies. A creative career planner who can develop a project may be able to obtain an internship or part-time job with agencies even if no formal internship program exists or if they have filled their quota.

LOCAL GOVERNMENT

Some local units of government have established internship programs. Usually, however, the process is much more informal, meaning it is up to you to take the initiative. A mid-sized or large metropolitan area will have a number of different agencies, and a large municipality will have dozens of municipal and county units of government, commissions, and regional agencies. Start at home, realizing that local governments like to hire their own citizens. Because it is so close to the issues, local government is an excellent place to gain practical work experience.

NONPROFITS

A very informal internship process prevails in the nonprofit sector, although some of the larger organizations such as the National Wildlife Federation and the Wilderness Society offer structured internships in their Washington, D.C., offices. Paid positions are not common. Think locally: There are many nonprofit environmental organizations at the local level, and your work will probably have more substance.

CORPORATIONS

Although many corporations have formal intern programs, few focus on the environment. Check with the company's personnel or human resources department, but don't stop there. Using the skills and resources mentioned in this chapter, try to get the names of people who work in the environmental department. If you're interested in a large corporation, seek out local plants or facilities where you could work. See if they have an environmental health and safety staff. At the plant level, you may find that they have never used an intern and haven't even considered the idea; be prepared to assess their needs and create your own position. In these cases, specific projects with tangible end products are going to get their attention. It might be administering a training needs survey that the environmental manager has never found time to do, or organizing a data base. A good question to ask is, "What projects have been sitting on your back burner for more than three months that I could take the lead on?"

CONSULTANTS

Most consulting firms are small, with fewer than 15 on staff. Few have formal intern programs. They are also very dynamic operations, always looking for business and staffing for projects. If you call them the day after they land a big contract you may be in luck; if you visit the day they finish that project you might see laid-off staff leaving the office. Consultants are used to working with a variety of staffing situations and may be more open and flexible to part-time and internship arrangements. The downside is that they rarely have a lot of time for managing or training interns. Your task, therefore, is to convince those who have the hiring power that you have a service to offer and are worth a small investment of their time. Take some initiative and do some research. A check of the local Yellow Pages under "Environmental and Ecological Services" will likely yield 15 or 20 firms in a large metropolitan area. Your professors or professional association contacts may know of some opportunities. Also check the *Consultants and Consulting Organizations Directory* (Gale Research), which is cross-referenced to list environmental consultants by geographical area and consulting activity.

SALARY

Whether you are paid on your internship depends on the demand in your field, the resources of the organization or agency, and your level of experience and education. While a paycheck would be nice, remember that this is part of your education, and your learning, not salary, should be the foremost consideration. Dave Buchanan of the Student Conservation Association, Inc., observes, "We have people who jump at a national park position that pays close to minimum wage for passing out parking stickers. At the end of the summer, what advantage do they have over the individual who took a volunteer position working with a natural resource manager collecting and analyzing data for a resource management plan?"

You may find that it is easier to get paid for your second or third internship experience. If you must earn some money, try to save up to take a summer off, or spend a few hours a week volunteering in your free time.

NATIONAL ENVIRONMENTAL INTERNSHIP PROGRAMS

There are two major nonprofit organizations devoted to developing internships in the environmental field. They are The CEIP Fund, under whose auspices this book was written, and the Student Conservation Association.

THE CEIP FUND

The CEIP Fund arranges short-term, paid positions in environmental fields for college students or recent graduates. CEIP has four branch

CEIP/Pacific Northwest Associate retreat, Seattle, Washington. CEIP retreats provide an informal way for associates to meet one another.

offices (Boston, Seattle, San Francisco, and Cleveland) that develop and administer internships in 17 states.

Sponsoring organizations include public agencies at the federal, state, and local levels, corporations, private consulting firms, activist groups, and nonprofit organizations. CEIP's role is largely that of a matchmaker, finding the best applicants for positions based on sponsors' needs.

CEIP associates, as the interns are called, can come in and perform well with minimal training and supervision. A key part of CEIP's job is to ensure that an internship is both educational and challenging for the associate, and productive for the sponsor.

As applications are received at CEIP, they go through a screening process. CEIP refers applicants to sponsors for review and the sponsors decide whom to interview. Interviews are frequently conducted over the phone. Three areas emphasized in the application process are (1) direction (knowing your career goals and what you want to do now), (2) experience, volunteer work, research, and class projects, and (3) strong references.

STUDENT CONSERVATION ASSOCIATION

The Student Conservation Association is a nonprofit organization that develops over 1,000 resource management positions every year in federal, state, and private parks and natural lands across the country. They have two programs. The first, the High School and Advanced Work Groups conducted in spring and summer, annually involves about 300 students. Volunteers serve in coeducational groups of six to twelve participants with one or two adult supervisors. These groups spend between three and five weeks working on a project while living in a tent base camp. One of the weeks is spent on a backpacking hike or in some other exploratory activity.

The second program, the Park, Forest, and Resource Assistant Program, operates year round and is open to anyone 18 years of age or older who has graduated from high school and has been out of high school for at least one year. About 750 positions per year are offered with resource, recreation, forest, wildlife, and fisheries management agencies and with educational programs and research projects in many fields. Positions, which usually last 12 weeks, include a travel grant, free housing, stipend for food and basic living expenses, and uniform allowance. The Student Conservation Association also publishes *Job Scan*, a monthly publication containing at least 100 job listings ranging from the executive to the internship level. Each issue also includes a feature article written by a professional, along with a calendar of events.

KEEP IN MIND . . .

Much of the advice on structuring volunteer work, given earlier in this chapter, is relevant to internships. An internship, however, is generally more focused on the goal of obtaining practical work experience and exploring career options, while also providing a service to the organization you are working with. These are some pointers on making your internship a rewarding experience:

- Explore numerous internship possibilities—as many as possible— concurrently. Projects for interns are not usually first priority, and development of these internships can drag on and often fade out as other projects take precedence. Be diplomatic, but try to pin down organizations and supervisors on decision dates.
- Think carefully about what you want to gain from an internship: Professional contacts, work experience, visibility in a particular organization? What skills do you want to develop?

- The most successful internships focus on one or two specific projects, are well supervised, run on a schedule, and have an end product. Approach your internship as you would a job: work with your supervisor to develop a work plan and set of goals. When prospective employers ask your internship supervisors about your abilities, these are the areas they will ask about. Be wary of unstructured internships.
- Set up a regularly scheduled meeting with your supervisor, ideally once a week, to evaluate your progress and get feedback. Insist on sticking to this schedule.
- Anticipate that you will be doing some mundane tasks: photocopying, typing, and running errands. If this takes up more than one third of your time, however, you have been brought on as an office assistant, not as a preprofessional intern.
- Keep a journal of your accomplishments and copies of your work. Before you leave, get a letter of recommendation that you can use in future job applications. If possible, develop working relationships with more than

PROFILES

Pam Irvin, Water Resources Research Technician, Cape Cod Planning and Economic Development Commission, Barnstable, Massachusetts

"An internship is really an extension of the learning process. You are there because you want to learn more about a particular field of work. People understand that you're going to ask more questions than you would if you were on a 'real' job. They're eager to help you learn.

"Working for the Cape Cod Planning and Economic Development Commission (CCPEDC) gave me excellent fieldwork experience. The commission provides technical assistance on water quality protection, solid and hazardous waste management, and demographics to 15 communities in Barnstable County, Massachusetts.

My project identified sources of groundwater pollution on land adjacent to the town well and from residential and commercial activities. We also assessed both current and future risks. The commission chose Chatham because this small town is surrounded on three sides by the ocean and has a limited water supply.

"I completed a master's in natural resources management, planning, and policy at the University of Michigan School of Natural Resources. I decided at that time that I'd like to take a few years and get my feet wet before I dived into a permanent position. The position that opened up

one staff person so that if your supervisor should leave, there will still be someone who can speak to future employers about your work and accomplishments.

- There is an unwritten code that says interns should be willing to go the extra mile to get the job done. Many before you have adhered to this code, and your internship will, in part, be evaluated based on your willingness to come in on a Saturday or to go to an evening meeting. This also allows you to get the most out of your work experience. One reason interns are appreciated is that they bring enthusiasm and new blood to an organization. Don't be afraid to show some excitement for your work.

- Spend some time getting to know people at your company and also at other organizations. Ask them about their work and tell them about your professional aspirations. If your work is solid, who knows where this may take you.

---

through CEIP with the CCPEDC was a great opportunity. I was able to do fieldwork within a community. This kind of work is good background for policy work.

"My tasks included conducting a land-use inventory of a square-mile region around the public water source. We mapped the land-use patterns. This information was plugged into a risk assessment formula that indicates what problems will occur in the future based on today's conditions. We came up with a nitrogen loading projection and documented underground storage tanks. Our report will be used by the town of Chatham in its planning process to support regulatory action.

"In the process, I gained experience with maps and learned how to meet with public officials and other members of the community. There was an incredible attention to detail in the

mapping process, from traffic patterns to the kinds of dish soap used by a restaurant.

"It was a pilot project. Because it went well and produced solid information, I was hired for another nine months to do the same kind of work in a neighboring area. This time the land-use inventory I worked on was just part of a more comprehensive study that included a much larger area than before and a number of wells.

"I've done two short-term jobs now and I'm ready to move on to permanent work with its associated responsibilities. Ideally, I'd like a job that combines both fieldwork and policy work. We need more people making effective *policy*. But behind every policy there needs to be the fieldwork.

"My long-term goals are to work with wetlands, but the field is so specialized it isn't suited for interns.

These projects were perfect for intern involvement. In fact, I'm so eager to see others have the same kind of intern experience that I've remained an active CEIP alumna. I've offered to talk to anyone in the program. I'd like others to learn the way I've been able to."

Jerlena Griffen, Magazine Associate, California Tomorrow, San Francisco

Jerlena Griffen used her internship with a nonprofit organization to test her choice of a career and to learn as much as she could about California's sociological, political, and environmental issues.

"California's open, multicultural character always attracted me. After I got my master's in counseling from Western Illinois University, I moved there. The magazine associate position with California Tomorrow was the perfect opportunity to fulfill my personal goal of learning as much as I could about California.

"The object of the internship was to assist with the 25th anniversary edition of the organization's magazine, *California Tomorrow.* The issue celebrates California Tomorrow's new focus on the state's population and cultural diversity. My position was funded by a special grant from the San Francisco Foundation through The CEIP Fund's Environmental Grants program.

"I worked with the magazine's editors in both Los Angeles and San Francisco coordinating the section that dealt with what the environment means to the average citizen in the state. I organized interviews with people all over the state and did a lot of interviewing myself.

"As a minority liaison, I focused on the 'slow growth' movement that is sweeping California. California annu-ally receives one fifth of the world's immigrants. California residents have grown increasingly concerned about how growth will alter the quality of life in the state. Towns and counties use ordinances and initiatives to adopt stringent growth regulations. There's concern that this movement is elitist and very possibly racist. The 'slow growthers' think progressively in one sense, but they don't yet have a handle on issues such as affordable housing and recognition of the many different ethnic populations within the state. I attended several slow growth conferences and reported back to California Tomorrow on the issues covered (housing, development, water, and growth's effect on the environment).

"I produced material for the chapter in the magazine that dealt with the interconnectedness of minority and environmental issues; this was the first time I was published. Because I was writing about real people—and what I was writing was going to be seen by real people—editing was crucial. In fact, what I wrote was eventually incorporated into someone else's chapter. But that's what editing is. It was a good experience for me to see my writing transformed that way and to understand why.

"I was able to take advantage of the position to learn what I wanted to learn about California. I had the opportunity to spend two days in the state capital, meeting with key people involved with the environment and with minorities. I met with legislators and lobbyists. I became familiar with the politics of the state and particularly with environmental politics.

"A university provides a sheltered environment. In this position, I was able to get out, travel around the state, meet people, find out about the state's geography, educational system, sociopolitical structure, and environmental issues and learn more about the multicultural aspect of the state.

"*Environment* is a large word that means something different to each person. It includes much more than marsh ecology and air quality. It includes people, people's lives, the way people live. Really coming to grips with that during the internship justified my choice of multicultural education as a career. I really tested what I was learning."

Aubrey Smith, Research Associate, Environmental Technology Group, BP America's Research and Development Center, Cleveland

Aubrey Smith learned that an internship can be one of the best ways to find out what kind of work you really enjoy. He also wound up with a permanent position with BP America, having proved his talents on the job.

"Too many students choose careers without having enough information on what's available and what they really like doing. For me, internships provided a fantastic opportunity to learn more about myself and my fields of interest. It gave me hands-on training. I worked with professionals who were more than willing to answer my questions. They *expect* this. I found that as an intern, I could learn as much as I was willing to take the time to ask.

"I first worked as an intern the summer of 1986, just after I graduated in biology from Lane College. Through a program managed by The CEIP Fund for the EPA, I was selected to test current wastewater analysis technology and to develop wastewater treatment methods. We were looking for the most efficient means of analyzing and treating wastewater.

"After a year abroad at the University of Edinburgh, I again sought out a CEIP intern position. The research position in BP America's Environmental Technology Group was perfect for my increasing interest in doing original scientific research. This time, I worked in a laboratory and studied processes of biologically producing elemental sulfur. The experiments were complex and lasted for months. I maintained the experiments and cultures, collected data, changed parameters, and observed and reported the results. My reports were funneled through the system and would be integrated into the company's research files.

"Scientific research isn't something that just occurs between nine and five, Monday to Friday. Sometimes I stayed late or came in on the weekend when the experiment had to be taken care of or observed. You have to be dedicated to research even when you have to work overtime and when your results don't turn out the way you anticipated or hoped. There's a lot of pressure in research.

"An internship like this allows you to test out whether you really want to be a research scientist or not. It puts you to the test and also exposes you to new ideas and aspects of the work. I've been devoted to research ever since my involvement with research projects early in high school. I've always wanted to find out something new that no one knows, produce the unknown. When my experiment at BP America called for overtime, I wanted to see it through. It was exciting.

"It was a difficult decision to accept the permanent position with BP

BP America Laboratories, Cleveland, Ohio. Aubrey Smith's internship experience initiated his career as a research scientist.

America. I intend to get my Ph.D. and I would get through school faster if I didn't work full time. But, looking at BP America's program, which allows us to continue our education while working, I decided that it would be best in the long run, even though it meant I would take longer to get my degree. Now when I get my degree, I'll have plenty of work experience to back it up."

Tamara Adams, Laboratory Technician, Wastewater Quality Laboratory, Municipality of Metropolitan Seattle

The technical experience Tamara Adams gained in Metro's labs during two successive CEIP internships gave her important background for further work in environmental protection and helped focus her career interests.

"When I first got out of school with a bachelor's in environmental health, I didn't have a very clear idea of what I wanted to do. I also had little real-world work experience, even though I had worked as a research assistant in the toxicology lab at Western Washington University during my senior year. I thought an internship would make the most sense. I could get work experience without getting tied down to something I might find I didn't like.

"During my first intern position with Metro, I worked in the environmental lab studying the effects of sewage sludge on freshwater supplies. I collected water samples from streams and lakes near sites where Metro's sludge was applied for agricultural purposes. I tested the water quality of these samples.

"It was a great experience, so I signed up for a second internship with Metro, this time in their Wastewater Division. In this lab, I monitored the wastewater treatment process from start to finish. I took samples of sewage during all stages of treatment both inside and outside the plant. The purpose of this work was to monitor the efficiency of the treatment plant. I'd begin at 7:00 A.M. collecting samples. The rest of the day I worked in the laboratory, running experiments on the samples (biological oxygen demand tests, fecal coliform and bacteria counts), analyzing the results, and entering the data on spreadsheets.

"I had done this kind of lab work in school but I never could see any application of the work. At Metro, the numbers aren't theoretical. They mean something. They are a means to an end. I enjoyed the feeling that my work was real.

"After these two internships I feel I don't want to continue with laboratory work. I'd rather get into the planning end of the field. But I don't think I would have known that as clearly without trying the work. Now I know much more what I want to continue with in school.

"People here have been enormously helpful. They know you are an intern and are willing to help you out and give advice. Of course, I also had to deal with office politics. That's some-

Municipality of Metropolitan Seattle. Tammy Adams collects water samples adjacent to Metro's wastewater plant outlet in Puget Sound. These samples are used to test the efficiency of the plant.

thing you don't learn in school and yet it's a major part of any job. The staff at CEIP have been really good about visiting my project and helping me with my career plans. They've given me a base from which to start.

"I'm using the people I've met to help me locate a permanent position with Metro in its Planning Department. I'd like to get work and continue taking classes in environmental planning and technical writing toward a master's in environmental planning."

In Summary

To have a volunteer or internship experience that provides you with a valuable jump on your career, you have to make it happen. You have to carefully choose where you want to work. In many cases, you must take the initiative in designing your project. You must even assert your right to adequate supervision; organizations usually seek volunteers because they are short staffed, and professionals are legendary for underestimating the time and energy it takes to supervise interns properly. Go into positions accepting the reality that the success of your experience is going to depend to a large extent on your drive and commitment. Professionals love volunteers and interns who take initiative and risks. They are the ones who are eventually offered permanent positions.

Resources

DIRECTORIES

California Environmental Directory: A Guide to Organizations and Resources. Gale Research, 835 Penobscot Bldg., Detroit, MI 48226.

Community Jobs. Community Careers Resource Center, 1520 16th St., N.W., Washington, D.C. 20036.

Community Resources Directory. Gale Research.

Conservation Directory (annual). National Wildlife Federation, 1412 16th St., N.W., Washington, D.C. 20036.

Directory of Directories. Gale Research.

Directory of Environmental Groups in New England. Office of Public Affairs, EPA Region 1, JFK Federal Building, Room 2203, Boston, Mass. 02203.

Directory of State Environmental Agencies. Environmental Law Institute, 1616 P St., N.W., No. 200, Washington, D.C. 20036.

Directory of Volunteer Bureaus and Voluntary Action Centers. Volunteer—The National Center, 1111 N. 19th St., Suite 5000, Arlington, Va. 22209.

EARTHWATCH Expeditions. EARTHWATCH, 319 Arlington St., Watertown, Mass. 02172.

Encyclopedia of Associations. Gale Research.

The Great Lakes Directory of Natural Resource Agencies and Organizations (1984). Published by the Freshwater Society, for the Center for the Great Lakes, 435 N. Michigan Ave., Suite 1408, Chicago, Ill. 60611.

Helping Out in the Outdoors: A Directory of Volunteer Jobs in State and National Forests. Northwest Trails Association, 16812 36th Ave. W., Lynwood, Wash. 90836.

International Directory of Volunteer Work. Vacation Work, 9 Park End St., Oxford, England.

Volunteer! The Comprehensive Guide to Voluntary Service in the U.S. and Abroad. Council on International Exchange Services, Campus Services, 205 E. 42nd St., New York, N.Y. 10017.

ORGANIZATIONS

Americans for the Environment, 801 Pennsylvania Ave., S.E., Washington, D.C. 20003.

American Trails Foundation, c/o Ray Sherman, P.O. Box 782, New Castle, Calif. 95658.

Appalachian Mountain Club, 5 Joy St., Boston, Mass. 02108.

Peace Corps, Recruitment Office, 806 Connecticut Ave., N.W., Washington, D.C. 20526.

Volunteers in Overseas Cooperative Assistance, 50 F St., N.W., Suite 9000, Washington, D.C. 20001.

Volunteers in Service to America, 806 Connecticut Ave., N.W., Room 10100, Washington, D.C. 20525.

Volunteer—The National Center, 1111 N. 19th St., Suite 5000, Arlington, Va. 22209.

BOOKS

A New Competitive Edge: Volunteers for the Workplace, by Kenn Allen, Shirley Keller, and Cynthia Vizza (1986). Volunteer—The National Center (address under Organizations in this section).

How to Work with Groups: Guidelines for Volunteers, by Julita Martinez Stone (1983). C. C. Thomas.

MISCELLANEOUS

Independent Sector. A nonprofit coalition of 650 corporate, foundation, and voluntary organization members whose mission is to create a national forum for encouraging donations, volunteering, and not-for-profit initiatives that help the public to serve people, communities, and causes. Publishes *Americans Volunteer 1985; The Board Member's Book: Making a Difference in Voluntary Organizations; Effective Leadership in Voluntary Organizations,* by Brian O'Connell, the organization's president; *Youth Service: A Guidebook for Devel-*

oping and Operating Effective Programs. 1828 L St., N.W., Washington, D.C. 20036.

Volunteers in Technical Assistance. Private organization providing technical assistance to individuals and organizations in the United States and developing countries. Emphasizes helping local groups adapt, implement, and market technologies appropriate to their situations. Concerned with reforestation, soil conservation, renewable energy, and energy conservation. 1815 N. Lynn St., Suite 200, Arlington, Va. 22209.

INTERNSHIPS

The CEIP Fund. Contact the regional office in the area where you wish to intern. See National Environmental Internship Programs, earlier in this chapter, for a description, and this book's preface for addresses.

Student Conservation Association. Develops natural resource internships for students at various levels. See National Environmental Internship Programs, earlier in this chapter, for a description. P.O. Box 550, Charlestown, N.H. 03603.

Internships: A Directory of On-the-Job Training Opportunities for All Career Fields. Writer's Digest Books.

National Directory of Internships. Large section on environmental affairs. National Society of Internships and Experiential Education, 3509 Haworth Dr., Suite 207, Raleigh, N.C. 27609.

4   Breaking into the Environmental Field

THERE ARE a number of stages in the process of developing your career, including education, reflection, and self-examination. You cheat yourself if you don't allow yourself to explore. At some point, however, it is time to get a job.

There are few secrets to job hunting, and no new theories. Job hunting is hard work, plain and simple. Starting a career is a skill that can be learned by anyone. Given today's volatile work world, it is a skill that you will use many times throughout your career.

Throughout your job search, remember this: Act as if you are an environmental professional, and soon you will be one. Read the publications, participate in the associations, talk to the professionals, and do volunteer work. It sounds simple, but not many people do it.

There is at least one secret to getting your career off to a good start. It doesn't concern how to write the perfect résumé, nor is it the knack of uncovering hidden job openings. The trick lies in your attitude or outlook on the process: Are you going to approach it with dread and apprehension or with excitement and creativity? All the raw materials are present to encourage the first mind-set: After all, in the job hunt we enter the world of sales and we must make a lot of cold calls. We are selling ourselves, which makes that dreaded rejection all the more painful; they won't be rejecting a used car or a mutual fund, but *you*.

This fear can cause us to hang back in the career development process, to fantasize about someone doing it for us or knocking on our door with a job offer. With this attitude, we are tempted to take the first offer that comes our way, just to get it over with. Then, all we would have to worry about is being miserable for at least 40 hours a week.

Consider the alternative. This is your life, your career, and depending on your creativity and persistence you can do anything with it that you choose. Try to view all the decisions, phone numbers, and contacts that lie before you as proof of the unlimited opportunities—you are choosing a career in one of the most exciting and diverse fields, one that is undergoing constant change, with new options appearing every day. What can be more exciting than a job search, than picking and choosing where and how you want to focus your creative energy? As for the rejection, there are no answers here, except to say that if you let it stop you, it certainly will. Leaning on a support network of friends, mentors, and fellow job seekers can carry you through.

RESOURCES FOR THE JOB SEARCH

START WITH YOURSELF

The takeoff point for a discussion of resources is to look at your personal resources—your skills and strengths. A salesperson's best resource is familiarity with the product he or she is trying to sell. In this case, the product is you. You have already spent some time thinking about what it is that interests you in the environmental field. You may have also spent some time training to enter the field. Before you try to sell yourself to an employer, however, you must step back, take some time, and do a thorough inventory of your skills and attributes. Then, you have to figure out how to package and market them, how to communicate and demonstrate to employers that you have certain skills: "I am skilled in organizing events and people, as evidenced by my chairing the fund-raising committee of our student environmental group. Our fund-raiser netted $3,000 for our recycling project. I was responsible for coordinating the work of five volunteers on this three-month project."

Many career counselors instruct jobs seekers to visualize their next job in terms of skills rather than job title. It is beyond the scope of this chapter to spend much time on exercises to identify skills or tips on marketing them. Many books, including *What Color Is Your Parachute?*, contain such information. The essence of many of these exercises is to list as many skills as you believe you have acquired, the talents you were born with, and ways you have shown these skills. The next step is to list, in order, those skills you would like to use on your next job or in your career. These exercises are important: They help you decide what you might pursue and prepare you to answer tough interview questions such as "What would you bring to this job?"

WRITTEN MATERIAL, PEOPLE, AND EVENTS

After you know what you want and what you have to offer, the next step is looking for job opportunities, or building your options. Lee DeAngelis, director of Environmental Career Services for The CEIP Fund, says, "There are three main resources to use in learning about opportunities in the environmental field. These are *written material, people,* and *events.* Do not focus exclusively on one of these resources at the expense of the other two."

WRITTEN MATERIAL

Invest some time and money in the variety of written materials that will give you the pulse of the environmental field that interests you, familiarize you with the players, and alert you to job opportunities. This should not be too much of a burden, since you should enjoy reading about the field in which you have chosen to start a career. By the time you are looking for a job, you should already be tapped into the written network: your subscriptions to magazines and newsletters are coming in, your clippings file is bulging with contacts, your student membership in the trade association of your choice has helped you build up your environmental library from their special publications and annual directories, and the environmentally related publishing houses are sending you information about newsletters and special reports. Besides looking into the general resources listed here, you should also study those included in the Resources sections of the subject chapters that interest you.

Newspapers. Read at least one major metropolitan newspaper, especially the paper covering the geographic area in which you would like to work. This will give you the names of organizations, agencies, corporations, and individuals to contact in your job search. The *Wall Street Journal,* the *Washington Post,* and the *New York Times* are excellent sources for those who want to get a sense of national environmental issues.

Free Publications. Many government agencies and nonprofits and some trade associations publish free literature on environmental issues, activities, programs, business developments, and laws. These are often a good source of contacts, job openings, and events. Professionals in the field are very resourceful in finding these freebies to stretch their publications budget; ask each person you meet for the names and addresses of their favorite three.

Magazines, Journals, and Newsletters. There are hundreds of regular publications related to the environmental field. Some, like *Asbestos Abatement Report*, are very specialized. Others, like *Sierra*, cover the environmental protection and natural resource areas writ large. Try to look at both types. Many of these publications can be found in college or public libraries or are received by college faculty and staff. *Directory of Environmental Information Sources* (Government Institutes, Inc., 1988) lists over 200 U.S. and 50 foreign environmental protection–related publications. The *Conservation Directory*, published annually by the National Wildlife Federation, lists natural resources–related publications. All libraries have card catalogs or on-line directories, and many can locate publications available at other libraries.

Annual Reports and Miscellaneous Literature. Virtually all government agencies and nonprofits publish some kind of annual report. Public corporations have annual reports and financial disclosure (10-K) reports (required by the Securities and Exchange Commission). These can be excellent snapshots of a company, agency, or organization: who works there; what the company does; issues it is facing; past, current, and future projects and priorities; and some budget information. Realize, however, that organizations are trying to portray themselves in the best light possible with these documents. Even if these annual reports do not speak directly about a company's environmental work, they identify facilities, plants, and all other company properties, as well as the top one or two officials in health, safety, and environmental affairs. Avoid going into a job interview or even an informational interview without having read the company's, agency's, or organization's annual report. Your current knowledge about an organization demonstrates initiative and commitment.

Directories. A variety of directories will help you identify organizations, companies, consultants, agencies, individuals, and publications. Never assume a directory doesn't exist, no matter how specialized or even trivial the information might seem. Some of the environmental directories are listed at the end of this chapter, under Resources.

Data Bases. The computer age provides you with limitless access to information. You can do very specified literature searches in minutes that would have taken days or just been impossible if done by hand. Electronic bulletin boards are a source of information about events, publications, and job openings. Finally, environmental-specific job listing services are available on computer. A relatively small number of people, least of all students, have access to these data bases because of their cost and logistical considerations. Public and university libraries often provide subsidized access to data bases, and career placement offices may be tied to electronic job listing services. And yes, there are directories of data bases.

PEOPLE

People are your best resource in the job hunt, be they neighbors, classmates, professionals, experts, friends, or casual acquaintances. One of the cardinal rules of job hunting is that you go out of your way to tell *everyone* you come in contact with that you are looking for a job—and give as much specific information as possible on the type of job. Most of us love to help others, especially when it is as easy as giving someone a name or making a phone call. And since we all know many people, each time you tell someone, your list of names and potential contacts expands logarithmically. Just to jog your creativity, here are a few categories of people resources:

College Faculty, Staff, and Students. If you are presently or have recently been in school, talk to your teachers, advisers, career counselors, and fellow students. Many professors are actively engaged in outside research or consulting projects or are at least familiar with professionals in the field. They may be able to provide a key recommendation to an employer they know personally. Students from smaller colleges or programs should consider seeking advice from staff at universities with larger environmentally related schools or programs. These programs often have at least one person who does career counseling. Time permitting, such counselors will often accommodate nonstudents, especially if you express an interest in graduate study at their university.

Alumni. A key resource for students and job seekers are alumni of their departments and training programs. Many graduates are now working in your field of choice. They share with you a bond, having gone to the same school and had similar teachers, courses, and experiences. Hence, they are often willing to help later generations of students. Some programs actively track the careers of alumni and work to tap into this source of information, expertise, and contacts for the benefit of current students and recent graduates. The Cornell University Department of Agricultural and Biological Engineering, for example, has developed the Cornell Alumni Career Advisory Network and an alumni profile sheet to link students and alumni. If your school does not have such a program, you might advocate for the establishment of one.

Friends, Relatives, and Neighbors. Don't overlook the obvious. Think about how many successful job hunting stories you know that included such phrases as "My uncle put me in touch with a consultant who was working in Detroit." They won't know, however, unless you tell them very specifically, and repeatedly, what you are looking for.

Professional Societies. The best way to meet people who can help your environmental career is to get involved in the field by joining the professional societies. The professionals you meet can provide advice, furnish leads, and attest to your qualifications.

Volunteering. This is another way to build up a list of contacts while getting experience and learning about the field. See chapter 3 for information on where to find volunteer opportunities and internships.

EVENTS

In most larger cities, aspiring professionals can attend a variety of environmentally oriented conferences, seminars, and meetings. In fact, few professions have so many events, perhaps a reflection of the diversity and depth of the environmental field. These events are sponsored by government agencies at all levels, consulting firms, corporations, trade and professional associations, and nonprofit organizations.

Attending a conference as a job seeker allows you to meet people, in a way that may be less intimidating than making cold calls or visits. If you were hoping to get into the hazardous waste field, for example, what could be a better use of your time than to spend a day meeting people at a conference put on by the EPA to explain how consultants prepare bids for Superfund contracts? You'll make personal contacts and learn about opportunities, such as what types of work the EPA is going to contract out to consultants and where some jobs might be created as a result. Moreover, simply mentioning to an interviewer something you learned at the conference can only make a good impression.

If you are a student or aspiring professional attending these conferences you have little competition from your peers, since most of your fellow attendees are seasoned professionals. Professionals are impressed when they see students at conferences and are often willing to talk with you.

How to find out about these events? The same way you find out about written materials. See if your EPA region has an events newsletter, and look at the events notices in local newspapers.

INFORMATIONAL INTERVIEWING

You may find it useful to talk with people who are actually doing the work you think you would like to do. This is commonly called informational interviewing. It is an excellent way of "trying on" a job before you decide to go out and get one. If you go about informational interviewing in the proper manner you will usually get a positive response from professionals—after all, most people like to talk about their job and their work.

A word of warning: Don't tell professionals you want an informational interview when you are actually looking for a job. This will turn off employers; nobody likes to be deceived. So many have abused this type of interview that you probably shouldn't even call it an informational interview. Instead, merely tell them instead that you are doing research prior to making a career decision and would like a few minutes of their time.

Some tips for informational interviewing:

- Talk to people who are actually doing the work that interests you, not to those who hire these people. You are not looking for a job but trying to find out what type of job you are going to be looking for.
- Find these people using the resources outlined in this chapter. At the conclusion of each interview, ask for the names of two people doing similar work who might be willing to meet with you. Also ask this question if you are refused an interview.
- Tell these people you want only 20 to 30 minutes of their time, and don't stay any longer.
- Don't waste their time by asking questions that you could have answered on your own by doing research on the company or the profession, or by talking to somebody below them in the organization's hierarchy. You should be asking, "What do you like about this work?," *not* "What regulations do you have to deal with?"
- Thank them profusely—30 minutes is a big gift for a busy professional to give to a stranger. Always send a thank-you note, even if it is handwritten, and, later, apprise them of your progress.
- Finally, there is nothing wrong with coming back to these people when you are actually looking for a job. Just be upfront. They will probably already have a positive impression of you based on the initiative you have shown in your career search.

JOB HUNTING 101

If you do not know some of the basic job hunting strategies, your job search will be long, frustrating, and difficult. Hundreds of generic job hunting and career books crowd the market; some are gems, others fluff (see Resources at the end of this chapter for some recommendations). Ask fellow job seekers and career counselors what their favorites are.

What follows is the key advice gathered from these publications and from the collective experience of The CEIP Fund in helping young professionals establish environmental careers over the past 17 years.

It is most important to immediately demystify the process in your mind: Effective job hunting is mostly common sense, hard work, organization, and persistence. Don't let anyone tell you you haven't been in the real world. If you have ever worked or been through school, you have.

Take the time you need to find the right job. Career counselors note that the average career-related job hunt takes six months to a year. Ava Butler, a free-lance career consultant in Seattle, advises, "You need to look at your career as a long-term research project that always takes much longer and more effort than you want it to." Structure your life so that you aren't forced by economics or anxiety to take the first offer. Lay the groundwork months before you actually want to start a position. Put some time into your search; according to *What Color Is Your Parachute?*, two thirds of all job hunters spend fewer than five hours a week on the process, so it takes them two months to log just one week of full-time job hunting.

A strategy of blanketing employers with résumés and "To whom it may concern" cover letters takes an enormous amount of time and is probably not going to work. One study found that employers sent out one invitation to interview for every 245 résumés sent cold to their firm. Richard Nelson Bolles, in *What Color Is Your Parachute?*, outlines an alternative strategy based on personal visits, networking, creativity, and hard work. Thus, résumés serve to cement a building process that begins with conversations, contacts, and reputation. To get this process going in the environmental field, volunteer, join professional associations, attend conferences, read, and be aggressive in talking to people in your chosen field.

Even though résumés are given more importance than they deserve, spend some time on yours. Two good books: *Damn Good Résumé Guide*, by Yana Parker, which also talks about cover letters, and *Don't Use a Résumé . . . Use a Qualifications Brief*, by Richard Lathrop. If you are straight out of school, sticking to one page is sufficient; however, it is more important that you include all that is important than that you keep it to one page. Employers want to know as much about you as possible. Be crisp. Become an expert at tailoring résumés to specific jobs: Employers like it to look as if your whole life has been leading you to a particular position.

Cover letters are meant to highlight parts of your résumé that especially qualify you for the job, demonstrate that you have done your homework, and convey enthusiasm for this line of work. Don't *ever* have a misspelling or typo on your résumé, cover letter, or any other correspondence to an employer. "If they can't even get it right on a job application, what kind of attention will they pay to important details after we hire them?"

Ask questions at job interviews. It shows some interest and psychologically conveys the feeling that you have options, which immediately boosts your stock. Perhaps one of the biggest mistakes job seekers make at interviews is being so determined to come across as cool and professional that they don't show any enthusiasm. Employers like to hire upbeat, excited, and motivated people.

Always send a thank you to the interviewer and anyone else who talked to you or helped you in some way, including support staff. Input is often solicited from everyone who had contact with you. Reiterate any points you want to make about your interest and skills.

Very close to the week when they will be making their decision, call to express your interest. Many times a decision on whom to hire is a close call. Once it is down to a few qualified finalists, gut reactions are important. Showing interest in a professional manner could tip the balance in your favor.

If you do not get the job, send a letter to the lead interviewer expressing interest in future positions. You may want to call and ask about other job leads and ask them to circulate your résumé if appropriate.

In the best of times job hunting is frustrating. Lean on your support network of friends, mentors, and job hunting companions.

Lee DeAngelis of CEIP points out, "Employers are practical people. They are interested in what you can do for them, how you can help them solve their problems, and make their work life easier. They want employees who will fit in with their organization, other employees, and the people the organization serves. Finally, they want people who will take on their agenda and be productive and cooperative."

EMPLOYMENT AGENCIES AND RECRUITING FIRMS

Should you use an employment agency or similar organization in your environmental job search? Probably not. Employment agencies are specialists at placing people in high-demand fields. They focus on secretarial, data processing, and accounting personnel. Executive recruiting firms usually search for experienced, well-qualified people for organizations. Outplacement firms have contracts with organizations that are reducing their staff; employees who are being laid off are given preference in placement.

All these operations will eagerly seek your business—and some will want your money, too. However, for the environmental job seeker, it would probably be a bad investment. The exception might be if you are experienced in a high-demand environmental discipline such as environmental engineering, chemistry, hydrogeology, toxicology, or other technical specialties. In such cases, executive recruiting firms may be worth investigating, although you probably won't need much help finding a job. You may, however, want to consider employment agencies to place you in short-term jobs while you are looking for full-time environmental employment. Having a part-time job is a good way to allow yourself to take the necessary time for a thorough job search. It also pays a few bills. You may be able to arrange a placement in an environmental department or corporation, even if the work is not, at first, related to the environment.

MINORITIES AND THE DISABLED IN ENVIRONMENTAL PROFESSIONS

The environmental profession has done an admirable job of removing the barriers that kept women from joining its ranks. Unfortunately, the profession's record in increasing the percentage of minorities taking up environmental careers can only be called poor.

Why is this so? Without excusing the lack of a significant recruitment effort by the profession, we can cite many factors beyond the direct control of the field. One of these is the decline in minority students entering and graduating from college, no doubt owing in large part to rising college expenses. Another reason is that talented minority students at the high school and college levels are heavily recruited for the more traditional careers of medicine, law, engineering, and business. The environmental professions have not responded with adequate recruitment, nor have they done much to encourage or assist minority students in preparing at the high school level for postsecondary education leading to an environmental career.

Yet opportunities definitely exist for minorities in the environmental field. Many federal and state agencies have special recruitment programs aimed at minority applicants. Some also have internship programs for minorities starting in high school. Colleges and universities with environmental programs also are looking for more minority applicants. Reports indicate this country will soon face a shortage of qualified technical and scientific workers. Employers are looking at all options for increasing the numbers of these professionals. One way is to communicate that salaries in the environmental field are competitive with those in other professions being chosen by young minorities.

There is a growing awareness among minority populations that environmental issues are often of special concern to them, whether it is a community organization fighting a toxic waste dump on the South Side of Chicago or migrant workers worried about the harmful effects of pesticides on their children's health. The United Church of Christ's Commission on Racial Justice, for example, found that, nationally, communities with two or more hazardous waste sites have three times the percentage of minorities than those with no waste sites, and that three out of five Blacks and Hispanics live in communities that have illegal or abandoned dumps. Clearly, minorities have an incentive to follow environmental careers, but some encouragement from the profession is required to eliminate the obstacles. See the Profiles of Jerlena Griffen and Aubrey Smith in chapter 3 for examples of minority students who took advantage of special programs in beginning their careers.

Some who are physically challenged may rule out an environmental career because of their limited mobility. That would be a loss to the individual and to the profession. Jobs in the environmental field are as diverse as the work world itself—one does not have to be a backcountry ranger to work in this field. Many in the profession spend their time working to improve human interaction with and access to the environment, for example by providing access for the physically disabled to outdoor recreational facilities or designing mass transit systems that benefit the environment and the disabled. Who, after all, could design better outdoor recreation areas than someone who has first-hand experience with the wall of exclusion created by a six-inch curb?

This profession is in need of qualified professionals, and it creates its own handicap if it excludes, either directly or indirectly, any segment of the population. Consider the following professionals, profiled in *Able Scientists—Disabled Persons* (Foundation for Science and the Handicapped), who have not allowed themselves to be passed over and have aided the environment in the process.

- R. Kent Jones, B.S., who has multiple sclerosis, is a civil engineer with the Metropolitan Sanitary District of Greater Chicago. He directs the activities of his section from his wheelchair.
- Cynthia Dusel-Bacon, B.A., who had an arm amputated, is a geologist in the U.S. Geological Survey and uses a specially adapted microscope to study geological characteristics of rock slices.
- Odette L. Shotwell, Ph.D., with disabilities from postpolio, is an organic chemist at the Northern Regional Research Center, U.S. Department of Agriculture, in Peoria, Illinois, where she heads a department of eight specialists.

See pages 86–87 for more information on career resources for minorities and the disabled.

Resources

ENVIRONMENTAL JOB LISTINGS

Job Scan (monthly). Contains at least 100 job listings at all levels in environmental fields. Student Conservation Association, P.O. Box 550, Charlestown, N.H. 03603.

Environmental Opportunities (monthly). Listing of permanent, seasonal, and internship opportunities around the country, primarily in natural resource management, with nonprofits and government agencies. P.O. Box 969, Stowe, Vt. 05672.

The Job Seeker (biweekly). Listing of permanent, seasonal, and internship opportunities around the country, primarily in natural resource management with nonprofits and government agencies. Route 2, Box 16, Warrens, Wis. 54666.

Environmental Job Opportunities Bulletin (ten times a year). Listing of job openings with environmental groups, government agencies, nature centers, consulting firms, colleges, and universities around the country. Institute for Environmental Studies, University of Wisconsin, 550 N. Park St., Madison, Wis. 53706.

JOBSource. Computer program with a data base of current professional job vacancies. Specializes in natural resources, natural sciences, agriculture, and liberal arts. If you are a member of the American Fisheries Society or the Wildlife Society, see the listing for JOBSource under Resources in chapter 12. 418 S. Howes St., Suite D, Fort Collins, Colo. 80521.

EcoNet. International computer network serving the environmental community. Has 100 electronic bulletin boards on environmental topics, issues, services, events, news, and so on. One board is a job listing that is constantly updated. 3228 Sacramento St., San Francisco, Calif. 94115.

GENERAL CAREER INFORMATION

What Color Is Your Parachute?, by Richard Nelson Bolles (annual). A guide to career planning and job searches. If you don't own it, buy it—and read it. Ten Speed Press.

Don't Use a Résumé ... Use a Qualifications Brief, by Richard Lathrop (1980). There are many, many books on résumé writing. It would be difficult to do better than this one. Ten Speed Press.

Damn Good Résumé Guide, by Yana Parker (1983). Ten Speed Press.

The Way of the Ronin: A Guide to Career Strategy, by Beverly Potter (1984). A discussion of the new work world and the type of employee who will flourish: one who is flexible and willing to make horizontal shifts in career paths, focusing on transferable skills. American Management Association.

PROFESSIONAL ASSOCIATION

National Association of Environmental Professionals. Interdisciplinary professional society. Offers student memberships. Publishes newsletter (monthly) and *The Environmental Professional* (quarterly). P.O. Box 15210, Alexandria, Va. 22309.

DIRECTORIES

Encyclopedia of Associations (1989). Five volumes: volume 1 (three books), *National Organizations of the United States*; volume 2, *Geographic and Executive Indexes*; volume 3, *New Associations and Projects*. Gale Research.

International Organizations (1989). Focuses on associations that are nonprofit, international in scope and membership, and headquartered outside the United States. Gale Research.

Regional, State, and Local Organizations (1989). Lists local, state, and regional nonprofit membership organizations in the United States and its territories. Gale Research.

Association Periodicals (1989). Describes journals, magazines, bulletins, directories, and other publications issued serially by associations, societies, institutes, and other nonprofit membership organizations. Gale Research.

Directory of Directories (4th ed., 1987). A comprehensive publication whose subtitle explains it all: "An Annotated Guide to Approximately 9,600 Business and Industrial Directories, Professional and Scientific Rosters, [and] Directory Databases." Gale Research.

Consultants and Consulting Organizations Directory (1989). Organized according to consulting activity and geographic location. Gale Research.

DATA BASES

Directory of Environmental Information, edited by Thomas Sullivan and Richard Hill (1988). Lists and describes over 100 environmental data bases and data services, as well as information on government agencies, professional associations, and periodicals. Government Institutes, 966 Hungerford Dr., No. 24, Rockville, Md. 20850.

MINORITIES

The Black Resource Guide (1988). Lists over 1,500 national resources in 36 categories for Black persons. R. Benjamin Johnson and Jacqueline L. Johnson, 501 Oneida Place, N.W., Washington, D.C. 20011.

Directory of Special Programs for Minority Group Members: Career Information Services, Employment Skills Banks, Financial Aid Sources, edited by Willis L. Johnson (4th ed., 1986). Information on 1,700 general programs, 360 federal programs, and hundreds of others sponsored by colleges and universities. Garrett Park Press, P.O. Box 190-B, Garrett Park, Md. 20896.

JOB SEEKERS WITH DISABILITIES

Resource Directory of Scientists and Engineers with Disabilities. Intended as a resource for students with disabilities interested in careers in science and engineering. American Association for the Advancement of Science.

Able Scientists—Disabled Persons (1984). Published for the Foundation for Science and the Handicapped. J. Racila Associations, 2820 Oak Brook Rd., Oak Brook, Ill. 60521.

INTERNATIONAL EMPLOYMENT

The Job Seekers Guide to Opportunities in Natural Resource Management for the Developing World (1986). Describes organizations, opportunities, minimum qualifications, and procedures for employment inquiries. International Institute for Environment and Development, 1717 Massachusetts Ave., N.W., Suite 302, Washington, D.C. 20036.

Part II

PLANNERS AND COMMUNICATORS

5 The Planning Profession

Donna Killebrew, a biologist with the Snohomish County Public Works Department in Washington state, is overseeing a land development review and stream rehabilitation project as part of a statewide program to review watersheds and prevent and remedy pollution and development problems.

Gary Ellsworth, a planner with the Cuyahoga County Regional Planning Commission in Cleveland, Ohio, is conducting an inventory of physical deterioration of an industrial and commercial corridor as part of a corridor revitalization project.

Kent Fuller, Senior Advisor to the Director, Great Lakes National Program Office, is involved in planning, negotiating, and implementing the Great Lakes Water Quality Agreement between the United States and Canada.

Richard DiSanza, a waterfront planner with Emanuel Associates in Nyack, New York, is updating a master plan for the city of Stony Point, on the Hudson River, which will include an inventory of the city's resources, a description of citizens' priorities, and recommendations and policy development initiatives.

THESE PROFESSIONALS have very different jobs and careers. A major part of all of their jobs, however, is planning. Planning is a *process*, rather than an issue, so it can cross the boundaries from one environmental field to another. Since planners are often called on to integrate the technical and the creative, many consider planning to be a fusion of science and art.

Cleveland, Ohio. This redevelopment project involves converting a parking lot, once a city dump, into a popular waterfront attraction.

The American Planning Association (APA) defines planning as a "systematic, creative approach used to address and resolve social, physical, and economic problems of neighborhoods, cities, suburbs, metropolitan areas and larger regions." And what do planners do?

Jim Bernard, director of the Natural Resources Division of the State Planning Office in Maine, captures the essence of a planner's role when he says, "Planners are ideally agents of change; anticipating the consequences of proposed actions or, better yet, anticipating what will be proposed and responding in a proactive, rather than reactive, manner with policy and program initiatives."

Planning encompasses a number of different roles, including research, technical analysis, advocating social change, design, program development, and management and education. Most planners are involved in all of these activities at various points in their careers.

PLANNING AS AN ENVIRONMENTAL CAREER

Although many environmental professionals use planning as a tool in their careers, there is a subgroup for whom planning is a primary responsibility. Likewise, most planners, although they are not usually considered environmental professionals, must pay attention to environmental concerns in their work—from the development planner who conducts an environmental impact assessment as part of a housing development, to the transportation planner analyzing the effect of mass transit programs on the need for new roads, to the policy analyst who must consider access to recreation in devising economic development initiatives.

TYPES OF PLANNING AND PLANNERS

Since there is considerable overlap in the planning profession, categorization is somewhat artificial. Still, it is useful to divide the field of planning into several areas:

- Urban Planning. Urban planners work on such issues as transportation, housing, commercial and industrial development, infrastructure, neighborhood redevelopment, historic preservation, and the gamut of social planning issues. Urban planners work in cities and towns of all sizes.
- Regional Planning. Regional planners work on a larger geographical scale than do urban planners; their territory may or may not be based on political divisions (cities, counties, and states). The Tennessee Valley Authority, for example, which employs land-use, environmental, economic, and general planners, is based on a watershed.
- Policy Planning. Issues, rather than geography, define the territory of policy planners, who develop and implement policies in such areas as the environment and economics.

Environmental planning is a specialization practiced by urban, regional, and policy planners. Dick Booth, a program director in the City and Regional Planning Department at Cornell University, defines environmental planning as "the utilization of the world's resources to ensure human needs are served in a context that allows for long-term stability of the environment." This underscores the interdisciplinary requirements and challenges of the profession. Although environmental planning can be viewed as a specialization, concern for environmental matters should permeate all aspects of the planning process.

The impetus for making environmental planning a profession in its own right probably came from the National Environmental Policy Act of 1970. The aim of this Act was to formulate a national policy to ensure a harmonious relationship between humans and their environment. The substance of this legislation is the requirement that environmental impact statements be prepared for major federal projects. States have also required that these studies be carried out for their own projects. Much of the major environmental legislation calls for a planning phase in development projects, including the 1972 Coastal Zone Management Act, the Resource

Conservation and Recovery Act (RCRA), Superfund, and the Clean Air and Clean Water acts.

Environmental planners are working on environmental issues ranging from air quality to fisheries. Some planners, like Beth Nuss, an urban planner in Cleveland who is helping a suburb upgrade its park system, may work on environmental issues as one part of their work. Other planners, like the EPA's Kent Fuller, may focus almost exclusively on environmental issues.

If planning is such an integral part of the various environmental fields, what separates the environmental planner from any other environmental professional? The answer, according to Jim Bernard, is that "planners are those who, because of the way their job is structured, get to see the real picture and realize that the whole is greater than the sum of its parts. A staffer for a water quality agency would look at applicable regulations when issuing a permit to an industry discharging into a particular river; an environmental planner wants to know what effect that discharger is going to have on the ecology of the watershed and the gulf that it empties into."

WHERE WOULD YOU WORK?

Of the estimated 30,000 planners in the United States (Fanning, *Opportunities in Environmental Careers*), the APA figures that about two thirds work in the public sector, most with local units of government—on the level of city, county, or region—and the remaining one third work in the private sector. Federal and state government employ more policy planners and planners in the areas of housing, transportation, and environmental protection. The largest federal employers of urban and regional planners are the Departments of Transportation, Defense, and Housing and Urban Development.

Planners in large cities may specialize in such areas as zoning, historic preservation, and energy planning. Small-town planners might do it all, including rewriting a town's zoning regulations, updating a master plan, and working with developers. The Profiles and Case Study in this chapter should give you a sense of the different roles played by planners in various geographical areas.

Of the one third of planners employed in the private sector, the largest group works for consulting firms hired by local, state, and occasionally the federal government. Consultants in the planning field are not as numerous as in some other environmental fields, such as hazardous waste. Many planners, however, work for consulting firms that specialize in certain environmental issues. Moreover, many engineering firms used to have large planning departments, which were eliminated when federal funds for urban areas were cut in the 1980s.

Planners also work for banks and real estate development companies, architectural firms, market research firms, transportation companies, and nonprofit organizations and foundations working on zoning issues, master plans, development projects, and design. Utilities and large waste management firms hire planners to work on siting issues.

Planners with expertise in environmental matters are employed in all of the sectors discussed here. Such planners include the professional developing a solid waste plan for a municipality, the land-use planning consultant helping a small New England town cope with development pressures, and the state or federal employee formulating pollution control strategies.

TRENDS IN PLANNING

The decline in federal funds for cities has reduced opportunities in urban planning. There have been dramatic declines in federal funding of Community Development Block Grant programs, which in some areas have been slashed by more than 50 percent, and in other forms of revenue sharing and grants. This has affected employment in the public and private sectors: City and regional planning agencies have eliminated staff positions, and public consulting dollars are harder to come by.

Removal of a consistent funding base for urban planning has contributed to another significant trend: Opportunities in planning vary greatly by region. According to Gary Ellsworth of the Cuyahoga County Regional Planning Commission, "Planning jobs are most plentiful in areas that are in the midst of rapid growth or an economic boom." Look at regional economies when you are thinking about job markets. Areas that are now particularly bright for planners include California, which has more planners than any other state, the Sun Belt—especially Florida, Texas, and Arizona—and New England.

James Kastelic, also with the Cuyahoga County Regional Planning Commission, says, "Issues relevant to older urban areas include redeveloping and shoring up an aging infrastructure, and historic preservation. In addition, I believe planners are increasingly going to be tackling social issues—elderly, the poor, health care, and housing." Planners with a traditional planning education may not be prepared to work on these issues, which are often considered outside the realm of planning. Finally, with public support drying up and local budgets becoming tight, older urban areas are looking increasingly to public-private partnerships.

Another urban planning trend is the megalopolis, an area so large that no matter where you go development is pervasive. According to Evelyn Martin of the APA, "We see this on the East and West coasts; as one urban area ends, another begins. This creates many new demands on the planning professional, especially in the environmental and regulatory areas: air and water quality planning, solid waste disposal, energy planning. A related development is the decreased reliance on the central city. Formerly, jobs were in the cities and workers commuted from the suburbs, or bedroom communities. Many jobs are now being created in the suburbs, and employees are increasingly living in areas beyond the suburbs, known as exurbia, and commuting in to the suburbs. This creates a host of challenges for planners: transportation and environmental problems, intergovernmental conflicts, and social changes."

States are playing a larger role in policy planning. According to Mark Popovich, senior staff associate of the Council of State Policy and Planning Agencies, "This is a longer trend than new federalism—the transfer of authority from the federal government to states in the 1980s. This reflects that states are a major public resource: State government has become more professional, governors are becoming active managers, and state work forces are taking on a broader range of issues. I don't think this is going to change. Take the issue of storage of low-level radioactive waste. In the sixties the federal government, through the Department of Energy, might have just said, 'All right, we'll decide where to store this stuff.' Now, however, states are forming interstate compacts for long-term storage and will be responsible for management and oversight of these facilities. Some states also opted not to form compacts, which, to me, reflects the diversity of state involvement in policy issues." With this greater role in policy issues, states are using more policy planning tools, like data bases, to ascertain future trends, and they also need more policy planning professionals.

There is some consensus, however, that environmental planning, which had its golden age in the late 1970s, may be making a comeback. Dick Booth of Cornell asserts, "With all the environmental problems and development pressures, environmental planning is definitely a growth field. A great many of our graduates enter specific environmental planning fields: hazardous waste, solid waste, and energy planning, to name a few." Jim Bernard agrees: "Everywhere people are becoming more aware of the need for better water quality planning for groundwater, rivers, lakes, streams, coastal areas, and the Great Lakes. Water resources can be considered a bottom line, because ultimately it limits growth in a particular area.

"In addition, in many areas, especially the coastal states, developmental pressures are being felt, resulting in a dilution of the quality of life. Here in Maine, the legislature has responded with comprehensive legislation mandating land-use planning in every county. That has instantly created 13 new planning jobs at the state level and who knows how many local and consulting positions." In short, environmental planners are concerned with everything that is scarce and everything that causes a problem in our relationship to the natural environment.

As in other planning areas, much of the initiative in environmental planning is occurring at the state level. Bernard says, "In environmental planning, the state level is where I want to be. At the local level you don't have as much latitude because you do so much trench fighting and have so many political boundaries to contend with. This makes working on environmental issues, while very important, very difficult at the local level. At the federal level, it's just as bad, but for different reasons; you get locked into regulations and more hierarchy and, recently, political volatility. Given this vacuum, it is the states that are carrying the ball."

Paralleling the increase in planning at the state level, regional planning in natural resources and environmental issues, which was at a high point in the late seventies and early eighties, is yielding to watershed-based and interstate planning. Instead of a few counties joining forces, an entire state or several states become involved in an issue. Many see this type of arrangement as a more pragmatic response to the realities of politics and natural resource management. For example, the New England Interstate Water Pollution Control Commission works on a wide variety of surface water and groundwater issues for the six New England states and New York. Susan Redlich, groundwater coordinator for the commission, helps these states coordinate their groundwater monitoring and regulatory activities.

Almost every interstate agency is concerned about hazardous waste, water quality, solid waste, and groundwater, but the focus of these agencies varies depending on the area and its environmental, geographic, and economic circumstances. Interstate planning in the Rocky Mountains or the Ozarks varies dramatically from planning on the Atlantic seaboard.

GETTING STARTED

The single most important factor in getting your first planning job is to have some practical experience, several internships if possible. In addition to experience, skills, and contacts, this gives you references from people who have seen you do the kind of work you now want to get paid for. Fifteen years ago that wasn't so common; now it is a virtual prerequisite for the field.

Evelyn Martin, Director of Professional
Development, American Planning
Association

If you want to be an environmental planner, a strategy that is hard to beat would be to obtain an undergraduate degree in the sciences or environmental studies, find some environmentally related work for a few years, and then get a master's degree in planning from a program that is accredited by the Planning Accreditation Board and that has some environmental emphasis you wish to pursue.

> Jim Bernard, Director, Natural
> Resources Division, State Planning
> Office, State of Maine

There are many different types of planning positions and ways in which planning is integrated into a career. Consequently, there are many ways to enter the field. You could obtain an undergraduate degree in planning, geography, urban studies, environmental studies, or natural resource management, and get a job if you came from a good school and had a lot of experience and a certain amount of luck. Another route, which is usually the surer way to success, has already been outlined: Acquire an undergraduate degree, some work experience, and a master's degree in planning. Most interviewed recommended that if you intend to pursue a master's in planning, you are better off using your undergraduate years to diversify and build a foundation in another area, such as the sciences, economics, political science, or communications. Finally, professionals are often promoted into planning positions based on their experience and knowledge of specific issues, such as hazardous waste or watershed management.

What skills, then, are needed for a career in planning? There appears to be some disparity between the skills that many consider necessary and those they see planners actually using—or not using—in their work. John McNulty, executive director of Partners for Livable Places, is most vocal on this issue. "There is a dearth of creativity in local planning departments today," he asserts. "There are too many report writers and pencil pushers who never take the lead. They are being bypassed by economic development departments and nonprofit organizations. We need to create a new type of professional who knows how to manage change. This is not done by churning out planners who focus on computer modeling and data crunching, but by training planners with a diversity of skills, including communications, law, economics, environmental issues, coalition building, politics, historic preservation, architecture, zoning, and mediation."

Planners' tools are their ability to think and reason, to identify problems and goals, to analyze, and to evaluate and develop a plan of action—that is, to implement. Professionals acknowledge that these skills take time to develop. That is precisely why internships and other forms of work experience are so vital to starting out in this field.

There are ways to develop some more specific skills that you can take to a prospective employer. Pursue a specialty within an academic program: a four-course sequence in environmental planning or an independent transportation project. Other skills that could help you get your foot in the door include graphic design, cartography, experience with census data, architecture, knowledge of zoning law, and demonstrated computer literacy and writing ability.

It does not appear that one sector is better than another for entry-level positions in this field. Rather than targeting consulting firms or state governments based on job prospects, a better strategy would probably be to look at areas of the country where planners are finding work—keeping in mind that openings occur even in the tightest markets. As the APA's Evelyn Martin says, "Once you get your first planning job, you've got it made." Your first job will likely be assisting upper-level planners with their projects by gathering data—in the field and the library—and maybe by doing production work, such as cartography, technical writing, paperwork, and production of graphics. Of course, it is entirely possible that if you are hired by a small town or consulting firm you could be thrown right into your own projects. All the more reason to complete independent projects and internships in school.

Although it is not a stated requirement for most jobs, the best positions usually go to those with master's degrees. This degree does not always have to be in planning, but could be in such areas as public policy, resource management, urban studies, economics, or resource economics. (As always, there are many exceptions for those who are creative and resourceful.) The Planning Accreditation Board (PAB), affiliated with the APA, accredits programs leading to degrees in planning. Ten of the approximately 30 undergraduate programs in the United States are accredited by PAB; 60 of the 100 master's programs get PAB's seal of approval. PAB looks for course work in theory and history, an emphasis on physical planning, economic organization, administration and government, and communications, and a final project that ties the course work together. Getting a degree from a school not accredited by PAB does not prevent you from being a practicing planner, but the lack of accreditation should cause you to look closely at the school's curriculum (something you should do anyway). If you are interested in environmental planning, make sure the school offers adequate course work and opportunities for independent study in that area.

SALARY

The demand for planners varies significantly from region to region, as do salaries. What follows are average figures. Those entering the planning field with B.A.s will receive starting salaries between $14,000 and

$20,000. Entry-level positions for those with M.A.s will pay about $18,000 to $24,000. An APA salary survey in 1985 found that:

- Planners with urban and suburban public agencies earn more than their counterparts in rural or exurban areas. In general, the larger the jurisdiction the higher the salary.
- Median salaries are the highest in the Pacific region; planners working in New England showed the highest percentage increase in median salaries between 1983 and 1985.
- The age of working planners is increasing, the number of minorities in the field decreasing, and the ratio of women to men increasing.

CASE STUDY

Cuyahoga County Regional Planning Commission

Cuyahoga County, Ohio, contains 59 communities ranging from Cleveland, with its sprawling industrial sector, healthy downtown, and struggling inner-city neighborhoods, to unincorporated townships and exclusive suburbs; the county encompasses industrial corridors, the third-largest urban park system in the country, and developments on the shores of rebounding Lake Erie. In short, Cuyahoga County runs the gamut of urban planning challenges.

To provide for coherent countywide and local planning, the Cuyahoga County Regional Planning Commission was created in 1947 by the county and its municipalities with the aid of state enabling legislation. According to acting director James Kastelic, "The mission of the commission is to provide a variety of planning, coordinating, and evaluation services to the county and member municipalities. This takes in innumerable functions and activities, including assessing the impacts of proposed developments on municipalities and the county, long- and short-range planning, economic development, zoning issues, helping communities secure state and federal grants, siting county facilities such as offices or treatment plants, solid waste management, airport construction, and coastal zone management."

Kastelic adds, "We are also involved in land-use issues, historic preservation, and natural resource and environmental planning. Our products are plans, studies, maps, and recommendations for whatever public body we are working for at the time. Funding comes from the county budget, municipal dues, and state and federal grants. By paying annual dues, municipalities in Cuyahoga County become eligible to contract our planning services at cost. In effect, we are a municipal consulting firm."

As recently as 1983, the commission had a staff of 12 planners, but because of state and federal cutbacks they are down to five planners and three administrative support staff. Planners' jobs are graded from 1 to 4, with a planner 4, or managing planner, being the highest-level professional. Kastelic notes, "We try to hire people who are flexible and can continually broaden their focus, working on a variety of projects, tying in their skills and experiences—that is how you climb in this business. However, within an agency people do begin to develop some specialties. For example one of our planners tends to focus on community development, another on economic development. Another planner has more of a cartographic background. Finally, one of our managing planners works more on physical environment projects, and the other is more zoning oriented— this works out well for the agency.

"As the acting director and deputy director, I divide my time into supervising existing work and finding ways to bring in more money and projects. I would characterize my day-to-day activities as quite hectic. About half of my time each day is spent reviewing the various projects our staff is involved with, reviewing the work, making sure we are on schedule and within budget.

"The other half of my day is spent drumming up projects. A community may call with a prospective project and I or one of the managing planners will meet with a municipal council, planning commission, or mayor to discuss their project. Then they will ask me to put together a work proposal. This can range from a simple study, such as the impact of a small housing tract, to a major overhaul of their zoning code.

"It's important to keep in mind that, like most planning agencies, we are an advisory, not a regulatory, body. We give advice and it is up to the county or municipality whether they act on it. This can be frustrating. Then there is the political arena to contend with. Planners try to stay unbiased and out of the political fray but can't always avoid it.

"The satisfaction of this job comes from seeing a project to fruition, from planning to implementation. This usually takes several years or longer. Or from having developed information on, say, vacant parcels of land, which down the road bring business and jobs into a community. Work in this field, while chaotic, is also incredibly diverse: We work with a large number of communities, with many different kinds of people, and never do the same project twice."

Kastelic started with the commission 15 years ago as a planner 1 and has held virtually every planning position in the agency. His undergraduate degree is in urban geography from the University of Kansas, his master's in urban planning from Kent State University. He is currently working toward a Ph.D. in planning, also at Kent State.

The Brookpark corridor revitalization effort is a good example of one of the commission's ongoing projects. The original proposal was written in 1986, and the agency got started in fall 1987 with funding from the county, four local communities, and the Cleveland Foundation. The Brookpark corridor spans nine miles and is the most heavily traveled nonfreeway artery in Cuyahoga County. It serves 350 commercial and 100 industrial properties, an airport, the NASA research center, and Cleveland's two largest manufacturing employers, the Ford and Chevrolet plants. Over the years the corridor has experienced progressive blight and deterioration, with an increase in junkyards, outdoor storage areas, pornographic theaters, and neon signs.

Kastelic says, "We are working with four neighboring communities, a citizens' organization, and local businesses to develop strategies and recommendations to revitalize the corridor. First, we had to do an inventory of the properties on the corridor. We also identified problems on the corridor through physical surveys and surveys of property owners and businesses to get their recommendations. Another component of this project is a commercial market analysis—what types of businesses might be attracted to this area and what types of assistance would be useful.

"One of the major goals is the formation of a local nonprofit development commission to work on implementation of our recommendations and to have an ongoing presence to strengthen the corridor. In addition to making physical improvements, we hope to attract a high-technology office park, hotels, and other amenities."

Gary Ellsworth, a planner 1 with the commission, is also working on the corridor project. "I am involved with a lot of the graphic and surveying work. I started by spending about one and a half weeks documenting commercial and industrial property, noting addresses and such, so we could get an accurate field map. Then, I went back and conducted a survey on conditions: parking lots, signage, building facades and curbs, and setback lengths. This will be turned into graphics, mostly sketches and mapping, and will likely include a current land-use map, a recommended land-use map, a map of property, and maybe a traffic map.

"Each of us is writing a chapter of the study; mine will be on conditions of deterioration. As with all our projects, we try to bring people into the process and spark as much interest as possible so that implementation has a better chance of occurring after we make our final recommendations. Sometimes you hit it, sometimes you don't.

"This is fairly typical of my role at the commission. I provide support for upper-level planners, doing a lot of the survey and graphics work and helping put together reports. Currently I am involved in various stages of five projects. These include visual windshield and walk-through surveys of neighborhoods to assess condition of housing stock and identify neighborhoods that are starting to deteriorate, and environmental review records, abbreviated environmental impact statements, for proposed developments. The work varies considerably from week to week and day to day. One project will heat up for a while, and then the weather will turn nice and I'll be off trying to get surveying done for another project.

"This is very dynamic. I spent two years doing flood insurance mapping for a private company—very production oriented and predictable; I knew exactly what I would be doing each day. Here, you come in and are never sure what you're going to dive into. You also must work cooperatively with other planners and staff to get projects done, getting the benefit of their specialties and experience—we do a lot of leaning on each other here. It's also interesting to know what's going on in the community."

Environmental and natural resource planning makes up a large part of the commission's work. Projects are treated both as discrete entities, such as a solid waste study, and as integrated parts of all planning activities. For example, planners might assess the impact on air, water, and land of a particular development. Other projects include master plans of park systems, plans for improved coordination of recreational services for the elderly and the disabled, studies of the environmental aspects of developing a former landfill facility, and plans for resource recovery, recycling projects, and coastal management.

Beth Nuss, a planner 2 who has been with the commission for two years, discusses a park improvement project she has been conducting. "Some time ago Rocky River, a western Cleveland suburb, did a master plan for their parks. We are going back now and, one park at a time, are making improvement recommendations based on their stated needs. I'll obtain an aerial photo, then make a site visit to get an idea of the condition of the facilities. Then I make a map of the existing facilities and my recommendations for improvements. In the most recent park, for example, I recommended removing deteriorating tennis courts, adding parking space, and fixing up some ball fields. At another facility they have a hillside erosion problem and I will recommend they plant ground cover to stop the erosion and, I hope, save trees whose roots have been exposed.

"In general I'm out of the office about one third of the time, more than I thought I would be before starting this job. That, in addition to the diversity of projects, allows me to be pretty independent and keeps this job interesting."

Among upcoming urban planning challenges, Kastelic says, "Zoning and development issues are becoming increasingly important and contentious. In an area such as northeast Ohio, where growth has been slow, these issues are challenging because development in one area could have a negative effect on stability in adjoining areas. It is also necessary to maintain existing public infrastructure development. In areas of rapid growth—like Florida and New England—zoning and development issues revolve around such contentious issues as orderly growth, suburban sprawl, natural habitat depletion, and the core question of when enough is enough. In all areas of the country, historic preservation is rapidly gaining in popularity and requires the work of planners with relevant backgrounds.

"Infrastructure planning will be another priority. This is a combination of upgrading and replacing existing infrastructure and adding new infrastructure because of development—in a future that promises shrinking federal and local dollars. Solid waste management is also a planning issue with significant ramifications. What are the impacts of construction of resource recovery facilities, transfer stations, recycling operations? What are the constraints on developing land that was previously used as a landfill?"

Because of competition in the field, Ellsworth advises, "Go to the best school you can find and try to get a master's. I have a B.A. and master's in

PROFILES

Ken Buckland, Town Planner and Administrator, Planning Board, Falmouth, Massachusetts

This profile gives you some idea of the diverse roles that a small-town planner must play as well as the issues arising in an area undergoing rapid growth.

"Falmouth is a small coastal town of about 27,000 people, with the potential of doubling in population over the next few years. As the town planner and administrator, I work with the planning board in trying to ensure that this growth occurs in a positive manner.

"I take the input and policy direction from town meetings and the planning board and integrate them into an overall plan for the town. For a specific development project, once I have done an initial survey of the parcels of land involved, I look at how the design will be incorporated into the particular neighborhood and estimate impact. This analysis encompasses everything down to soil and vegetation. After completing the survey, I ask the board to request project proposals from developers. As these are received, I review the designs and plans, checking for such details as how the plan will fit on the site according to soil and water maps and what impact the project would have on traffic and services. Usually, I spend about a third of my

geography, both from Bowling Green State University. In addition, internships are probably more important in planning than in many other fields—you just won't know the work until you get hands-on experience. As far as skills, take a lot of design and maybe a smattering of architecture. Rendering skills are one of the qualifications that will get you your first job in this field."

With a B.A. in urban studies from Cleveland State University, Nuss proves there are other ways to get started. "During school I was an intern at a local municipality's planning department and after graduation stayed on as a temporary employee until I heard about an opening with the commission. A couple of areas I think students should learn about: census data—know what it means and how to use it; zoning and planning law—there are many legal issues in planning; historic preservation—it is hard to find people who have a planning background and have some architectural and architectural history skills. Finally, knowing how to operate a personal computer and having some knowledge of various types of software will be very useful."

---

time getting a feel for the land and about half reviewing the proposed project and its impact on the community. The final step in the process is to negotiate with the developer, their consultant, and several board members on the specifics of development. This was the method used for developing locally needed affordable housing and picking a site for an ice rink.

"The role of chief planner and administrator for a small town is very diverse. I like the involvement at various levels. I do planning, and I also have a lot of direct contact with different people during negotiations and town meetings. Planning departments in larger towns tend to have upper-level people doing administrative and managerial work and lower-level people doing development reviews, specifications planning, environmental planning, and neighborhood planning. A generalist planner is not as common in a large town, and policy direction is provided more by boards, citizen groups, and elected officials, while the technical support is provided by the planning staff.

"The common thread, however, that runs through planning in any community is that development is affected by outside forces that are generally out of your control, such as the economy of the nation and the region or demographic trends. Consequently, as a planner you must be able to see broad issues as well as focus on the needs of individuals within the town, who ultimately make the decisions on use of their land and need for services. At the same time, aspiring planners must realize that the results of their efforts may not be seen for years.

"I found my first job somewhat by happenstance. After completing my M.S. in marine affairs, I called CEIP's Northeast office the same day the city of New Haven called to ask for an intern to develop a coastal plan for the city. Although I did not use CEIP for the job I took in New Haven, I feel the program was responsible for my first employment as a planner. From there I got a job in Stamford, Connecticut, as an environmental planner develop-

ing flood plans, a river walk, aquifer protection and soil-based rezoning proposals, and coastal plans.

"My next career move will be into a position as a consultant in a private firm, which I will be starting in a few months. As a town planner, I built on my experience in specific areas of planning and was able to diversify into all areas of town planning; as a consultant, I will be able to use these skills to benefit other cities and municipalities. It is this feeling of being able to do something for a community and raise the quality of its environment that keeps me going."

Richard DiSanza, Associate Planner/Waterfront Planner, Emanuel Associates, Nyack, New York

"Emanuel Associates is a firm of six consulting planners offering a wide variety of services, including master planning, zoning review, development proposal review, waterfront planning, and design studies. The firm's structure allows each associate to specialize in his or her area of expertise. I joined Emanuel last year to work primarily on waterfront plans.

"A waterfront plan is a guide for a city to protect and preserve its coastline. When developing a waterfront plan, we look at water-dependent uses like boat launches or industries that require a significant amount of water. Another aspect is water-enhanced uses, such as waterfront trails or parks, scenic overlooks, and mixed-use development. In all of these plans, public access is important.

"My most recent project was for Stony Point, on the Hudson, which

had developed a waterfront plan that sat around on a shelf for quite a few years and needed updating. I began by taking inventory of the area, analyzing the community's population, water resources, open spaces, scenic resources (both the positive and the negative), waterfront facilities, historical resources, transportation facilities, and public access. I then put together a public survey to establish more firmly what ideas the community had and how they would like to use their waterfront. The survey was a questionnaire that was distributed in two locations in the town by local volunteer groups (primarily the Boy Scouts) and then tabulated.

"This is a part of the development process which I feel very strongly about. Some planners don't like to be bothered by public opinion because they feel it takes too much time, but I believe it is critical to involve the community as much as possible. I use public opinion to develop a policy that communicates people's needs and desires.

"Environmental planning is definitely experiencing a resurgence. Much of this planning was initially spurred by the environmental movement of the sixties and seventies. Now, however, mainstream America is finally realizing they have to protect what they have left. Coastal planning, for example, is a major issue of concern.

"I started working for an environmental planning organization in a six-month volunteer internship program while earning my undergraduate degree. I had been debating whether to go into environmental law, but my internship supervisor was an attorney for the organization and I witnessed all the frustrations of his job. This helped me come to the conclusion that I would like to play a proactive rather than reactive role. The career debate then became a decision between landscape architecture and planning. If I had it to do over again, I would probably go with the landscape architecture because planning is much more quantitative, with a technical orientation, and doesn't involve much design work—which is what I like. This was something I didn't really find out until I was working with a community doing urban planning, conservation planning, and preservation planning as part of my curriculum in graduate school at the University of Virginia. The community I was working for offered me a job as a planner of subdivision review and city zoning, but I went to work for the state of New York in-

stead. The pay was lower, but I liked the fact that I was doing some design work.

"While working with the state, I was responsible for developing public access to sites on the Hudson, which included obtaining additional lands for the public as well as designating scenic areas. I was under contract with the state, and as the project neared its close, I didn't foresee the position opening up into anything permanent. I had done public sector work, which was very bureaucratic, and it didn't seem to me that the people were doing all they could do, which bothered me. I decided to try the private sector. I've found that the private sector's main interest is in producing, and you must be careful that you don't compromise your values. I've stood up for what I believe in and have been known to refuse projects, which causes some heat. I guess I'm still looking for the middle of the road—a combination of good work and prosperity.

"The best advice I could give an aspiring environmental planner would be to leave your options open; don't settle for something just because it is comfortable or pays well. I have seen a lot of people do this, and they are the first to become dissatisfied with their work. Stress what you want to do and *get experience*—it's a great bargaining tool. More specifically, it is important when interviewing that you become aware of the philosophy of the principal planner and that of the firm you are interviewing with. For example, if you have strong environmental concerns, you probably wouldn't be well received in a firm that emphasized development interests."

Peter LaBrie, Planning Coordinator, Department of City Planning, City and County of San Francisco

Planning jobs with local units of government make up a large proportion of planning positions. Peter LaBrie's work is different from that of professionals at the Cuyahoga County Regional Planning Commission in that he works for a unit of government that has the power to implement the plans he develops.

"For planning purposes, San Francisco is divided into six districts; I am currently responsible for leading a team effort to prepare a comprehensive plan for the southeast section of the city called the South Bayshore Conservation and Development Program. This district, which is a mixture of industrial and residential areas, had a comprehensive plan done back in 1969.

"We are currently revising this plan according to the following elements: land use, transportation, housing, commerce, industry, urban design, recreation and open space, energy conservation, community facilities, and public health and safety. The plan, when approved, will set forth objectives, policies, and implementation actions for shaping development in the district over the next 10 to 20 years.

"We began the process by reviewing the old plan and then conducted a survey of each parcel of land and building in the district. In addition to this, our research included demographic analysis of the population and employment trends. The result of this research was the production of an issues report (a combination of statistics, narrative, and graphics) which is then submitted to various citizens' groups for public comment on the issues facing South Bayshore. From here the report enters the plan development stage.

"During a typical work week, I spend one to one and a half days in the field looking at sites; a couple of days analyzing data and writing reports; a day acting as liaison to property owners, community groups, and representatives, and a day meeting with other planners. Although other planners in this division play the same role as I, because of the physical and economic variety in districts, their planning takes on assorted characters. The poorer, less developed areas raise the issue of compatibility with indus-

IN SUMMARY

Planning is a diverse profession—it may be only a part of your work and career, or it may be your primary work objective. Further, environmental planning is only one subset of the field. The need for planners is increasing as environmental and natural resource issues become more technical and

try. The north section, located by the bay, is very touristy, the variables there being intense retail, dense buildings, land use, and pedestrian rights. In the inner city, the planning issues are height of buildings, traffic, and congestion. In suburban areas, we focus primarily on housing.

"I received a B.A. in political economy and a master's in city planning from the University of California at Berkeley. It was during my junior year that I began seriously thinking about a profession. I liked academia but didn't want to teach, so I oriented myself toward planning, which I thought was a good balance between theory and practice. I went to New York City for an internship in 1964 and have been a planner ever since. The status of the profession probably peaked in the late to middle seventies under the influence of various activist movements but has since declined as planning has lost its priority in government funds allocation. Nevertheless, environmental issues, land use, and transportation have become important issues, which has helped to sustain the field.

"Planners are concerned with the future and with ecology in an integrated and holistic way. Planners have to think ahead about the relationship of people to all aspects of their environment: natural, built, and hu-

man. This broad perspective has been threatened in recent years by the increasing specialization in the field, as more and more planners are confining their training and career options to specific areas such as housing, environmental law, transportation, urban architecture, and so on.

"I like working at the city level because it is closer to the end result. Environmental work for the state requires too much paperwork and is too remote. The challenge of urban planning is to mix science and art in your work. Take, for example, South Bayshore, which is a poor, industrial area, and how challenging it would be to try and bring out the positive aesthetic environment and space while maintaining the functional use of the buildings. Incorporating all the elements into your work is the satisfaction of planning.

"The best advice I can give for someone hoping to becoming a planner is to get an interdisciplinary background in hard sciences and the humanities. You want to have a broad background and resist getting tunnel vision or becoming rhetorical. To be a good environmental or urban planner you have to be policy oriented. Lately, planning has become too legalistic. A diverse education and background can help keep you flexible."

interrelated. The planner who will do well in the future, whether in environmental planning or in another field, will have a broad outlook allowing for the integration of many disciplines, good basic planning skills, and possibly an area of specialization gained through experience or graduate study or both. This is a tall order, but it is in keeping with the challenging nature of the profession.

RESOURCES

American Planning Association. The largest professional organization in the field of urban and regional planning, with 21,000 members and 45 regional groups. Subgroups include one for environmental planners, which publishes a newsletter. Student membership in APA includes the magazine *Planning* (monthly) as well as membership in a state chapter. Other publications and services include *Planners' Salaries and Employment Trends, 1987* and *JobMart* (semimonthly), a job listing service. 1776 Massachusetts Ave., N.W., Washington, D.C. 20036.

Urban Land Institute. Publishes *Land Use Digest* and *Urban Land* (both monthly). 1090 Vermont Ave., N.W., Washington, D.C. 20005.

American Society of Consulting Planners. Publishes newsletter (monthly). 210 Seventh St., S.E., Suite 647, Washington, D.C. 20003.

Metropolitan Association of Urban Designers and Environmental Planners. Publishes occasional newsletter. P.O. Box 722, Church Street Station, New York, N.Y. 10008.

American Society of Landscape Architects. Publishes *Landscape Architecture News Digest* (monthly). 1733 Connecticut Ave., N.W., Washington, D.C. 20009.

Association of American Geographers. Publishes *Professional Geographer* (quarterly), newsletter (ten times a year). 1710 16th St., N.W., Washington, D.C. 20009.

Partners for Livable Places. Publishes *PLACE* (bimonthly). 1429 21st St., N.W., Washington, D.C. 20036.

Guide to Graduate Education in Urban and Regional Planning, by Carl V. Patton and Kathleen Reed (5th ed., 1986). Association of Collegiate Schools of Planning (available through APA).

6　Environmental Education and Communications

Michelle Roest is the school recycling education coordinator for the city of San Francisco, where she writes curricula for children in kindergarten through 12th grade, works with teachers, promotes environmentally oriented activities and field trips, and works in the classroom.

Frank Corrado, founder of the Chicago-based Communications for Management, produces videos that train community organizations to apply for technical assistance grants as part of the Superfund program of the U.S. Environmental Protection Agency (EPA).

Ed McCrea, with the U.S. Fish and Wildlife Service's Office of International Affairs and president of the North American Association for Environmental Education, is involved in international educational and technical assistance programs in India and Pakistan.

Don Swann, director of interpretive services for the Metropolitan District Commission in Boston, administers and provides support to 25 year-round and 30 summer interpretive staff and is responsible for all educational materials developed by the staff.

ALTHOUGH ENVIRONMENTAL educators work in a wide range of settings, they share one objective: To foster public awareness of and concern for the environment, and to motivate people to work toward the solution of current environmental problems and the prevention of future ones. Further, as Thomas Levermann, president of the Alliance for Environmental Education, Inc., remarks, "Education is ideally a tool that all environmental professionals use in their work. Our environment 20 years down the road will be the product of the education we are doing today."

The definition of environmental education is a subject of some controversy, especially among the educators themselves. Levermann suggests, "Environmental education is explaining interrelationships and effects in our environment: Does a developer understand the impact of the proposed development? Is the corporate executive aware of hazardous waste issues? Environmental education is the dairy farmer explaining milk production to city kids; it is a well-written article or a good picture." In these pages, environmental education is broadly defined to include conservation education, nature study, issues-oriented education and environmental education in the formal classroom setting, as well as the realm of mass communications and public relations.

WHERE WOULD YOU WORK?

Although many positions in this field are unique to a particular organization, agency, or company, there are some broad categories of workplaces that may be helpful to you in narrowing your search for a niche in environmental education.

TRADITIONAL SETTINGS

Many environmental educators work within the traditional education system at every level from primary school to graduate school. A smattering of school systems employ designated environmental educators, but in most the work is done by science teachers. Some states have environmental educators who work statewide to help schools develop environmental curricula and to produce support materials. (Many schools go to private or local nature centers for their environmental education needs.) More environmentally focused teaching slots are available in colleges and universities.

NATURE CENTERS AND INTERPRETIVE CENTERS

Interpreters or naturalists work at nature centers, museums, and zoos. The bulk of these centers are funded by local governments and park districts. Privately operated centers are common and are growing in popularity. Next come interpretive centers operated by state parks; these tend to be farther from urban areas and offer more seasonal positions. This is also true of federal interpretive positions, which can be found with the National Park Service, the U.S. Forest Service, the U.S. Fish and Wildlife Service, and the Bureau of Land Management.

COMMUNICATIONS AND PUBLIC RELATIONS

Think for a moment about where the general public gets the bulk of its environmental education. Realistically, it probably comes more from the media and the work of various other communicators than from nature centers or professors. While somewhat set apart from others in this field, communications professionals are a key component of environmental education in this country. They include journalists for newspapers and trade association and organizational publications, but also some less visible communicators, such as public information officers and community relations personnel who work for all levels of government, corporations, and consulting firms. Backing them up are a variety of researchers, writers, and production staff. An increasing percentage of these jobs are in the electronic media: radio, television, films, and video.

NONPROFIT ORGANIZATIONS

Nonprofit organizations play a large role in environmental education. Education of the public and policy makers is usually one of the major objectives of these organizations, which range from large national outfits like the National Audubon Society to community groups promoting neighborhood gardens. They approach environmental education from virtually all perspectives and work in the schools, with the media and policy makers, and in any other forum that will help them reach the public.

ISSUE-ORIENTED SETTINGS

This catch-all category covers those who educate on specific environmental issues. This might be a full-time job or, more likely, only part of a person's duties. Included in this group are those working for a variety of government agencies from local departments of health, to state departments of natural resources, to the Soil Conservation Service. They educate the public on such topics as recycling, potential hazards of pesticides, and depletion of the ozone layer. This category also includes those who provide environmentally related training, such as federal employees who train local air pollution control personnel and consultants who develop and administer employee training programs pursuant to worker and community right-to-know programs.

ISSUES AND TRENDS

Michael Zamm, director of environmental education for the Council on the Environment of New York, sums up the attitude of many environmental educators: "There is a lot happening in the area of environmental education, but there is a feeling our time hasn't come yet." Environmental education is a continuously evolving discipline that has always included nature study, conservation education, and outdoor education. Like most environmental activities, environmental education got a boost from the activism of the sixties and seventies. The field also became more complicated and diverse as the public pushed for more education on issues related to science, technology, and the environment.

Much of the public education funding that flowed in the sixties and seventies has dried up. The Environmental Education Act of 1974 was never renewed and the Environmental Education Office of the Department of Health, Education, and Welfare stopped making grants in 1981 and eventually was abolished, as were many education programs in other federal agencies. However, the field is still left with its diversity. Ed McCrea, president of the North American Association for Environmental Education, points out, "One of the factors that makes the promotion of environmental education difficult is that we are made up of five or six subgroups that do not speak with a single voice and hence present a fuzzy image to the general public."

Environmental education has not become a part of the formal educational structure—a separate discipline. Michael Zamm says, "Environmental education is so interdisciplinary it often gets lost. It includes the sciences, the social sciences, and the arts. Therefore, the ideal situation is for every teacher to infuse environmental education into their lesson plans. Without some kind of formal mechanism, however, this depends on each individual teacher." As the operator of a nature center in Ohio observes, "A local school has three fifth-grade classes. One teacher brings her class out four to six times a year and gets the kids involved in ongoing projects. I've never seen the other two classes."

Most interviewed believe there will not be a substantial change in the near future in the way environmental education is taught in the formal educational system. If you want to teach environmental education in primary or secondary schools you are probably going to have to integrate this into a career as a biology, chemistry, or even social studies teacher. Change will likely come informally and slowly; environmental education proponents are focusing their efforts on raising teachers' general level of awareness and education on the issues. While no state certifies environmental educators, some states, like Wisconsin, require educators to take environmental courses as part of their training.

If you are bound and determined to focus on environmental education in the classroom, look at opportunities outside the structured educational system. There are many encouraging and interesting developments in this field. Many private, nonprofit organizations are working with school districts to provide environmental education and are working to promote environmental education to the rest of the public. See the Case Study on the Council on the Environment of New York as an example of some of the creative ways groups across the country are promoting environmental education. Another example is the Alliance for Environmental Education, whose member organizations are working to establish a National Network for Environmental Education; by the late 1990s, they hope to have as many as 100 regional training centers for environmental educators. These would be based at universities, would train teachers and the public, and would eventually become self-supporting.

Colleges and universities are also wrestling with the issue of how best to teach environmental issues. Dr. Arnold Schultze of the University of California at Berkeley remarks, "Even at the college level there is a tendency to act as if the natural world can be organized into specific disciplines like biology and chemistry. It would be more useful to take the world as it is, fully integrated, and structure interdisciplinary environmental education accordingly. There is still a feeling among many that an interdisciplinary education leads one to be a jack-of-all-trades and a master of none. This is unfortunate. Thus, if you want to teach at the college or graduate level you are going to have to stake out a specific field and become an expert . . . But don't forget the rest of the world."

At the federal level, environmental education is structured differently and given different priority in the various agencies. "Besides reduced funding to contend with, there is also a philosophical opposition to teaching environmental education, the attitude that environmental education is the responsibility of the states," says one federal employee. "There are still jobs in various agencies and departments, but without a lot of support and funding from above, education must happen *in addition* to other responsibilities." Federal agencies that employ full-time environmental educators or include environmental education in certain job descriptions include the Bureau of Land Management, the Army Corps of Engineers, the Soil

Conservation Service, the EPA, the U.S. Forest Service, and the U.S. Fish and Wildlife Service. This list may not be complete and does not include those agencies involved in park management and interpretive services; see chapter 13 for a thorough discussion of such agencies.

If, in fact, it has been decided that environmental education is a state responsibility, most states have not responded by hiring environmental educators en masse. As mentioned earlier, some states have small staffs that work with educators on environmental education. There is also more and more issues-oriented education. Most state governments, for example, are hiring staff to educate citizens and local units of government on solid waste issues, particularly waste reduction and recycling. Other educators work in state EPAs and natural resource departments, usually holding other responsibilities besides education. Interpreters often work for state park systems; although most of these jobs are seasonal, parks near population centers are increasingly offering year-round programs.

One area of significant growth in environmental education is at local nature and interpretive centers, both publicly and privately funded. "Many communities are setting aside land for nature centers," says John Ripley Forbes, founder of Natural Science for Youth Foundation, an organization founded in 1947 to help localities set up and operate nature centers. He continues, "Take Atlanta, for example, with a metropolitan area of 2.2 million people. They had one nature center only a few short years ago. Now they have six, and I envision they need and will eventually have 15 to 20. One reason for this is the importance of the centers to our youth. With all the problems kids are having these days, communities are looking to programming at interpretive centers as one way to help."

Don Swann, director of interpretive services for the Metropolitan District Commission in Boston, a state agency, has seen his agency go from hiring its first full-time interpreter in 1983 to expanding to a current full-time staff of 25 year-round interpreters. "I see two major reasons for this growth. First, agencies are beginning to see interpretive staff as an important way to call attention to the parks and to build a park constituency. In addition, we are facing some serious environmental problems, which will give rise to more hiring of interpretive and educational staff."

Paul Franzen, president of the National Association of Interpretation, ranks the sectors in terms of hiring of interpretive staff: "Way out in first is the local level: municipal, county, and regional park systems, and also private nature centers. Second come state parks and the private sector: cruise lines, amusement parks, theme parks, and so on, although these private sector jobs are often low-paying and seasonal. Finally, though employment is down now, I wouldn't rule out the federal sector. We are becoming a leisure society and the federal government is eventually going to have to respond."

GETTING STARTED

The field of environmental education is extremely diffuse, with many different sectors offering a wide range of jobs: the parks and recreation establishment, the educational system, nonprofits, and every level of government. Many of these positions are unique to a particular agency or organization and many must be created by the individual. A lot depends on being in the right place at the right time. Despite the rewarding nature of the work, it is hard to plan for a career in environmental education. You can start by joining national and local professional organizations as a student, reading the literature, talking to everyone in the field, and actually getting involved in the field.

Ed McCrea, President, North American
Association for Environmental
Education

Environmental educator is a job title that includes many different jobs. There are interpreters, journalists, science teachers, professionals involved in curriculum development, those in the nonprofit sector, and numerous environmental professionals for whom education is but one of several job responsibilities. Further complicating the matter, support for environmental education varies from sector to sector and region to region.

Professionals are, however, making careers in this field, and for those who wish to join them they advocate persistence and flexibility. Don't expect the field to get any neater in the near future in terms of job classifications. If anything, environmental education will be carried out by an increasingly diverse group of professionals. Local nonprofit and governmental education and interpretive efforts are growing, despite constant funding challenges. People on this cutting edge are developing new ways of interacting with the public and the formal educational system.

How can you prepare for the change and uncertainty seemingly inherent in environmental education? First, you should possess a combination of scientific, education, and communications background and skills. Professionals seem almost evenly split on the question of which area to focus on, with a slight edge going to communications and education. "You need to take some education courses, learn about the philosophy of education, what a teacher goes through on a daily basis, some of the tricks of the trade," notes Tom Levermann. "In the final analysis, however, all your knowledge is of little worth if you don't know how to translate and communicate it to people. Paralleling this, you need to ask yourself: *'Do I like working with people?'* The only way to know, of course, is to get out and see." Don Swann of the Metropolitan District Commission backs this up: "When I hire someone I look for enthusiasm and a demonstrated commitment to the field, *plus* communications skills: Can you talk to people and can you write? Of course, you must have some natural history background, but that usually isn't what makes up my mind."

A master's degree is not essential to getting started in this field, but it may be useful later in your career. One option is to structure an undergraduate education that covers the sciences, especially biology, perhaps as your major, with a strong emphasis on education, the liberal arts, and communications. You could also earn an undergraduate degree in science and a graduate degree in education. Some of the undergraduate degrees commonly pursued to prepare for a career in environmental education are biology, botany, zoology, environmental studies, communications, natural history, natural resources, and outdoor recreation. If you want to teach in a formal educational setting, you must also meet state licensing requirements.

On top of this, give yourself an edge with some skills that will set you apart from other applicants when you apply for your first job. These can include a specialty within the field—such as competence in history, habitat restoration, or a specific environmental issue—or knowledge of graphics, photography, art, writing, or curriculum development. Finally, recognize that educators are performers, and take any chance you can to work in front of people or use creative ways to entertain and educate. Finally, get a variety of experiences, like summer jobs, internships, and volunteer projects, to demonstrate your talents and your commitment to the field.

When looking for your first job, be aware that there are regional considerations that affect the job market. Paul Franzen notes, for example, that interpretive work in the West and Pacific Northwest is often connected with public lands, so that such federal agencies as the Bureau of Land Management and the Army Corps of Engineers hire more environmental educators. Interpreters in the Midwest and New England, on the other hand, more often work at public and private nature centers.

Professionals advise job seekers to look at the local level for their first job, primarily because that is where much of the hiring is done. There is also a lot of turnover because the pay is very low. To find local and regional jobs, put your professors to work for you in giving you contacts and leads. Be prepared to work seasonally, ideally while you are still in school. One option for seasonal entry-level positions is interpretation and education in the private sector, at amusement parks, theme parks and villages, and other tourist attractions. This gives you essential experience in working with the public.

"One frustrating reality of this field is that you tend to get promoted out of environmental education," comments Ed McCrea. "It seems that many people will do this for eight to ten years and then say, 'I need to get a real job.' There aren't that many rungs of the ladder to climb in environmental education, not so many high-level jobs. You must be conscious of this likely career path earlier in your career so you can plan for it. There are two ways to do this. One way is to focus on the few areas where there are managerial positions and aim toward these positions; your best bet is probably private nature centers, since an environmental education professional often runs the show. Another path is to recognize you are likely to leave the education focus behind as you are promoted and take business and management courses so you are ready to be a park manager or division administrator. I give this advice hoping that this situation changes during your career. We need people who make lifetime careers out of environmental education."

COMMUNICATIONS

Getting started in the field of environmental communications is similar in many ways to starting out as an environmental educator, but there is some advice specific to this area. If you are interested in environmental journalism, recognize that the jobs are scarce at daily papers; the *New York Times* has only one environmental reporter. Trade association publications and the environmental press present much more opportunity. Frank Corrado, founder of Communications for Management and former public affairs director for EPA's Region 5, counsels, "Although jobs may initially appear scarce to the job hunter, be patient. There is a crying need for journalists who are scientifically trained. Technical writing and environmental risk communication are also growing fields for scientifically oriented journalists."

According to Corrado, government agencies and consulting firms that hire public information officers tend to consider an environmental studies or hard science background and experience working with nonprofit environmental organizations to be at least as important as training in communications or journalism. "Sure, you need the writing and communications skills and need to know how the media work," he acknowledges. "But the focus these days is on community relations more than on the press. The two career routes I recommend are working for a local paper for a few years, preferably in a small town where you can cover a wider range of issues, and working for a citizens' environmental organization."

Both the private sector and government are increasingly contracting with consultants for public relations work. This includes media relations, community outreach, image advertising, and production of printed material for public use. For example, many government consulting contracts, such as those under the EPA's Superfund program, require a community involvement component. Much of this work is done by general public relations firms, but some firms specialize at least in part in environmentally related work.

SALARY

While environmental education is one of the lower-paying environmental fields, salaries are becoming more competitive. "On the interpretive end, employers are finding they can't attract enough committed individuals to the field when they are only offering five-fifty an hour and no permanency," observes Paul Franzen. "Therefore, the pay scales are definitely rising." General environmental educators can expect to start off in the range of $15,000 to $22,000, with pay varying mostly by geographic location. Interpreters start between $10,000 and $22,000, with private nature centers falling at the low end of the scale, the federal government somewhere in the middle, and state and local public interpreter's positions at the high end. Journalists and communications specialists also find entry-level salaries to be on the low end, ranging from $16,000 to $22,000. Private public relations and consulting firms pay somewhat higher starting salaries.

CASE STUDY

Council on the Environment of New York

The nonprofit sector is heavily involved in environmental education. The nonprofit sector has traditionally taken on the task of educating the public and policy makers on a whole spectrum of issues. Nonprofit organizations lead the way in introducing environmental curricula in the schools, providing informal education opportunities, initiating issues-oriented environmental education, and building a constituency for environmental education. A career in environmental education may well include a stint in the nonprofit sector, and because of the diversity and creativity you may decide you don't want to leave.

The Council on the Environment of New York is a privately funded, nonprofit citizens' organization established in the Office of the Mayor in 1970 to do public policy and educational work on environmental issues. In 1975 the organization made a decision to change its focus to hands-on, grass roots involvement in New York's neighborhoods. This led to the council's current emphasis on four program areas: open space greening projects, farmers' markets, office paper recycling, and environmental education. Currently, the organization has a full-time staff of 19. This includes administrative personnel, program directors and staff, a publicity specialist, and a communications specialist. The council supplements the work of staff with consultants, interns, and volunteers.

The work of the council covers a range of issues and activities. The Open Space Greening Program has helped to establish neighborhood parks and green play areas adjacent to day care centers. This program has also helped community groups and residents to establish and maintain community gardens and open spaces, by lending tools, conducting training sessions, and selling gardening materials at cost. The Greenmarket is a system of markets that give regional farmers access to urban buyers. The Office Paper Recycling Service has designed and installed 120 programs, involving 45,000 individuals citywide. The Training Student Organizers Program works in 14 high schools and two colleges to teach students about environmental issues and organizing.

"The specific results of projects we work on are important and gratifying, such as seeing children playing in one of the beautiful neighborhood parks we helped establish," acknowledges Lys McLaughlin, executive director of the council. "However, we are also very conscious that these are vehicles for a more basic mission, which is to promote environmental awareness among New Yorkers. This is our focus, and our work is evaluated from that perspective.

"Education means many things. Over the long run it may mean changing the syllabus for schools in the state of New York so 15 years down the road we have a more environmentally educated adult population. On a more immediate level, all our programs, from gardening to the Greenmarket, aim to involve people and to increase the importance of environmental issues in their lives.

"As an organization, we carry this out in a number of ways. We have a formal environmental education program, and we integrate education into all of our programs—education of the public, the media, and policy makers. Our staff is constantly speaking at various meetings and conferences and leading training sessions. Further, we produce a whole array of pamphlets, press releases, public service announcements, posters, and studies, which are targeted toward specific audiences ranging from the media to the real estate industry to schoolchildren. We also make use of volunteer expertise. Our Noise Abatement Committee, for example, is made up of dedicated and knowledgeable people who generate publicity on noise on their own. This is a constant and ongoing process.

"My job as executive director is to keep things moving and focused. In the nonprofit sector you must deal with the often frustrating reality that there is too much to do. I, for example, can get very depressed if I look at several environmental problems at once, but when I sharpen my focus to specific projects the future looks much brighter.

"The key functions of nonprofit management are fund-raising and administration of programs and people. This entails an extremely unpredictable workday, with each day's activities ranging from the very heady—talking to the chairman of our board about a potential new project—to the very mundane—can we afford a fax machine. Today, for example, I went over a list assembled by a volunteer of corporations we could approach for funding, talked to a couple of program directors, tried to find an agency that would publish a brochure we are developing on asbestos, worked on our employee benefits package, met with public relations staff on publicity for the Greenmarket, and tried to get our aging phone system fixed.

"How did I prepare for this field? I studied classical civilization at New York University! Then I worked for a public relations firm for five years, where I learned a lot about publicity and nonprofits, as most of the clients were museums. While on a sabbatical, I was canoeing on a river in Canada that was scheduled to be dammed up. Then and there I decided I wanted to work for the environment and see how green I could make my native city. Returning to New York, I knocked on every door I knew; six months later I started at the council as communications director, later became assistant director, and in 1978 became executive director."

Although education is integrated into all activities of the council, for Michael Zamm it is his primary activity. Zamm is the council's director of environmental education and is responsible for the Training Student Organizers Program.

"The goals of the program are to teach students the skills needed to plan and carry out environmental projects in the school and community, to increase students' environmental awareness and concern through direct involvement in local environmental improvement efforts, and to develop students' leadership ability and sense of effectiveness as citizens capable of constructive action," says Zamm. "To achieve this we have four full-time staff members who work with students and teachers, prepping them on issues and helping them develop action-oriented projects.

"We try to pick issues and projects that mean something to the students: nuclear waste, water, greening, preservation of monuments, and other urban environmental issues. Our staff works with teachers and students for one or more terms in the classroom, helping them pick a project, supervising its completion, as well as conducting lessons and organizing issue-related field trips."

Student projects have included surveys, such as a recent one on parents' knowledge of lead poisoning; water petitions to state legislators; graffiti prevention and mural campaigns; recycling drives; energy conservation workshops; park redesign; alley, pond, park, and beach cleanups; and letter writing campaigns.

"A good example of a participatory project was at James Madison High School," Zamm explains, "where students enrolled in the law program chose to investigate the New York City noise pollution codes and how citizens could be involved in enforcement and development of regulations. Their project goal was to coordinate a panel of experts who would discuss possible policies and actions for alleviation of the noise problem. They recruited various public officials and experts to participate in a public forum and were also responsible for promoting the event. Students have written press releases and flyers, and they've been guests on local college radio stations to discuss environmental issues they have studied.

"The goal of our environmental education program is to make better citizens out of the students through an education process that culminates in an event or result. At the same time, they get a strong educational experience in using cognitive skills such as reading, writing, communication, cooperation, and problem solving.

"As director of environmental education, I supervise the overall program, troubleshoot with staff, and train new people. I have four sites of my own to supervise, and I also do fund-raising. The fund-raising requires a lot of proposal writing to banks, corporations, and boards of education, as well as a lot of negotiation. I usually spend two days a week in the office doing administrative work. The other three days I spend in the field working on my own projects, with other staff, or in meetings.

"My sense is that the profession of environmental education is going to be up and down for the next five years. I don't anticipate a lot of school systems hiring environmental educators per se, but I believe the issues are becoming a bigger part of the regular school curriculum. Further, there is quite a proliferation of nonprofits engaging in environmental education efforts either in conjunction with school systems or separately. Look into museums, environmental organizations, and nature centers.

"To best prepare for this field, I would recommend an undergraduate degree that emphasized hard sciences, biology, or environmental chemistry. Fifteen years ago the background of many environmental education professionals was eclectic, but that may be changing. I would then recommend a graduate program that had some combination of environmental studies and education. Entry-level jobs range from state departments that hire naturalists to nonprofits such as the council to the larger nonprofits, which probably pay as well as if not better than government agencies."

Education is also the major objective of the Office Paper Recycling Service. Sheila Millendorf, director of the recycling service, discusses its operation: "We recruit offices for waste paper recycling through publications, direct mailings, recommendations from current clients, workshops, conferences, and published articles.

"In addition to the actual recycling, education is a critical component of this project. When discussing the recycling program with participants or potential clients we make connections to the waste disposal problem in New York City and what their recycling can do to alleviate the problem. Our pragmatic approach to a seemingly overwhelming problem is quite successful in terms of consciousness-raising. I might add that next year the New York Department of Sanitation plans to hire 50 to 70 staff to work in its Office of Recycling.

"As director of the program, I make policy decisions, meet with potential clients, continue to design programs, supervise a staff of four, direct the tone of the program, and do outreach, marketing, and education.

"Since the goal of this program is to educate the public, we attempt to get all sectors involved, including colleges, hospitals, nonprofit organiza-

PROFILES

Barb Post, Naturalist, Cleveland Metroparks System

This profile will give you a feel for the work of a naturalist and show how to prepare for the interpretive field.

"The Cleveland Metroparks System was established with state enabling legislation in 1917 and is a separate body, run by appointed commissioners, which has taxing authority. The system includes 19,000 acres, 12 reservations, and a zoo with an aquarium. We have about 400 employees, about half of whom work at the zoo. I am one of 14 full-time naturalists who work for Metroparks.

"As a naturalist, the prime focus of my job is education of the public, helping them learn about the natural envi-ronment. I work with school classes, the Boy Scouts, handicapped and elderly groups, garden clubs, and individuals. To best educate people about the environment I believe you must get them out in it. So I lead a lot of hikes or wade around the marsh with people. However, you don't have to go on a hike to teach; we use whatever resources are available. This may include anything from a straight lecture format to putting on a skit. Increasingly, naturalists are going out into the community to reach people.

tions, large businesses, multitenant housing facilities, and municipalities.

"I have an associate's degree in fine arts and my background in private industry was in project planning, development, and public relations. Before coming here, I was an account executive for a toy manufacturer and was responsible for creating and developing new toys, so I knew how to bring a concept to fruition. I've been here now for nine years. When I'm interviewing people, I look for basic characteristics: perceptiveness, an inquisitive mind, someone who is articulate and energetic, likes a challenge, is creative, outspoken, a good listener and speaker. These characteristics are as important to many employers as formal qualifications."

Many nonprofits work on environmental education projects. For a list of these organizations, start with the annual *Conservation Directory*, published by the National Wildlife Federation. See also the *Encyclopedia of Associations* (Gale Research) to find out about other organizations. Your most up-to-date and relevant information, however, almost always comes from personal contacts; ask professionals which organizations work on the issues that interest you.

"One big event we use to promote the parks is our annual Fall Fest, or Pioneer Day. It's kind of our mass education day. We have pioneer crafts and food as well as nature exhibits. I have an art background so I used this skill in the Fall Fest program: The event gets people to the park whom we might not otherwise see, which brings up another role of the naturalist: to promote and build support for the parks.

"My special project is the restoration of a marsh located at the nature center where I work. (Each park has some specialty, such as meadowlands or Indian heritage.) We decided to create a wetland ecosystem for educational purposes. Interestingly enough, people were initially up in arms: In their eyes, we were tearing down the park to put in a swamp. This is tied into some of the stigma about wetlands. Now, they have come to see it as part of their park.

"To shed a little of the mystique about the work of a naturalist, I should note that I have a desk—which I spend a lot of time at—and a phone, which also gets a lot of use. This job requires a lot of writing and planning as well as setting up interpretive engagements. It is not all fieldwork.

"My undergraduate degrees are in art and biology. At the time, people thought that was a strange combination. Now it seems complementary: Biology taught me to be analytical; art helps me to be creative. From there I got an M.S. in biology with an emphasis in botany.

"To be a good naturalist, I think there almost has to be a bit of an actor in you. You are constantly in front of people—many different kinds of people. I would advise students to get experience working with different people and see how they relate to people. Go walk around the woods and take people with you. If you find this boring, that's a sign. I remember the first day I had to spend an hour with a group of kids, I didn't know how I was going to fill the time. Now I can say hello for 30 minutes.

"You also need the science background. Go with a hard science. My biology background has been quite valuable. Even if you're not going to explain the subtleties of a plant species, the more you understand, the better you can teach. I sometimes wish I had more education courses, although my teaching assistantship in graduate school has helped. Any fieldwork skills you can pick up through school or volunteer work will be useful when you look for your first job.

"As for getting started, my advice is to do the best you can to get established in the field before you get out of school. Having somebody know you and your work is going to aid you tremendously in getting your first job. Beyond that, realize that you may have to start off with seasonal work. Knowing this ahead of time might prevent you from becoming overly discouraged. Think about work in various sectors. I like the local park system because I feel we get a lot of variety. In the national park system you have a lot more people coming through on a one-shot deal, and you may find yourself giving the same presentation every night for a month."

Nancy Pearlman, Executive Producer, Host, and Director, Educational Communications, Inc., Los Angeles

This profile gives you some idea of the nature of environmental communication and education work in the electronic media.

"Educational Communications, Inc., a nonprofit organization, was established in 1958 to promote educational and scientific purposes for the public welfare. This has evolved into a specialization in environmental media programs for nonprofit groups. We view education as learning both within and beyond the established academic structure—learning that helps the individual fulfill his or her own needs and the needs of society.

"Educational Communications has two major media projects in which I am involved: 'Environmental Directions' and 'Econews.' The award-winning 'Environmental Directions' is a weekly half-hour interview-format radio series covering an entire range of problems affecting the earth's ecosystem. It is the only regular broadcast of its kind on environmental issues offered in the United States and Canada. These programs provide up-to-date information presented to the public in an enlightening and entertaining manner. The subjects discussed include air and water quality, land-use planning, wilderness area creation, and resource conservation, combining regional, state, national, and international viewpoints to enhance the analysis of even local issues. The guests include environmental activists, business representatives, scientific experts, government officials, and other knowledgeable people from around the world.

"The Emmy-nominated 'Econews' is a regularly scheduled news, interview, and documentary series specializing in the issues of our environment as they affect citizens in their communities. Millions of homes and viewers are reached by distributing programs through both Public Broadcasting stations and cable channels. The format includes news briefs segments, film and video clips, and lively discussions and interviews with guests. Topics and guests are chosen to represent several sides of an issue so as to present a balanced program.

"Being executive producer, host, and director involves fund-raising, coordinating crews, working on content and program ideas, interviewing, and supervising technical operations. Being a nonprofit organization, we do not have the staff to cover all of these roles and as a result everyone has to know a lot about everything to make it work.

Santa Monica, California. Host Nancy Pearlman and special guest Peter Strauss filming the ACE-nominated television special "Gem in the Heart of the City," a documentary on the Santa Monica Mountains National Recreation Area. Photo courtesy of Nancy Pearlman.

"I learned broadcasting from the bottom up. The technical aspects I picked up by going in and practicing with the equipment. I've found that the more you know about the technical aspects of broadcasting and production, the better producer you are. You learn by asking questions. Above all, adopt the attitude that your job, no matter what the level, is meaningful. Even the simplest things, such as holding cue cards, are extremely important in making the show a success.

"Before working in broadcasting, I had been doing environmental administrative work for various organizations and was a guest on several talk shows to discuss environmental issues. I realized I could control and direct interviews, and I also saw the potential of using radio and TV to reach a larger audience. I had been a member of several professional organizations, committees, and groups that wanted to educate the public on environmental issues and attempted

to do so by conducting conferences and classes, but those forms of education generally attract only those that are already knowledgeable. I realized that radio and TV were the most effective media for reaching those who were not converted. It is a challenge to make solemn, hard-hitting information fun, exciting, and interesting.

"I pretty much created this position; jobs in this field don't just happen. The best way to enter this field is to do volunteer work and internships, which will give you the opportunity to produce works of your own so you have a portfolio to show to potential employers. We had a crew member who used to volunteer every night and weekend on top of a full-time job: He took this experience and is now running his own television channel. This work is not for those who want a nine-to-five job; you must be willing to live, sleep, drink, and eat journalism and broadcasting to succeed."

Mary McColl Nielson, Public Information Specialist, EPA Region 10, Seattle

To call the communications field simply public relations is to leave out much of the story. Professionals in this field strive to communicate between a particular agency or company and the general public, the media, and other relevant agencies and organizations.

"Continuing reauthorization of major pieces of environmental legislation such as the Clean Water Act and Superfund emphasizes the need for individuals within the EPA to work with the public and explain concisely how EPA action on various environmental issues will affect the individual, the economy, and the community. EPA

public information specialists serve in a variety of ways to interpret federal environmental laws and regulations so the public will understand and support them. My duties are defined further by the Freedom of Information Act. This law gives the public access to a wide variety of public documents. Information on water and air quality, landfills, waste management, and hazardous waste sites is of increasing interest to local governments, health professionals, industry, unions, and financial institutions. Finally, public forums and presentations require me to use writing, speaking, and video skills. To perform my job, I have to know the law, administration process, and EPA systems.

"I work extensively on task forces and work groups, promoting environmental education and improved information management. This includes developing and implementing public forums or brown-bag lunches for public interest groups, which creates a forum for exchange among diverse groups and the agency. As an additional role, I serve as small business ombudsman, assisting small businesses with regulatory information and a guide to state and federal resources.

"The other side of my job is to furnish other EPA managers with information on questions and concerns of the public and media. This is done in two ways: anticipating public and media reactions to EPA action, and being proactive in providing facts and interpretation. You must be flexible and adjust to the needs and concerns of the public; things change quickly and the public interest changes accordingly. Above all, this requires that you have a genuine interest in what you are doing and an appreciation of your overall objective, which in my case is to provide a two-way link between the agency and its many constituencies.

"I have a B.A. in sociology with a minor in journalism, which I followed up with graduate work in public administration. My social work background has been of tremendous help in dealing with a variety of people—office holders, technicians, citizens. I would say in this field there is a need for generalist backgrounds. It is easy to get tied to one area when you have a scientific or technical background. However, some technical background or know-how is necessary to be able to translate information for the public use.

"Preparation for this type of work should include a lot of experience in concise writing—take journalism courses and practice writing. Read beyond your own profession to understand how it relates to the rest of the world. Take other classes than those related to your major. See your education as a continuing process. Develop an awareness of computer skills and language as a tool. A bachelor's degree in the arts and sciences is appropriate; there isn't as much of a push for MBAs anymore. Other skills to develop? Ability in writing, speaking, publications, and videos. Ability to view assignments or projects as opportunities to be creative. Manage solutions, not problems.

"Take your leisure time to stop and think about where the future is heading in the next five to ten years. Project yourself into the future. Take the opportunity to gain experience from internships; business gains just as much from these opportunities as you do—they get your fresh insights and creativity. I'd like to add one final commercial for public service: There is a role for strong, creative, responsible people in government. Consider doing it for even a short time. With that experience you are more valuable to private enterprise."

IN SUMMARY

Ed McCrea, president of the North American Association for Environmental Education, asserts, "This field has to prove itself useful. Besides paying lip service to environmental education, managers and administrators must come to see environmental education as a tool to get things done—whether it is the manager of a fishery or a local solid waste coordinator. That is the only way I believe we are going to build the kind of constituency that will give environmental education its rightful place in the environmental and educational community." This is good advice for the profession and for the student embarking on a career in it. The field is diverse, and support for environmental education is spread thin. Therefore, a good way to direct your career in this field is to decide what type of education is useful and needed and then to find or create a position that fits the bill.

RESOURCES

Alliance for Environmental Education, Inc. A coalition of organizations that works at the regional, state, and national level to promote environmental education. A recent initiative is an effort to establish a National Network for Environmental Education to consist of regionally based, self-supporting education and teacher training centers. Holds a national conference; publishes *The Alliance Exchange* (quarterly). Box 1040, 3421 M St., N.W., Washington, D.C. 20007.

North American Association for Environmental Education. Membership includes elementary and secondary educators, university environmental educators, and government and private sector personnel involved in environmental education and communications. Sponsors annual conference and workshops, lists internship and employment opportunities in *The Environmental Communicator* (bimonthly), and otherwise works to promote environmental education. P.O. Box 400, Troy, Ohio 45373.

Natural Science for Youth Foundation. Works to help localities establish and maintain nature centers. Also the professional organization for personnel of nature centers and small nature museums. Provides training for nature center management at its annual conference; publishes job opportunities bulletin (bimonthly) and *Nature Science Center News* (quarterly), as well as a directory of natural science centers. 11 Wildwood Valley, N.E., Atlanta, Ga. 30338.

National Association of Interpretation. The consolidated Association of Interpretive Naturalists and the Western Interpreters Association, which merged in 1988. Sponsors annual conference and Interpretation Management Institute, has regional chapters, and publishes *Journal of Interpretation* (bimonthly). Employment services include Dial-a-Job (303-491-7410) and Dial-an-Internship (303-491-6434), which are updated weekly. Printout of the week's listings costs $3. P.O. Box 1892, Fort Collins, Colo. 80522.

Educational Resources Information Center (ERIC). See Resources, chapter 2, for description.

Part III

ENVIRONMENTAL PROTECTION

7 Solid Waste Management

Until recently there was always another hole or gravel pit the county could buy. Now the public wants to know where the waste is going. Tremendous challenges, tremendous opportunities.

J. B. Cox, Special Assistant for
Resource Recovery, U.S. Department of
Commerce

IN 1987 NATIONAL attention was focused on the hapless international journey of a barge filled to the brim with municipal waste that had been generated in Islip, New York. The town of Islip had to scramble when it ran out of landfill space and couldn't find another landfill willing to accept its waste. One of their solutions was to contract to have some of it carted off in a barge to points unknown. They thought that was the last of it—for that batch anyway. Unfortunately for Islip, the contractor could not find a state or country willing to accept the waste. The now infamous garbage barge was in the news for several weeks, searching for a final resting place.

Cartoonists and comedians had a field day. The incident, however, brought to public attention what experts have known for some time, and politicians are beginning to realize: We are drowning in our garbage. Putting in place economically and environmentally sound solid waste disposal policies will no doubt be one of the most taxing challenges facing municipalities in the coming decade.

For centuries most cities piled trash in open dumps and later burned trash in these dumps or in crude incinerators, as did many commercial establishments and residences. In the late 1960s the Clean Air Act put an abrupt stop to this practice. Chicago, for example, was forced to close three of its four incinerators, eliminating its major waste disposal option.

Landfilling was the next answer. The dominance of this option, however, appears to be short-lived. Most pre-1970 landfills, built without environmental safeguards, are leaking large amounts of contaminated liquids into surrounding water supplies—4 million gallons per day at the Fresh Kills landfill on Staten Island, New York. Leaking municipal landfills are creating an environmental dilemma some experts say may surpass that of hazardous waste.

Half of the nation's 15,000 landfills will be closed by 1995; 3,500 have closed since 1979. As existing landfills reach capacity or are closed for environmental reasons, public opposition has made it virtually impossible to site new landfills, regardless of environmental safeguards instituted. At the same time, Americans are generating more waste—from 2.9 pounds per person per day in 1960 to almost 5 pounds in 1988.

There is a growing consensus that a combination of strategies will provide the most effective long-term solution to the solid waste dilemma. This includes waste reduction, recycling, resource recovery (burning of garbage to produce energy), and secure landfilling of the remaining waste.

Municipalities, however, will have to act quickly and decisively. A study by the Worldwatch Institute estimates that half of the cities in the United States will have exhausted their landfills by 1990. A major restructuring of solid waste management practices and policies will be required. This overhaul will include various governmental units working on cooperative waste disposal options, the establishment of recycling routes, and the designing of waste-to-energy facilities. People in the United States also need to take responsibility for the garbage they generate.

WHERE THE ACTION IS

The Department of Commerce's J. B. Cox points out, "The changes in this field will create challenges and opportunities for many types of environmental professionals in all sectors. One could get involved from almost any discipline; the field needs engineers, environmental scientists, economists, political scientists, managers, marketing personnel, entrepreneurs, journalists . . . the list goes on and on. Hands-on experience, whether it is internships or independent research projects, will be the biggest asset in getting started in this field."

Go to where the problem lies and you have also found the location of the opportunity. For solid waste, this means at the local level, hometown USA. This is ultimately where the solutions to solid waste management problems must be developed and carried out. Further, although the issue has more immediacy for the East and West coasts and New England states, there are few areas of the country that can afford to avoid this issue for long.

FEDERAL GOVERNMENT

To date, the federal government has left responsibility for solid waste disposal to states and municipalities, engaging only in limited solid waste data collection and distribution and technology transfer. Consequently, there are few solid waste employment opportunities at the federal level. Some experts, including Frank McManus, editor and publisher of *Resource Recovery Report*, believe this may be changing. "Congress is going to push the federal government into a more active role in solid waste. This will likely include research, technology transfer, data collection and analysis, and possibly regulation."

Federal regulation already has affected this field. Federal Clean Air Act regulations closed most pre-1970 incinerators and prompted a shift to landfilling. There have been efforts to tighten regulations on incinerator emissions. Further, the U.S. Environmental Protection Agency (EPA) is considering whether to classify incinerator ash as a hazardous waste—a move that would make the ash ten times as expensive to dispose of as the solid waste from which it was generated. In sum, federal jobs fall under the broad headings of research, planning, and related enforcement activities.

STATE GOVERNMENT

Being closer to the problem, states have taken a more active role than has the federal government. Most state governments are engaged in some form of statewide solid waste planning. Michigan, for example, requires municipalities and counties to develop five-year solid waste management plans, which must be approved by the Michigan Department of Natural Resources; New Jersey and Rhode Island have required that mandatory recycling programs be established at the local level.

State activities have gone beyond planning to include establishment of regional facility siting authorities, mandatory recycling of beverage containers, efforts to stimulate regional markets for recyclables, and legislation to restrict the flow of waste into a state. States also have the authority to determine environmental criteria for municipal landfills. For example, almost half the states have special regulations regarding disposal of incinerator ash. Positions created by this state activity include planners, communications and education experts, lobbyists, program managers, recycling experts, and enforcement personnel.

LOCAL GOVERNMENT AND PRIVATE SECTOR

It is at the local level where solid waste management decisions ultimately must be made, financed, and implemented. The workings of local government are often very politicized, and this seems particularly true in the area of solid waste. Milan Kluko, a consultant with Envirodyne Engineers, who assists municipalities with solid waste management plans, observes, "Waste disposal is very parochial, very political, and *very* emotional. Those entering this field should be well aware of this. However, it is at the local level where the action and I think the fun is—both in the public and private sector."

THE SOLUTIONS

RECYCLING

Many municipalities are embarking on a comprehensive solid waste planning process, beefing up planning staff and hiring outside consultants. These plans usually include recycling and sometimes include waste reduction efforts. "Recycling is a bona fide part of any integrated waste management strategy simply because the potential to reduce the amount of garbage entering the waste stream is significant," asserts Connie Leach, project director the New Hampshire–Vermont Solid Waste Project. Japan has made recycling the cornerstone of its waste disposal effort, reducing by 65 percent the volume of garbage that must be landfilled or incinerated.

Franklin Associates estimates a possible recycling rate in the United States of 20 to 25 percent by the year 2000. Some communities are aiming much higher. Seattle recently initiated a citywide curbside pickup program of recyclables and aims to recycle 50 percent of its waste stream by the turn of the century.

James Frey, vice president of Resource Recycling Systems in Ann Arbor, Michigan, says, "Most municipalities are set up to handle waste in a very conventional manner, landfilling and sometimes incineration, and the big waste management firms are structured accordingly. The costs of these two options, however, are increasing rapidly and causing municipalities to incorporate cost-saving measures such as recycling."

West Coast Salvage and Recycling, San Francisco, California. WCSR's "can line" separates and weighs aluminum cans.

Programs must be tailored to the unique characteristics of the area served and range from state or locally mandated separation at the household to drop-off centers to separation after collection—often at resource recovery facilities.

Recycling programs obviously need staff with recycling credentials. New Jersey, for example, only recently mandated that each county hire a recycling coordinator. Now, each New Jersey town is required to have personnel with recycling responsibilities. This is happening across the country, and consulting firms are hiring to keep pace.

A number of recycling specialists are emerging. These include entrepreneurs, market development experts, personnel to educate the public on recycling programs, communications experts, and recycling program administrators and planners. As Leach points out, however, "You can study natural resource management, but there is no recycling major I am aware of. One can enter the profession with a variety of educational backgrounds, but your real educational training must come in the field."

INCINERATION

Not all solid waste can or will be recycled. Thus, many municipalities that are facing imminent landfill shortages are considering resource recovery, or waste-to-energy facilities. These facilities burn garbage and generate electricity or steam as a by-product. In the United States, about 5 percent of the waste stream is burned, a figure that may grow to 25 to 35 percent by the year 2000 (by contrast, Japan burns 50 percent of its waste). Revenues for firms designing and operating these plants are projected to grow at a rate of 10 to 20 percent per year over the next decade.

This option, however, is not a panacea for municipalities. Resource recovery facilities are enormously expensive to start up, and construction usually takes more than five years. Given concerns about toxic heavy metals and dioxin emissions, the public often opposes these facilities as vehemently as it does landfills. Moreover, the 10 percent remaining volume in the form of ash is difficult and expensive to dispose of. In an incident rivaling that of the Islip garbage barge, Panama and seven states refused to accept a barge containing tons of incinerator ash from Philadelphia.

"Resource recovery is an immature industry with new companies springing up every month," says Frank McManus. "There is no formal training or stringent qualification for entering the industry, although a background in engineering, especially civil, or environmental science would be useful. The industry desperately needs creative people." Planners, scientists, and economists are needed to conduct feasibility and siting studies; financial personnel to capitalize these projects; and scientists and engineers to design, construct, and operate them.

LANDFILLING

Landfilling of municipal waste is not going to disappear when the current generation of sites reaches capacity. Even those municipalities that have the financial and technical resources as well as the political will to enact ambitious recycling and resource recovery programs will have remaining waste—either incinerator ash or noncombustible material. This will be about one third of the original waste stream, according to Dan Nelson, district manager for the Arbor Hills Sanitary Landfill of Browning-Ferris Industries of Southeastern Michigan, Inc., located outside Detroit.

New landfills will, however, be required to meet very strict environmental criteria such as multiple liners, leachate collection systems, coverings, and wells to monitor surrounding groundwater. As a result, says Nelson,

"The cost factor means that the landfill business will increasingly be dominated by large companies that have the tremendous capital needed to site a landfill.

"On-site as well as design staff must have a stronger technical background," he adds; "this is a new development in the field." Nelson has a master's degree in environmental engineering, and an operations manager at the landfill has a degree in public health. These are two of the best fields of study for those interested in design, construction, and management of municipal and hazardous waste landfills. In locations where the new landfills are an option, municipalities and counties have an increased demand for planners, engineers, public health specialists, hydrologists, and community involvement personnel.

GETTING STARTED

You can enter the solid waste management field from almost any discipline, but hands-on training is practically a must. Over the long haul, a master's degree enhances your career prospects considerably in this field, but it is not a prerequisite to landing a first job or being successful. In a new field such as solid waste, careers are made more by the ability to find solutions and get things done, not by degrees. Most professionals advise students considering an advanced degree to work for several years after college to lend more focus to their graduate study.

While a master's degree is not essential, an internship or some form of related work experience is considered vital. As any creative student knows, this experience can be obtained while still in school through a steady progression of research, independent study projects, volunteer positions, and summer jobs or internships. Help set up a school recycling project, intern at the local planning agency, do an independent project on local waste disposal projections (with original research). That is how you will get your first job.

Although you can start a career in solid waste management from almost any discipline, there are some courses of study that tend to foster skills particularly useful in the field. Civil, environmental, mechanical, and electrical engineering, possibly with additional work in public policy and management, are the most valuable degrees, especially for those who want to work for waste management companies and consulting firms. Public health is a popular major for those aiming for local government as well as the private sector. A planning or environmental science degree, with a resource management background, would lead you toward state and local employment. If you are interested in recycling, environmental science or natural resource management are useful disciplines.

Focus on developing, packaging, and marketing basic transferable skills, like analytical thinking, communications, project development and implementation, economics, and management. This is true for preparation in all fields, but particularly in a field changing as rapidly as solid waste is.

Be flexible and open minded about your first job. You are gaining experience and probably won't be designing resource recovery facilities. More likely you will be working to publicize a pilot recycling project, tracking down and entering data for a consulting firm, fielding consumer calls for a local planning agency, or double-checking regulatory paperwork for a disposal firm. Try to understand how your work fits in to the larger picture; focus on learning all you can and meeting everyone possible. This is all part of laying the foundation for your career.

SALARY

Starting salaries in the solid waste field vary according to sector, academic degree, experience, and region of the country. For consulting firms and the private sector, a graduate with a B.A. or B.S. can expect a salary ranging from $16,000 to $30,000, with $19,000 to $24,000 being the starting range for most. Engineers fall at the top end of the scale, as do persons with a broad range of skills, such as a combination of computers, planning, and life sciences.

Starting salaries in state government are a little lower but are fairly competitive with the consulting field. Expect around $20,000, maybe a little less. For entry-level jobs, this does not vary greatly according to your undergraduate degree. There is great variety in salaries at the local level. Generally, however, municipalities are strapped for cash. Someone with a B.A. or B.S. will probably start at around $16,000 to $18,000, maybe higher if the position is difficult to fill. Finally, starting salaries in the nonprofit sector are about $15,000 to $20,000.

CASE STUDY

Chicago's Solid Waste Crisis

Chicago has found itself quickly approaching the day when there will be no such thing as "out of sight" for its solid waste. The same scenario is being repeated across the country. In this case study we look at a range of professionals who get involved in solid waste management issues, from planners to consultants to community activists, to see how they work within the highly politicized arena of local public policy.

The southeast side of Chicago was once the center of industrial activity rivaling West Germany's Ruhr Valley. Much of the industry is gone, but the waste remains: 51 disposal sites, including sanitary landfills, on-site settling ponds, and sewage treatment plants. Concerned residents have begun to organize against continued dumping in this now economically depressed community.

In 1982, mayoral candidate Harold Washington was confronted by residents while campaigning on the Southeast Side. They were upset by plans to construct a privately owned municipal landfill in their community. Washington pledged, if elected, to put a hold on these landfill plans and set a citywide goal of recycling 25 percent of the waste stream by the year 2000.

In a historic election, Washington became Chicago's first Black mayor. Subsequently, he and his City Council rival, South Side alderman Edward Vrdolyak, fell over each other in their haste to enact a legislative moratorium on landfill expansion in the city. This only brought to a head a crisis already in the making. Chicago generates almost 5,000 tons of garbage daily, 20 percent of which is incinerated, the remainder stored in landfills that will probably reach capacity by 1990.

Seizing the momentum, environmental, recycling, economic development, and community groups throughout the city formed a citywide Coalition for Appropriate Waste Disposal (CAWD). According to Sue Lannin, a Sierra Club volunteer and cochair of CAWD, "This coalition came together over a realization that it wasn't equitable to continue dumping on the Southeast Side, but a force outside of City Hall needed to move the city toward implementation of an environmentally and economically sound waste disposal policy."

This coalition has met on a regular basis for more than five years, holding as many as several meetings a week. A diverse group of member organizations has provided staff time to work on the various subcommittees and projects. Robert Ginsburg, Ph.D., the research director of Citizens for a Better Environment, is the other cochair of CAWD. Ken Dunn is the president and operations director of the Resource Center, a nonprofit organization that employs 25 people on several curbside and buy-back recycling programs. Rennie Heath represents Southeast Chicago Development Commission, a nonprofit that pursues economic development opportunities for Chicago's South Side. Much of the leadership and labor also comes from volunteers of member organizations.

CAWD receives funding from a local foundation to employ staff from the Center for Neighborhood Technology (CNT), a local technical assistance and policy organization, part time. Woullard Lett, environmental projects coordinator for CNT, and Kathy Tholin, assistant director of CNT, are the primary CAWD staff. Activities of the coalition have included research, press conferences, public meetings, meetings with government officials, and demonstrations.

The wheels of public policy have moved slowly. In Chicago many city departments are involved in various aspects of waste disposal. Streets and Sanitation has direct responsibility for collecting and disposing of municipal garbage; Public Works designs and constructs public structures, including incinerators, landfills, and transfer stations; the Department of Planning looks at issues in the overall context of the city; and Economic Development weighs the economic impact of various options. Of course, major policy and funding decisions must be approved by the City Council.

According to Charles Williams, director of energy management with the Chicago Department of Planning, "Our department finally became involved because no one seemed to be doing any planning on what the city was going to be doing with its waste come 1990. Using our planning and technical staff, we did some research and wrote some white papers outlining the issues involved. The mayor's office, responding to citizens' efforts, began to read this as a political issue that could explode in their face. A public process was their answer."

In 1985, on the eve of the third landfill expansion moratorium, the administration announced the creation of the Mayor's Solid Waste Task Force to recommend a waste disposal strategy for the city. This 60-plus-person task force included representatives of six city departments, waste management firms, trade associations, recyclers, community groups, and environmental organizations—from engineers to businesspeople to activists. The objective was twofold: to draw on the expertise inside and outside of government and to try to reach some consensus among the involved parties.

Commenting on the process, Sharon Pines, then on the staff of CAWD, says, "Most of the real work was done in the various subcommittees: Finance, Recycling, and Resource Recovery. As chair of the task force's Recycling Subcommittee, I had to mediate between a contentious assemblage of technocrats, bureaucrats, politicos, community interests, and the private sector—each with its own agenda."

Milan Kluko was a consultant with the Department of Planning at the time. "A lot of work went into this process—by both staff and task force members. My role was to provide technical research for the subcommittees and to report their findings back to the city. I think it was an important education process for both the city and outside interests."

After months of work, many draft reports, and a lot of meetings, some semblance of consensus was reached. Recommendations were presented to the mayor, calling for the city to establish a waste management strategy with the following priorities: reduction, recycling, incineration, and, finally, landfilling.

The coalition has not been enthusiastic about the speed with which the city is implementing the task force's recommendations. City officials acknowledge the slow pace, but point to political and bureaucratic problems. "We are trying to fit innovation into a structure that is highly resistant to change," comments Dave Robinson, director of environmental services for the Department of Streets and Sanitation. "It's not like the private sector. We must contend with politics, unions, budgets, and personnel shortages. At the same time, while the public participation process is necessary, it sure slows us down—there are too many chefs in the kitchen."

Recyclers have not waited for the city to act. In the fall of 1987 they formed the Chicago Area Recycling Industry Council. This council works to promote the industry regionally and now has more than 50 dues-paying businesses, recyclers, scrap dealers, and waste management organizations, and a full-time executive director. Pines, now staff director for the City Council Committee on Energy, Environmental Protection, and Public Utilities, points to a mandatory recycling ordinance before her committee as another indication of future change in waste disposal practices.

Dave Robinson talks about some of the changes championed by the city: "We are attempting to create a pattern of recycling programs that fits the recommendations that came out of the mayor's task force. We are instituting an office paper recycling program in city buildings, a composting program, tire shredding, and promotion of biodegradable plastics in packaging, and we're writing procurement legislation to encourage the city to purchase recyclable materials. Other programs include a diversion credit program to compensate recyclers for each ton they divert from landfills, and tax abatement to promote a recycling industrial park in an impoverished West Side community."

"Almost six years after the initial fireworks, the city appears to be poised to take off on these issues," according to Woullard Lett of CNT and the coalition. "As much as anything, it was the escalation of the crisis that ultimately motivated them. Waste Management, Inc., reduced by 75 percent the volume of city garbage they will accept at C.I.D., a major landfill for city waste, and upped the tipping fee considerably. The city is now scrambling to truck much of its waste downstate and is having a particularly hard time finding a disposal site for its incinerator ash."

A consulting firm will soon be brought in to help the city further develop its solid waste management plan. Discussion continues on construction of another landfill on the city's Southeast Side—a move sure to meet with strong opposition. Finally, various incinerator scenarios are also being debated, yet these generally take a minimum of five years to site and construct and will no doubt be fought every step of the way. In other words, it is likely to get worse before it gets better in Chicago.

The Chicago example is probably more the norm than the exception for urban areas nationwide. Fundamental change is occurring in the way

PROFILES

Connie Leach, Project Director, New Hampshire–Vermont Solid Waste Project, Claremont, New Hampshire

The number one attribute for advancing in this field is the ability to get things done on the ground floor and to be flexible. Connie Leach's one-of-a-kind position is one of many that have cropped up in the solid waste field as each municipality responds to the unique nature of its solid waste situation.

"The New Hampshire–Vermont Solid Waste Project was created by 28 communities in Vermont and New Hampshire that banded together to take a regional approach to solid waste issues—for example, by siting one landfill rather than 28. The three components of our task are to develop recycling programs, to operate a 200-ton-per-day waste-to-energy facility, and to construct an ash residual landfill. We are governed by a board of supervisors and an executive committee. Funding comes from a user fee system in the 28-community region. Currently, two people are on staff: an accountant/secretary and I.

"My responsibilities include making sure trash gets to the facility, promotion of recycling, overseeing construction of the ash landfill, and developing the district's budget. A typical day could start at 7:30 A.M. and last till 9:30 P.M. It is common to have several meetings scheduled each day with one of the consultants or engineers working on the project or with one of the 28 representatives from a member municipality. Many evenings are dedicated to meetings with selectmen, recycling committees, or the board of supervisors. There may also be meetings with statewide organizations I am involved with, including the Vermont Technical Advisory Committee on Solid Waste and the New Hampshire Resource Recovery Association.

"Work time not scheduled with meetings or answering phone calls is dedicated to correspondence, developing media strategies, and keeping up on the literature. Related to construction of the ash landfill, there are designs to review, financing issues, and legal advice needed to answer appeals from those in opposition to the project. Recycling requires that a great deal of time be dedicated to educating waste generators on the need to separate their recyclables. This ongoing

Americans view and treat municipal waste. Change can be painful and difficult. As this case study shows, professionals from all sectors and with varied backgrounds are desperately needed to help municipalities successfully tackle this issue.

---

task includes a publicity campaign, public speaking, and work with local recycling committees.

"When you have a limited staff, common to nonprofit and public projects, employees must possess diverse skills and be self-motivated. Work at the local level is very time consuming. Also, working in the trash field can be emotionally stressful, since there is no one solution that is environmentally benign. Someone is always unhappy with the solution that is implemented; it's always in somebody's backyard. As a result, it is not uncommon to see dedicated professionals burn out after a few years.

"My undergraduate work was in the liberal arts with a focus on environmental studies. I had set up a recycling program at my college, so I was able to land a job as a recycling coordinator for a solid waste district. Later, I went back to school at the University of Michigan to get a master's in natural resources by writing a thesis on solid waste management. While in graduate school I had several internships to get more field experience and received a grant to study solid waste management and recycling in Western Europe.

"Solid waste management is a growing field, particularly in the area of recycling. Firms building resource recovery facilities will have to build in a recycling component to market their facility to municipalities. Trash haulers are also getting in tune with recycling and will be initiating such programs as designating recycling routes and pickup schedules for recyclables. There is much work to be done in the area of market coordination and development. Entrepreneurs will be looking at creative uses for recyclable products. Though once distinct, hazardous and solid waste management strategies are becoming closely linked. Waste minimization and recycling are important components of an integrated waste management system.

"People ask what kind of training you need for this job. My training came on the job and in the field, aided by formal studies in natural resources. Technical skills are important for some facets of solid waste management, particularly in designing and operating facilities. However, people with strong management, public speaking, and communications skills are equally important. If I were to hire someone today to assist me, I would look not only at his or her formal schooling but also at the practical experiences that indicate organizational and communications skills and an understanding of environmental issues."

Dan Nelson, District Manager, Arbor Hills Sanitary Landfill, Browning-Ferris Industries of Southeastern Michigan, Inc.

Landfilling is not going to disappear, no matter how much recycling, waste reduction, and incineration we do. The landfill field is changing; the level of academic preparation and experience needed for this field is rising steadily. Besides engineering, landfill work calls for skills in management, business decision making, and media relations.

"I am responsible for managing the 900-acre Arbor Hills Sanitary Landfill, which handles two thirds of Detroit's trash, or 10,000 cubic yards per day. Part of the landfill is currently under construction. I am also responsible for the details of construction work, marketing, public relations, and building a competent staff.

"Each day when I come to work there is a new challenge to meet, which makes this job very exciting. Today, for example, there is a local township board meeting and a local garbage forum (at the same time). I will interview consultants who are preparing a proposal to do some work for us and will be reviewing other consultants' reports. Later in the day I hope to be talking with my boss in Baltimore concerning some long-term development issues such as land acquisition, access rights, and shared maintenance agreements. Of course there will also be the more mundane day-to-day tasks such as paying bills. Other projects this week will include an interview with a TV station, an industry association meeting, and lobbying on some state legislation. I generally have evening commitments two to four evenings a week.

"Our full-time staff hovers around 25. In addition to myself, this includes an accounting manager, a clerk, a secretary, a record keeper, two or three mechanics, 10 to 15 operators and laborers, an operations manager, and two supervisors. We are grooming these supervisors for possible future positions as district managers or operations managers. One has a degree in public health, which is a new trend in the landfill industry. On-site managers are becoming more technically oriented as the new generation of landfills is becoming very sophisticated. I am a professional engineer with a master's in civil and environmental engineering, which is uncommon but will probably be the norm in the future.

"After graduate school, I spent two years with a research lab at the Army Corps of Engineers, four years consulting on landfill design, and three years with PRC Engineering working on resource recovery. My last position was at Waste Management, Inc., where I was a staff engineer at their international headquarters. My desire for a line job led me to my present position with Browning-Ferris Industries."

Milan Kluko, Senior Environmental Scientist, Envirodyne Engineers, Chicago

Milan Kluko turned school projects into the beginnings of a career—a common way to get started in this field. Since this interview Kluko has joined American Ref-Fuel, a waste-to-energy vendor in Houston, where he is manager of business development, another indication of the fast pace and job progression available to young professionals in this field.

"I am a senior environmental scientist in charge of coordinating Envirodyne's solid waste and resource recovery. Envirodyne is a multidisciplinary engineering firm involved in a variety of solid waste–related projects in the Chicago area. Our current projects include working with the Chicago Department of Public Works to update their data base on waste generation figures for the city; landfill operation and monitoring; providing technical assistance for lobbying efforts in the area of solid waste; and working in several Chicago-area counties on feasibility studies for recycling, waste-to-energy facilities, and general solid waste planning. This latter project will entail supplying much information to the public through presentations and forums.

"A typical day for me includes reviewing the status of all our solid waste contracts to make sure the proper work is being carried out on schedule, reviewing work for accuracy, examining the analysis developed by project team members, and writing final reports. In other words I spend a lot of time in meetings. A good chunk of my time also involves making presentations on our projects and talking to the press. Generally, I'm out of the office about two days a week. I also spend time with professional organizations such as the American Planning Association and the American Society of Civil Engineers. Finally, as with most consulting jobs, there is a lot of planning and marketing—following up on leads, planning work load and timelines.

"I got my undergraduate degree in geography from the University of Illinois at Chicago, and my background is in physical geography and hydrology. I suppose you could call me a geomorphologist. I started consulting while still in college pretty much by accident. While growing up, I had spent a lot of time hunting in Will County, south of Chicago. Over the years I began to notice a lot of changes in a local waterway as a result of development. I decided to study this and began doing floodplain mapping and measuring stream levels and sedimentation. At the same time a nearby drainage district official was looking for someone to analyze the impact of development on drainage in their township. He talked to the chairman of our department and I was in business.

"From there I took an internship through CEIP with the Chicago Department of Planning, where I was hired to study wetlands and drainage issues on the Southeast Side of Chicago. At this time the solid waste issue was coming home to roost in Chicago and I found myself serving as a technical consultant for the newly formed Mayor's Solid Waste Task Force.

"Our company hopes to be involved in helping the city develop its solid waste management plan. This would be extremely satisfying for me, working on a project that initially started my career.

"This is a hot, wide-open field and there is no one right way to get started. I have seen this field diversify significantly since I got started in 1984. You can't go to school to study garbage. Therefore, an internship is particularly important. One area of demand in solid waste is for project managers, in the public as well as private sector. In consulting, the normal progression seems to be that your first few jobs are spent in the research mode. From there you progress to report writing or assembling the data. Ultimately, you are involved in activities such as project management and development. Most often, you won't start in consulting but will cut your teeth at the state or local level. Local work will be very hands on, product oriented, state work a little more esoteric, such as examining and promoting alternative technologies.

"As far as general skills are concerned, work on your communications skills, get a master's degree in a different discipline from your undergraduate degree, take environmental, planning, and analytical courses, and remember that everything these days is done on computers."

IN SUMMARY

Don't stop with the Profiles and other information in this chapter. Individuals like those featured here work in your community. Each community's solid waste situation is a little different, requiring a different mix of professionals. Talk to them. How did they get started?

There is much to be done in the area of solid waste management and a great need exists for creative people of all backgrounds. This field is wide open.

RESOURCES

National Solid Wastes Management Association. Publishes *Waste Age* (monthly); has local chapters, conferences, seminars; offers internships. 1730 Rhode Island Ave., N.W., Suite 1000, Washington, D.C. 20036.

Resource Recovery Report (monthly). 5313 38th St., N.W., Washington, D.C. 20015.

The Management of World Wastes (monthly). Communications Channels, Inc., 6255 Barfield Rd., Atlanta, Ga. 30328.

Resource Recycling (seven times a year). P.O. Box 10540, Portland, Ore. 97210.

Recycling Today (monthly). GIE Publishing, 4012 Bridge Ave., Cleveland, Ohio 44113.

Solid Waste Report (weekly). Business Publishers, Inc., 951 Pershing Dr., Silver Spring, Md. 20910.

Solid Waste & Power (bimonthly). HCI Publications, Inc., 410 Archibald, Kansas City, Mo. 64111.

8　Hazardous Waste Management

IN THE 1980s hazardous waste management became *the* environmental issue. This was the result not only of infamous hazardous waste dumping incidents such as Love Canal, New York, and Times Beach, Missouri, but also thousands of lesser-known leaking toxic dumps and landfills. This ushered in what many refer to as the second generation of environmental issues. Public concern was warranted and is increasing as we learn more about the extent of the toxic waste. Consider the following:

- In 1980 the U.S. Environmental Protection Agency (EPA) estimated there were about 400 major abandoned hazardous waste sites in the United States; the Office of Technology Assessment says that 10,000 sites may be discovered over the next 50 years, and others place the number as high as 20,000, or an average of 400 per state. These dumps often contaminate surface water and groundwater supplies and can create significant toxic air pollution problems.
- The United States produces over 254 million tons of hazardous waste per year, or one ton per person per year.
- As of 1985 less than 1 percent of abandoned hazardous waste sites had been cleaned up, and costs are soaring. Superfund, the major federal cleanup legislation, received a total $1.6 billion appropriation for 1980 to 1985. It is estimated that the cleanup of the Superfund site at Adams City, Colorado, the Rocky Mountain Arsenal, will cost over $1 billion. The Department of Defense and Shell Chemical Corporation shared operations at this site.

This chapter will discuss the extent of the hazardous waste problem, the regulations and measures being adopted to combat this dilemma, the types of careers and skills needed to enter this developing and expanding field, and how best to prepare for and start a career in what is broadly called hazardous waste management.

THE DILEMMA

Unfortunately, the first generation of environmental legislation, embodied in the Clean Air and Clean Water acts, may have inadvertently contributed to the current hazardous waste site dilemma. A significant portion of waste is diverted to landfills as a result of efforts to reduce waste discharges into the air and surface water. Air pollution devices such as scrubbers produce large amounts of wastes; wastewater treatment facilities produce hazardous sludges. The shift to incineration of municipal wastes will produce large volumes of ash that contains heavy metals and may be classified as hazardous by federal and state legislation.

Now many of these hazardous waste dumps are leaking into the groundwater, and the air emissions near landfills can be a significant problem. This is another example of the common cross-media pollution, or environmental shell game, which is slowly coming to the attention of policy makers. There is concern that new hazardous waste treatment practices such as incineration and dilution into water supplies will merely exacerbate this trend.

Where does the hazardous waste come from? The chemical industry, particularly the organic sector, accounts for about 68 percent of all hazardous waste generated, with the metals and related industries (electroplating and metal finishing) contributing 22 percent of the waste stream. Although these large-scale generators are increasingly regulated, users of their products continue to add hazardous wastes to the stream. These users include small businesses such as dry cleaners, jewelry manufacturers, and automotive service centers, many of whom are now becoming subject to regulation.

Those in the field are quick to point out that hazardous waste and municipal solid waste are inextricably linked. It is only in the past two decades that we have attempted to separate disposal methods for hazardous and nonhazardous waste streams. Previously, most industrial waste was dumped on the site where it was generated—if a stream or body of water wasn't handy. Later, the waste was dumped and often burned with municipal garbage.

RESPONSE OF THE FEDERAL GOVERNMENT

The major federal legislation regarding hazardous waste is the Resource Conservation and Recovery Act (RCRA) and Superfund. RCRA regulations revolve around classifying hazardous waste and setting standards for its disposal, whereas Superfund focuses on cleanup of existing hazardous waste disposal sites.

Passage of RCRA in 1976 signaled the federal government's entry into the regulation of hazardous waste disposal. The heart of RCRA is to classify wastes as hazardous and require their disposal in designated facilities, and to establish a cradle-to-grave system for tracking hazardous waste from the point of generation to its ultimate disposal and 30 years afterward.

RCRA was significantly amended by the Hazardous and Solid Waste Amendments of 1984. Changes included increasing several-fold the number of generators (businesses) under regulation, setting a schedule to ban land disposal of over 400 hazardous chemicals, encouraging source reduction efforts, developing a process for classifying wastes and determining whether they are hazardous, and formulating regulations pertaining to industrial underground storage tanks.

There are, then, two kinds of hazardous waste: waste that is Hazardous with a capital H because it is so deemed by the government, and waste that is not regulated because of its low volume or diluteness but that is in fact hazardous. Municipal landfills, although not licensed to accept regulated hazardous wastes, in practice contain large amounts of hazardous waste from household trash, small nonregulated generators, and illegal dumping. This will present a significant challenge to future environmental professionals.

While RCRA focuses on regulating hazardous waste disposal, Superfund legislation is aimed at cleaning up abandoned and inoperative waste sites. There is little disagreement that the original legislation (entitled the Comprehensive Environmental Response, Compensation, and Liability Act, or CERCLA) was woefully inadequate, considering the scope of the problem. Between 1980 and 1985 the law brought about long-term cleanups at only 14 sites nationwide—out of an estimated 2,000 to 10,000. It is hoped that the Superfund Amendments and Reauthorization Act of 1986 (SARA) will rectify some of the early problems (see the Case Study for further discussion of Superfund).

State legislatures have established their own superfund programs to supplement federal activity. However, many at the federal and local level consider Superfund a necessary evil. Dr. Rebecca Head, hazardous substance specialist for Washtenaw County, Michigan, says, "For some time to come federal and state governments will continue to focus on cleanup and will be spending big bucks in that area. I would hope, however, that they will move toward a more proactive role, such as providing assistance to industry and enforcement to prevent future superfund sites." Some states are already beginning to move in this direction, as we will see later in this chapter.

Anyone interested in pursuing a career in hazardous waste management needs to understand the importance of being familiar with the legislation and regulations. "There are several reasons that regulations are important," remarks Deborah Flynn, an environmental planner with the consulting firm of Dames & Moore in Seattle. "Obviously, legislation certainly drives the jobs in this field, but also remember that people drive the legislation. The legislation serves as a pulse for people's attitudes and concerns regarding hazardous waste." Understanding the plethora of federal, state, and local regulations is an important part of a hazardous waste professional's job. It is with some justification that an environmental consultant, in promoting his services at a recent conference, likened the job of a multistate corporate environmental affairs coordinator to "walking a tightrope blindfolded while being fired at."

If legislation and liability drive jobs, they also drive changes in environmental disposal practices. Here again, there are parallels with the solid waste industry. Largely because of the staggering prospect of cleaning up existing hazardous waste dumps, federal and state regulations discourage and in some cases are beginning to outlaw land disposal of these wastes. Also falling out of favor are strategies such as deep well injection and dilution. Public concern, or the not in my backyard (NIMBY) syndrome, has resulted in the closing of existing facilities and created an atmosphere in which, as Resources for the Future, a nonprofit research organization, reported, not one hazardous waste facility was sited in the United States between 1980 and 1986.

Options for approaching this dilemma fall into two broad categories: (1) finding new ways to treat hazardous waste generated and (2) devising methods to reduce the amount of hazardous waste generated in the first place. Under the first strategy, one of the leading options is high-temperature hazardous waste incineration. This is being actively pursued, although critics point to its expense and speculate that, once again, we may be merely shifting the problem to another media—this time, the air. Other treatment technologies include oxidation, biodegradation, and more secure landfilling techniques.

The second strategy has met with far more excitement and, with the support of industrial trade associations, appears to have momentum on its side. Measures would include waste reduction, recycling, reuse, and concentration. The congressional Office of Technology Assessment released a report in 1987 that estimated that in the next few years half of hazardous waste generated in the United States could be eliminated by using existing technology. There are, however, no federal regulations mandating waste reduction. Right now the movement—deemed too slow by many—is toward encouragement, assistance, and incentives.

JOB OPPORTUNITIES IN ALL SECTORS

> *Hazardous waste issues are creating jobs at the federal, state, and local levels and with consulting firms and industry. Tell them you are interested in hazardous waste and suddenly they want you to come in and talk to them.*

> Deborah Flynn, Environmental
> Planner, Dames & Moore, Seattle

All employers in this field, whatever the sector, are scrambling to find employees who can help them solve hazardous waste problems. Although many types of professionals are needed for these efforts, some of the specialists in high demand include hydrogeologists, to trace groundwater pathways for contaminants; quality control and quality assurance people who have chemistry and systems backgrounds, to evaluate and manage projects; risk assessment workers; public and environmental health professionals; environmental engineers, to design systems and processes to reduce, recycle, and treat hazardous waste streams; lawyers and records management personnel; managers with technical backgrounds; and environmental chemists and environmental toxicologists.

FEDERAL GOVERNMENT

Federal legislation drives regulation and cleanup activities in the area of hazardous waste. Each of the EPA's ten regions has divisions charged with administration and enforcement of Superfund and RCRA. Recent reauthorization and expansion of both pieces of legislation have boosted activities, and hence EPA hiring, significantly. Phillip Millam, chief of Region 10's Superfund Branch, comments, "Our office has doubled in two years and is now growing at a rate of about 10 percent per year. I expect this to continue for at least the next several years."

The federal government is also engaged in researching treatment technologies, toxicity of waste streams, and waste minimization technology. While federal government hazardous waste activity is centered on the

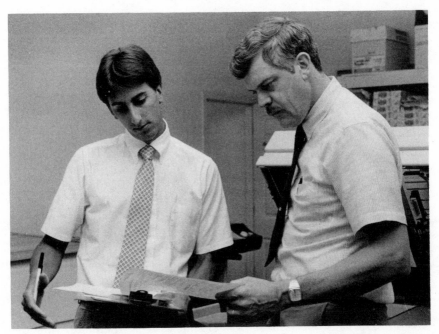

Hanover, Massachusetts. Mike Szerlog reviews new regulations governing the disposal of hazardous wastes with local print shop owner Bob Parmenter.

EPA, hazardous waste–related positions in both research and cleanup exist in virtually every government agency, from the Department of Defense to the National Park Service. The major governmental employers of hazardous waste professionals include the Occupational Safety and Health Administration, the Departments of Defense, Energy, and the Interior, and the Army Corps of Engineers. Ironically, the federal government, specifically military installations and production sites for military equipment, has many major leaking hazardous waste sites, including some of the most costly Superfund sites.

Any federal job search should include a thorough exploration of agencies other than the EPA. A good place to start is at Federal Job Information Centers located in major cities. Contact agencies and departments directly for job information as well as fellowships, cooperative education agreements, and internship information.

Consulting Firms

Consulting firms come on the heels of the federal sector because they do much of their business either directly with the federal government or with industries being regulated because of federal legislation.

The federal government, although responsible for overseeing remedial action at Superfund sites, hires consultants to do most of the work. This includes initial feasibility studies, testing, lab analysis, designing solutions, actual cleanup, and even coordinating public participation. Superfund funding increased fivefold in 1986, and a commensurate long-term increase in demand for consulting services is expected.

Companies hire consultants to help them understand and comply with federal, state, and local hazardous waste regulations. There are some Superfund-related activities, including compliance with community reporting requirements and emergency response planning provisions. Most of the work, however, stems from RCRA regulations. Large companies need assistance in complying with evolving RCRA regulations, and many smaller companies that were brought under regulation by the 1984 RCRA amendments are turning to consultants rather than hiring staff.

There is much diversity in the consulting field, in terms of both firm sizes and specialties. Some firms take on a company's entire waste problem: air, water, hazardous waste, worker training, and legal and technical aspects. Other, more specialized firms may be called in to analyze one of several hazardous waste streams. Personnel needs, therefore, vary depending on the work of the firm. Consulting firms are primarily interested in experience and demonstrated skills in project development and management, whereas the government, especially at the state and federal levels, often uses rigid hiring criteria and extensive testing of applicants. Deborah Flynn points out that the head of Dames & Moore's hazardous waste division in Seattle has a B.A. in psychology but was hired because "he had the skills." These aren't just any skills (see Getting Started), but examples like this illustrate two important points: (1) In a developing field, educational criteria are not formalized, and experience and skills are often obtained on the job, and (2) nontechnical skills, such as project management, communications, and the ability to bring projects in under budget and on time, are valued in a field like hazardous waste because of its focus on projects rather than products.

STATE GOVERNMENT

More and more, states are doing the federal government's bidding by serving as the principal implementers and enforcers of federal environmental statutes. States are the first line of RCRA enforcement, and many states have hazardous waste legislation that goes beyond RCRA. Illinois, for example, is one of a number of states phasing in a ban on land disposal of liquid hazardous wastes, the largest category of hazardous waste. Further, most state legislatures have established and funded their own superfund programs to supplement federal activities and to clean up sites not on the National Priority List.

States are involved in and often have final authority over the thorny issue of siting hazardous waste facilities. They take the lead in developing emergency response plans in the event of toxic releases. Many states are going beyond the federal focus on cleanup and are trying to prevent future superfund sites; more than 33 states have waste minimization efforts. Minnesota, for example, provides on-site and telephone waste reduction consultation, a waste reduction resource bank, and research grants for waste reduction projects.

LOCAL GOVERNMENT

All hazardous waste is generated in some municipality or county, and all of it, except what is dumped in the ocean, comes back to roost in our backyards. Thus, despite a complicated web of federal and state regulations, we are still talking about a local issue. "People are increasingly aware of and concerned about hazardous waste issues in their communities," acknowledges Rebecca Head. "This, combined with a decentralization of environmental issues, is resulting in more activity at the local level."

Much of this local involvement centers on responding to hazardous waste issues specific to a community and on supplementing the state and federal regulatory structure. "Many issues can best be tackled by local units of government," asserts Lee Botts, deputy commissioner for environmental protection for the city of Chicago's Department of Consumer Services. "Federal and state regulations regulate big generators and are geared to postincident response. We are looking at prevention and thus have programs such as taking inventory of abandoned facilities and vacant lots to discover contaminations. We also respond to such issues as fly-by-night dumping and violators acquiring old buildings and stuffing them with hazardous wastes." Botts adds, "I head up a staff of 55 persons, most of whom hold positions that have been created in the last few years. Job titles include environmental control samplers, director of toxic pollution control, and environmental coordinators—essentially the gamut of professionals needed to develop and implement various hazardous waste detection and response programs."

County governments get in on the action as well. Washtenaw County in Michigan, for example, is implementing its own community right-to-know ordinance, establishing emergency response teams, collecting household hazardous waste, starting a groundwater mapping project, and providing waste reduction assistance to area businesses.

PRIVATE SECTOR

Hazardous waste activities in the private sector can be divided into two broad categories: first, those companies that generate hazardous waste in their production operations, and second, firms that transport, treat, and dispose of the waste other companies produce.

Simply stated, at the generation end, companies need personnel who can help them comply with environmental regulations in a cost-effective manner. For larger firms, this may translate to an entire environmental affairs department complete with lobbyists, lawyers, engineers, health specialists, and plant-level staff. Mid-sized companies have significantly smaller staffs. Marcella Colling, profiled later in this chapter, is an environmental engineer, responsible for all environmental issues—air, water, and hazardous waste—at a mid-sized steel company in Michigan. Smaller companies often use consulting services, although changes in regulations are causing some increased in-house staffing.

A related and overlapping field that is growing rapidly is known as industrial hygiene. These professionals are primarily concerned with worker safety and toxins in the workplace. They often interact with environmental staff; in many cases industrial hygiene is one of the responsibilities of an environmental affairs coordinator. State regulations and those promulgated by the federal Occupational Safety and Health Administration are relevant to this field.

As noted earlier, there is a trend toward reducing the amount of hazardous waste generated in the first place. This includes waste reduction, waste separation and concentration, material recovery, and waste exchanges. According to many experts, this is an engineering issue that, more often than not, involves redesigning production processes. Thus, those with both an environmental and a management or production background are in high demand.

Driven primarily by hazardous waste regulations, an entire industry has sprung up to transport, treat, and dispose of hazardous waste. The research firm Arthur D. Little, Inc., estimates this will be an $8 billion market by 1990, $13 billion by 1995. Some are new companies, and many have evolved from and are part of businesses dealing with other waste streams such as solid waste. They range from mammoth international companies like Chemical Waste Management, Inc., and Browning-Ferris Industries to local firms specializing in the treatment of a waste stream from a particular industry, such as metal finishing. Many of these firms continue to orient their operations toward land disposal of hazardous

Michigan Department of Natural Resources, Lansing, Michigan. Trina Swygert analyzes organic waste compounds taken from water samples to be tested in the department's environmental lab.

waste. Others are working on developing new treatment and detoxification methods and moving into areas such as waste reduction and recycling.

There are many opportunities with these firms, including testing companies' waste streams, regulatory analysis, research on waste treatment technologies, design and operation of landfills and other waste treatment facilities, and selling the services of these companies.

NONPROFIT SECTOR

Neither government nor the private sector brought the issue of toxic hazards to the forefront of public concern. This was the result of grass roots efforts and national environmental organizations. Lois Marie Gibbs, a resident of Love Canal, New York, led the fight in her community when toxins from an abandoned dump began leaking into basements and appearing in school yards. This was the nation's first widely publicized toxic disaster. Gibbs went on to form the Citizen's Clearinghouse for Hazardous Wastes, Inc. (CCHW), with five offices nationwide. She attributes the success of her effort to organizing, not lawsuits, and CCHW operates under a philosophy that environmental public policy is 90 percent politics and 10 percent science.

National organizations such as the Natural Resources Defense Council, Inc., the Sierra Club, Environmental Action, Inc., and the National Wildlife Federation work extensively on hazardous waste issues. As the environmental movement matures or ages (depending on your perspective) these organizations are increasingly hiring technical staff such as scientists and economists to bolster their arguments.

The real story as far as the nonprofit sector is concerned, however, is the strengthening of grass roots organizations and, hence, increased staffing of these groups at the state, regional, and local levels. Hazardous waste is usually only one of many issues that nonprofit environmental organizations work on at the state and local levels. These organizations are looking for people who understand how public policy is formulated, can communicate, and know how to organize people into action; a technical background, while extremely useful, is probably of secondary importance. The jobs are there, even though the competition is tough and the financial compensation, while improving, is often below that of business and government.

GETTING STARTED

There is great demand for many types of professionals in the hazardous waste management field. As with the solid waste management profession, you can enter the field with just about any educational background and the right hands-on experience. Those with technical backgrounds such as chemistry, engineering, and hydrology are in great demand, as are professionals with knowledge of related air and water quality issues.

In a new and expanding field, practical experience takes you far. Obtain some of this experience while still in school through internships, independent projects, and research. Good experience for the hazardous waste field would include demonstrated laboratory and field skills, projects that showed a grasp of relevant legislation and the workings of federal, state, and local regulatory processes (SARA, CERCLA, RCRA, Title III, manifest forms, cradle-to-grave, right-to-know—all of these terms and acronyms should mean something to you *before* you go in for your first interview), computer projects, technical writing, and any work in a government office or regulatory agency.

You can get a job in hazardous waste with a B.S. and even a B.A. Because of the technical nature of the jobs, however, graduate and technical degrees are more important than in the solid waste management field. Chemistry, biology, geology, and engineering are some basic undergraduate degrees. Environmental studies, environmental science, or liberal arts majors should take as many hard science and engineering courses as possible. Learn about hydrology, toxicology, public health, economics, public policy, and statistics.

After you work for a while you will see the range of specialties available to you and can target any further study accordingly. The more popular areas of graduate study include engineering (especially chemical and environmental), public health, toxicology, public and business administration, chemistry, hydrology, biology, planning, and industrial hygiene. Don't make the mistake of counting yourself out of the field because you aren't working toward or haven't obtained the right degree. There is a niche for just about anyone in this field. Course work, skills, and experience are almost always more important than the degree, provided, of course, that you present yourself effectively.

If you have a B.A. or B.S., your first job is likely to include a lot of fieldwork and lab work, tracking down data, data entry, helping out on various projects, and possibly some writing. You will be a technician of sorts, not 100 percent heady stuff, but remember you're learning some basic and important skills, and everyone has to start somewhere.

After being in the field for some time, you may wish to take an examination to become a certified hazardous materials manager. This exam is administered by the Institute for Hazardous Materials Management in Rockville, Maryland, and tests for theoretical and practical knowledge of hazardous materials management. Hazardous waste specialists are certified by the National Environmental Health Association in Denver.

SALARY

Starting salaries for those with a B.S. or B.A. are generally comparable to those in the solid waste management field. In the consulting field, salaries are somewhat higher, starting at between $22,000 and $26,000. An M.S. or M.A. could bring $23,000 to $35,000 to start. This reflects both higher demand and the more stringent credentials required by this field.

Starting salaries in established waste management companies or companies that generate hazardous waste tend to be a little higher, with a range of about $22,000 to $27,000, with engineers occupying the high end. With an M.S., you could start at $30,000 or higher.

The federal government is a significant employer in the hazardous waste field. If you have a B.A. or B.S., you'll start at about $17,000, with an M.S. around $23,000.

CASE STUDY

Superfund: Cleaning Up Generations of Mistakes

Few environmental statutes have received as much public attention or have been as politicized as Superfund, the nation's hazardous waste remediation program. Passed in 1980, when little was known of the extent of abandoned hazardous waste sites, the legislation received little support from the Reagan administration. Foot dragging and politicizing of the program eventually led to the resignation of EPA Administrator Anne Gorsuch Burford and the imprisonment of Rita Lavelle, EPA's top hazardous waste official.

While unfortunate, these events, coupled with a regular disclosure of new hazardous waste spills, galvanized public support for a strong national cleanup effort. This was reflected in the 1986 rewrite of Superfund, the Superfund Amendments and Reauthorization Act (SARA), which strengthened the Act tremendously and increased funding fivefold.

SARA brought about a number of changes that aspiring professionals should note because of their impact on the types of skills in demand in this field. First, SARA focuses on seeking permanent solutions and alternative technologies for Superfund remediation projects rather than merely moving the hazardous substances to other landfills, which may eventually leak. Second, the act includes an extensive new regulatory structure for underground storage tanks. Finally, Title III, the Emergency Planning and Community Right-to-Know Act of 1986, requires communities to improve their emergency planning procedures for chemical accidents and mandates that industries report the presence of hazardous substances to community authorities.

If you're considering entering the field of hazardous waste cleanup and wondering if there will be anything left for you to do, rest assured that federal and state remediation activity is not going to cease when SARA expires. The most wildly optimistic figures estimate that 500 sites might be cleaned up by 1992. The Office of Technology Assessment estimates that 10,000 uncontrolled sites might be discovered over the next 50 years, with cleanup costs reaching $100 billion. In addition, the U.S. Department of Energy estimates it should spend $150 billion for cleanup of hazardous wastes at its weapons-production facilities. The Department of Defense says $11 billion to $14 billion are needed to clean up hazardous waste pollution at 5,000 sites on U.S. military bases. This means long-term growth for the industry. According to EPA documents, the current federal need is for civil, sanitary, and environmental engineers, chemists, biologists, public health specialists, geologists, hydrologists, and soil scientists.

What follows is a look at some of the professionals and projects at the Superfund program in Region 10 of the EPA, based in Seattle. Following this look at the federal aspects of Superfund, we look at Environmental Toxicology International, Inc., a private consulting firm working in the area of hazardous and toxic waste.

EPA REGION 10, SEATTLE

Phillip Millam is chief of the Superfund Branch for Region 10 of the EPA, which includes Alaska, Idaho, Oregon, and Washington. "I serve as the program manager of the Superfund remedial, removal, enforcement, and Title III efforts. The biggest responsibility of my staff of 40, however, is the Superfund remediation program. Currently 55 sites are listed on the National Priority List (NPL) in Region 10; 41 of these sites are being investigated or cleaned up.

"The staff divides into Superfund teams to work on specific projects. The site management team may consist of engineers, lawyers, toxicologists, biologists, and generalists—those who have a wide variety of technical and managerial experience. The educational degrees of these persons vary widely, but each individual must be able to work in a team environment. Cleanup of a site typically takes two to five years from start to finish. We also work with the Army Corps of Engineers, community groups, state agencies, and contractors."

Sally Martyn is one of Region 10's Superfund site managers. "I am responsible for tracking, organizing, and managing the activities at two Superfund sites. When a site is placed on the NPL, EPA starts the Superfund process with a remedial investigation. The purpose of the investigation is to characterize the extent of contamination and the potential for migration, both off-site and throughout the site. On my end, this means scoping out the work, managing contracts and contractors, and working with whatever other agencies are involved. We also work closely with any nearby communities.

"After characterizing the problem, a feasibility study is conducted to evaluate cleanup options. For contaminated soils, these options could include capping the site to contain the hazardous material, removing the soils, treating the soils, either on or off site, and so on. Before completing the study and writing a record of decision, EPA solicits public comment on the validity of the characterization and evaluation. Finally, the cleanup action is initiated. My responsibility is to keep all parts of the project moving forward, on schedule. Consequently, most of my time is spent communicating and coordinating with all parties involved.

"I frequently turn to EPA's Environmental Services Division for assistance. This pool of experts includes hydrologists, hydrogeologists, biologists, geologists, soil scientists, and other specialists. I think site managers frequently draw on these personnel when difficult technical questions arise or when aspects of the projects require expert review."

Millam observes that the Gramm-Rudman-Hollings Act, or Balanced Budget and Emergency Deficit Control Act, "may put a crimp on federal hiring, but I see three avenues of potential growth related to the EPA. They are EPA contracts with private engineering and consulting firms (mostly to implement Superfund), new or expanded EPA regulations that have budgets for implementation, and state-funded superfund programs, which are on the increase."

A few Superfund-related personnel that are in demand include hydrologists, records managers, paraprofessional assistants, environmental lawyers, financial analysts, quality assurance personnel with chemistry backgrounds, environmental engineers, and environmental paraprofessionals or technicians with two-year degrees in hazardous waste disposal practices.

"There are numerous mechanisms for getting involved in this field," Martyn says. "I have chosen the government route. The private sector, specifically consulting firms, is another way to go." On working for the federal government, Millam admits, "It definitely has an element of frustration. Unrealistic congressional deadlines, low salaries, and high expectations of the press and public top the list. However, I still think I have the greatest job. I am continually fascinated by the work and am surrounded by competent and extremely dedicated people."

ENVIRONMENTAL TOXICOLOGY INTERNATIONAL, INC., SEATTLE

The EPA is a relatively small employer in the hazardous waste field. Many more employees work for consulting firms that contract with the EPA, state government, and the private sector. Environmental Toxicology International, Inc. (ETI), based in Seattle, is one of these firms. According to Dr. Kathryn Kelly, the president and founder, ETI focuses on assessing the health effects of environmental problems, and training workers to deal with hazardous waste emergencies. Her firm has clients in both government and private industry. The firm assesses the health effects of Superfund sites, proposed incineration facilities, and many other sources of contamination.

"Passing by Love Canal on my way to graduate school helped me decide what I wanted to focus on," relates Kelly. "I was disturbed by the general 'out of sight, out of mind' way of handling hazardous waste and wanted to do something about it. Preventing illness was what I wanted to be doing, so I made toxicology my focus. After working at several different places, I most enjoyed the challenges and diversity of opportunities offered by consulting firms."

ETI now has about 20 employees. These include toxicologists, chemists, biologists, community involvement specialists, risk assessment specialists, hazardous materials managers, and personnel concentrating on health and safety and emergency response.

Dr. Joyce Tsuji, an environmental physiologist at ETI, discusses one of her current projects. "A company owned an industrial site that it wanted to donate to the public. This site, however, had some polychlorinated biphenyl (PCB) contamination, both in the soil and in adjacent river sediment. This is a responsible company and wanted to clean up the site before making the donation. As is often the case, an engineering company had been called in first, and we were asked to analyze their sampling data. This is a challenge, since the data are not always adequate for assessing potential health risks. We were asked to estimate risk from the contamination for humans and also for the organisms in the river. We requested biota sampling and evaluated PCB concentrations in a worst-case indicator species, sculpins, which are bottom feeders.

"Even though this was a voluntary cleanup, the EPA was involved and recommended we expand the scope to include priority pollutants. This additional evaluation resulted in identification of high lead levels for a portion of the property. Actual cleanup is not handled by ETI. Our final product is a report estimating site risk and assessing the relative risks of different types of remedial activities, in this case dredging or capping PCBs in the river sediments.

"Other current projects include health risk assessments for proposed incineration facilities of all types. On these projects, we estimate the impacts of ambient concentration and deposition on human health and wildlife for different pathways, such as inhalation, uptake and bioaccumulation of chemicals in sport fish and in food crops, and ingestion of contaminated soil by children. These are multidisciplinary studies involving professionals with several types of backgrounds."

Kelly says that consulting firms do not usually require successful job applicants to hold a certain type of degree, and they often provide a lot of room for advancement regardless of one's degree because the hierarchy is less entrenched than in some other firms or in government. Further, entry-level jobs do exist in consulting for those with a B.A. or B.S. "We understand some people are gifted in various areas and may have the skills even if they don't have the degree. The major limitation is when the person must make a presentation or sign off on a project where the credentials of a graduate degree are important. Attributes that I look for are good judgment, intelligence, self-motivation, and dedication to producing the best possible results."

Bryan Graham was hired by ETI in January 1988. "This is my first job in the field. With a B.A. in geology, I consider myself lucky, since most consulting firms require at least a B.S. with its more technical course work. I really enjoy working for a small consulting firm because of the interaction with senior staff." Graham is assisting project teams conducting risk assessment studies for three incinerator projects in the Seattle area. "I research the chemicals and their interaction, compile existing ambient air quality data from various sources, do data entry, and write portions of reports. As part of one project, we are setting up a hotline to handle the public's questions on the proposed incinerator. I will be handling these calls. I am also helping to track deadlines and budgets on various ETI projects."

PROFILES

Marcella Colling, Environmental Engineer, Quanex Corporation, Mac Steel Division, Jackson, Michigan

In-house environmental staff in the private sector must possess a wide range of knowledge and skills, and often find themselves doing a juggling act. If you want to be a jack-of-all-trades, small to mid-sized companies are for you; if you want to specialize, consider a larger operation.

"I am environmental coordinator for a 230-employee facility and do related consulting for other facilities owned by our company. If you did this work for a big corporation you would probably specialize in, say, water treatment, hazardous waste, or air quality, but with a small to mid-sized company, such as ours, you are an environmental generalist; in other words, you do everything!

"One area at a time, then. Hazardous waste: I arrange pickup of waste, implement waste reduction efforts, replace old equipment, handle manifest tracking (the required paperwork for cradle-to-grave tracking of hazardous waste), talk to regulators, and am trying to figure out how we will deal with the new landfill ban contained in RCRA. Water: I handle National Pollutant Discharge Elimination System permits and make sure systems are working, gather samples, do some lab work, tabulate and write up results, fill out permits, negotiate with regulators, appear at commission meetings, and write special reports

Commenting on work in the consulting field, Kelly admonishes, "The consulting business is not for you if you desire an eight-to-five job. On the other hand, if you want a lot of diversity in your work and are highly motivated, there are no greater opportunities than in consulting." Tsuji adds, "There is probably more pressure than in government work. Your product is your performance, so the pressure is always on to keep performing. Personally, I like the excitement and opportunities in a small firm.

"My advice to students is to get a good handle on issues in the environmental field. While it helps to have a specialty, you should also generalize. We have interviewed people who had very valuable specialties but did not have the 'big perspective' on other issues. Without this larger perspective, our recommendations are of little use to the client, so good judgment is very important. Undergraduates often get jobs in consulting firms in a support role, work for a while, and then go to graduate school once they've found an area they want to research further."

and recommendations for improving or replacing wastewater systems. Air: I handle the permit process, talk to regulators, and take emission readings.

"In addition to these plant-level activities I also lobby through the Michigan Manufacturers' Association and am active in the local manufacturers' association. I serve as the representative of small industry on the state Emergency Response Commission, established by our governor under Superfund, and am a member of the county solid waste planning committee. These activities are all considered part of my job.

"To give an example of a specific project, we used to pay $4,000 to $5,000 per month to haul away waste oil. I started talking to maintenance staff and engineering about what a waste this was and, gradually, a plan

began to develop to install a settling tank and to use that oil for lubrication in other areas of the plant. I needed to get the cooperation of everyone involved and keep the idea afloat. We rigged this up using existing equipment and whereas we used to buy 20 55-gallon drums of oil per month, we haven't purchased oil in two years.

"I graduated with a degree in environmental science in 1979, and since there were no jobs I took a part-time job doing water quality planning at a regional planning agency. As the economy improved and more jobs became available, I was able to secure a position in industry. While working at Mac Steel, I have earned a master's in industrial technology.

"Initially, I had my doubts about working for industry, but now I love it. The job is very satisfying in that you have the opportunity to make improvements firsthand. Sure, sometimes you have to make decisions that aren't black and white: Do you shut down the plant if parts per million of oil goes from 10 to 11 in an hour? However, I do see a commitment on the part of industry to being good environmentalists, and I feel I can do a lot of good. Responsible companies never ask employees to break the law; they just don't do that. I feel I am improving the environment and instilling an environmental ethic among employees. They come to me and ask, 'What do I do with this waste?' They could have dumped it down the drain and no regulator would have known. It is also very satisfying to be part of a team effort. Finally, the money is good.

"Frustrations? There is still a male good-old-boy network in the manufacturing sector and some lingering resistance to environmental compliance—they do it, but their heart is not always in it. This is not true of more enlightened management. It can also be frustrating working with a tight budget. I sometimes would like to do a big study and get all the information, but I can't—the money or time isn't there.

"My advice to anyone who is interested in this field is to target the industry you want to work in and learn as much as you can about it: How do they work, what are the trends and manufacturing processes? You need this for interviews. Further, join technical and trade associations to keep up on the field and trends in the industry. Know chemistry and biology because regulation is based on science. Develop a love for reading law. You will be doing a lot of it."

Donald Macdonald, Environmental Compliance Officer, Chemical Waste Management, Inc., Sauget, Illinois

Donald Macdonald has an entry-level position in the hazardous waste management field, with one of the larger of the many firms that transport, treat, and dispose of hazardous waste. Here, he talks about the hands-on nature of his job and gives some advice on getting into the field.

"As an environmental compliance officer, I conduct environmental and health and safety assessments of our waste management facilities, primarily incinerators, landfills, and solvent recovery and deep well injection sites. I also audit outside companies if they handle our waste. As part of an assessment, I visit a site for two or three days to review federal, state, and local permits, look at paperwork, such as manifest forms, to ensure it is being filled out correctly, and conduct a systems check following waste from when it goes in to when it comes out of a facility. I might also check groundwater samples or any data relevant to a particular site.

"In a given day, I am exposed to almost every environmental law—hazardous waste, air, and water; federal, state, and local. I sit down with the general manager and environmental manager and we figure out how to resolve problems.

"This is one of several levels of Chemical Waste Management's internal environmental review system. We have an Environmental Compliance Officer Program Manual, which we follow in attempting to identify and act on issues and concerns before they become regulatory violations. I suppose I'm an 'internal EPA' of sorts.

"The satisfaction of this job is seeing that a company can handle hazardous materials in a responsible fashion—there is a structure for change when necessary. I deal with many types of facilities and issues, so I am getting a broad background and meeting many people. I suppose the biggest frustration is the travel, which takes up about 50 percent of my time. Also, I am responsible for six or seven facilities, so I'm never around long enough to get to know people as well as I would like. Finally, the hours are long, which is not too bad since I am finding the work very exciting.

"I have a bachelor's in public affairs and a master's in environmental science, with a concentration on hazardous waste management, from Indiana University School of Public and Environmental Affairs. I also took a lot of classes in economics, management, and law, recognizing that these would be important skills, especially later in my career.

"Through The CEIP Fund, I obtained two internships with the Standard Oil Company (now BP America) working on hazardous waste issues. It is fair to say that my internships made my career. In addition to the important experience and contacts, internships help you learn what you *don't* want to do as much as what you do want to do. The experience from the internships also helped me tremendously in getting this job. Even though it was my first job, I already had related work experience. This put me a cut above other applicants coming straight out of school. My advice in obtaining your first job is to get organized, set goals, do your homework, stay away from human resources departments, and take the time to get the job that is right for you. Be creative."

Lee Botts, Deputy Commissioner for Environmental Protection, Department of Consumer Services, City of Chicago

Lee Botts considered herself an environmentalist long before Earth Day. She has worked in the public and private sectors in a number of capacities. The hazardous waste work of Chicago's Department of Consumer Services shows the range of hazardous waste issues municipal governments are tackling.

"As deputy commissioner for environmental protection, I am responsible for a staff of 55 involved in everything from field operations to coordinating environmental programs with state and federal agencies to environmental policy and program development. This is the top environmental position in the city of Chicago, and basically, I had to create it. An earlier study I conducted while working for a nonprofit organization noted a lack of leadership on environmental issues within the city and recommended that the city strengthen its environmental efforts. Incidentally, this is true of a lot of jobs in the environmental field. They are often not easily categorized, and you must create them yourself with your objectives as the blueprint.

"My taking a position with a local unit of government in a way parallels the movement of environmental concerns. Environmentalism started at the local level with a concern for public health. Then conservation issues took the forefront and action moved to the federal level. Legislation was passed in many areas. In my case, I began working on environmental issues first as a citizen activist, then moved to regional and national issues. I chaired the Great Lakes Basin Commission, from 1978 until I was fired by James Watt in 1981.

"Back to Chicago: I was shocked to discover that Mayor Jane Byrne had abolished the Department of Environmental Control, an example of thoughtless budget slashing, especially when the federal government was returning environmental responsibilities to the local level. While federal standards and policies for environmental protection are essential, many of these issues can best be tackled by local units of government. Some projects we are working on involve safe handling of hazardous materials in ways not being dealt with under existing state or federal regulations. These laws regulate large amounts of waste and are geared to clean up after spills or environmental damage has occurred. We are looking at prevention and are inventorying abandoned facilities and lots for hazard contaminations. We are also responding to fly-by-night dumping as RCRA regulations go into place. As disposal costs increase, hazardous materials are being left in old buildings and in vacant lots or by the side of the road.

"Our new hazardous waste program

IN SUMMARY

Hazardous waste is the hottest environmental issue in the United States and will remain so for some time. The field needs creative individuals from all backgrounds—individuals who have specific technical skills, and just as important, those who see the larger picture. How can we cost-effectively mitigate the environmental hazards from the thousands of uncontrolled waste sites? How do we address the cross-media issues, so that solving a groundwater toxics problem doesn't create an airborne toxics dilemma? How does a country, and the world for that matter, continue economic progress, which necessarily includes manufacturing, and not threaten the health and very existence of its environment with the resulting toxic by-products? Those who have the vision and the nuts-and-bolts skills to tackle these questions will prosper in this field.

will require us to create 24 new positions. These jobs will include environmental sampler, environmental control inspector, environmental engineers, director of toxic pollution control, and environmental coordinator.

"Another goal of our new program is to work with other city departments and integrate our environmental programs with state and federal programs. Here one encounters some of the reality of municipal government: bureaucracy and inertia. It is important to have well-defined goals but be flexible in implementation and above all be patient. Local politics is another ever present reality. Accept this and carry on.

"There is no pattern as to how local governments set up environmental programs. Arrangements are all over the map, unlike state government where there is a pattern of separating pollution control and conservation. Urban environmental issues include ozone, with many cities needing to deal with their nonattainment of national standards and possible economic development penalties; chemi-

cal waste and hazardous materials as well as solid waste issues—all issues that are economic as much as environmental; and finally, an attitude change concerning pollution. In the sixties the question was whether to control pollution; now the question is how much control to exert.

"In my time you didn't get a specific education to work in the environmental field—that didn't exist. You formed or worked for an organization, continually broadening your scope of issues. That has changed. Many aspiring environmental professionals come to me for advice. The ones that aren't going to make it are those who say they want to get paid for doing good or saving the world. You need degrees and experience and you need to get practical. I strongly recommend experience before graduate school. As an undergraduate, try to get some science background. I have a B.A. in English and in my work I must interpret scientific information, which means I have had to educate myself and do a lot of reading."

RESOURCES

Hazardous Materials Control Research Institute. Professional organization. Publishes *FOCUS* (monthly newsletter), *Journal on Hazardous Waste and Hazardous Materials* (quarterly). 9300 Columbia Rd., Silver Spring, Md. 20910.

Air and Waste Management Association. Trade association for personnel in the fields of air pollution control and hazardous waste management. Publishes the journal *JAPCA* as well as various special publications. April issue of *JAPCA* each year contains a useful directory of companies and government agencies in these fields. Association operates a job matching and referral service at its annual meeting. P.O. Box 2861, Pittsburgh, Penn. 15230.

Chemecology. Covers health, safety, and the environment as it relates to the chemical industry. Subscriptions are free. Chemical Manufacturers Association, 2501 M St., N.W., Washington, D.C. 20037.

American Chemical Society. World's largest organization devoted to a single scientific discipline. Publishes over 20 periodicals, including *Chemical & Engineering News* (weekly), *Environmental Science and Technology* (monthly), and *Chemical Abstracts*. Also publishes materials on careers. Student memberships are available. 1155 16th St., N.W., Washington, D.C. 20036.

Citizen's Clearinghouse for Hazardous Wastes, Inc. A nonprofit, grass roots organization that assists, through research and publications, community organizations that are working on hazardous waste issues. Publishes *Action Bulletin* (four times a year). Maintains regional offices in Virginia, Louisiana, Alabama, West Virginia, and California. Publications catalog is available. P.O. Box 926, Arlington, Va. 22216.

Pollution Engineering: The Magazine of Environmental Control (monthly). Focuses on air and water pollution control and hazardous waste management. One issue a year includes a Yellow Pages–type listing of environmental instrumentation, equipment supplies, components, materials, and services. Pudvan Publishing Co., 1935 Shermer Rd., Northbrook, Ill. 60062.

9 Air Quality

AIR POLLUTION is quite egalitarian—it disperses rapidly to affect all living organisms, and it is a serious threat to the environment as a whole. By contrast, groundwater contamination, although dire enough in its own right, is a slow process, often measured in years; at any point along the way contaminants can be measured, analyzed, and cleaned up through remediation measures. Pollutants in the air, however, can disperse within minutes, and there is no possible retrieval. Some pollutants can accumulate in upper layers of the earth's atmosphere, changing our climate and causing irrevocable damage to the protective ozone layer. The disastrous gas leak at Union Carbide Corporation's Bhopal, India, plant in 1984, which killed and injured thousands, showed how toxic and uncontrollable atmospheric pollutants can be.

Despite the seriousness of the issues, ensuring healthy air quality might appear to be a fairly simple and straightforward proposition: Prevent pollutants, generated mainly in chemical reactions and combustion processes, from being released into the air. At one time, policy makers envisioned a relatively simple, albeit ambitious, regulatory agenda: Air pollution was seen mainly as a local problem, which could be solved by regulating the primary pollutants being discharged in an area or region, principally by big industries and automobiles. This was the essence of the major amendments to the Clean Air Act which were passed in 1970. In some respects, the strategy has worked quite well. According to the U.S. Environmental Protection Agency (EPA), the following reductions in pollutant concentrations nationwide were achieved from 1976 to 1985: lead in the air, 79 percent; carbon monoxide, 36 percent; total suspended particulates, 24 percent; nitrogen dioxide, 11 percent; and sulfur dioxide, 42 percent.

These are not, however, the gains policy makers, public health officials, and environmentalists hoped for back in 1970. Virtually every major metropolitan area is out of compliance for concentrations of ozone or carbon monoxide (or both), and unregulated toxic pollutants are now recognized as a serious health threat. Pollutants are also traveling long distances, crossing national boundaries, and combining in ways scientists don't fully understand to threaten human and environmental health. Even our homes can no longer be considered a safe refuge as studies suggest our indoor air may be more toxic than that outdoors, even in industrial areas.

In short, solving first-generation air quality problems has proved to be much more complicated than originally envisioned. On top of these unsolved problems, other threats to air quality, such as acid rain and depletion of the ozone layer, are growing in severity and scope.

CLEAN AIR ACT

The first Clean Air Act, passed in 1955, was replaced in 1967 by the Air Quality Act, which is still referred to as the Clean Air Act. Amendments such as those in 1970 and 1977 have strengthened the Act considerably. Presently, the heart of the Act is the requirement that the EPA establish national ambient air quality standards (NAAQS) for any air pollutant that may "reasonably be anticipated to endanger public health or welfare."

In 1971 EPA developed standards for six priority pollutants: ozone, carbon monoxide, sulfur dioxide, lead, nitrogen dioxide, and particulates. Each state was required to submit a state implementation plan, demonstrating how it would meet the standards within five years. State implementation plans include regulation of stationary sources (mainly industries) and automobiles. In the face of extensive noncompliance, Congress extended the deadline to 1982 and again to December 1987.

Most states have met air quality standards for lead, particulates, and nitrogen and sulfur dioxides, but virtually every metropolitan area is out of compliance with carbon monoxide or ozone standards (or both). Carbon monoxide is primarily attributed to vehicle emissions. Ozone, which is often equated with smog, is a secondary pollutant formed in the atmosphere by a chemical reaction between nitrogen oxides, volatile organic compounds (VOCs), and sunlight. Nitric oxides and VOCs are discharged by fossil-fueled power plants, industrial operations, and motor vehicles.

Both carbon monoxide and ozone present serious health problems and contribute to environmental degradation.

By law, regulators are supposed to levy such sanctions as construction bans and cutoffs of federal funds against metropolitan areas not attaining ozone or carbon monoxide standards. This is unlikely to happen. Instead, Congress is working on compromises in the rewrite of the Clean Air Act, which would require new state implementation plans with more realistic schedules for meeting these standards. This will continue to challenge state and local air quality officials who must look for new ways to further reduce emissions.

Although meeting NAAQS may be a headache for state and local air quality officials, acid precipitation, or acid rain, is the air quality issue attracting national and international attention. Scientists, utility officials, and policy makers have had great debates on the origin and effects of acid precipitation. Most agree, however, that sulfur and nitrogen emissions from power plants, smelters, and, to a lesser extent, automobiles combine with atmospheric moisture to form an acidic rain that increases the acidity of lakes and streams, reduces forest growth, affects crops, and may contribute to coastal degradation. Any solution to this problem will be expensive and could disproportionately affect the economies of certain regions of the country. Acid rain is the most controversial issue in the rewrite of the Clean Air Act.

Stratospheric ozone depletion and the greenhouse effect are two other global concerns. The culprits in depletion of the ozone layer are primarily chlorofluorocarbons found in aerosols, refrigerants, and plastic foams, which slowly rise to the stratosphere. There, they break down the ozone layer, the earth's shield from ultraviolet rays. The discovery that winter ozone levels in Antarctica have plummeted 40 percent has made this an immediate global issue. The greenhouse effect, caused by long-term buildup of carbon dioxide and pollutants like carbon monoxide emissions, which trap heat in the lower atmosphere, can result in a global warming trend, which could have disastrous social and economic consequences.

James Barnes, deputy administrator of the EPA, points out, "Global air pollution poses special kinds of control problems. The problems inevitably encountered when people attempt to coordinate research projects or control programs are compounded by international differences. Nevertheless, the United Nations–sponsored 1987 Montreal Protocol ozone agreement, the first international effort to control an air pollutant, indicates that air quality work and research on the international level are going to increase in the coming years.

Another major issue to be addressed by the Clean Air Act rewrite will be airborne toxic emissions. These include dioxins, cadmium, polychlorinated biphenyls (PCBs), and hundreds of compounds that are linked to cancer, lung disease, birth defects, and other diseases. Sources of these toxic emissions range from chemical plants, oil refineries, incinerators, and motor vehicles to dry cleaners and sewage treatment plants. The EPA, under the 1970 Act, was instructed to identify and regulate toxic air pollutants that present a public health problem. This pollutant-by-pollutant approach has not worked: In 19 years, standards have been set for only eight of hundreds of toxic chemicals. The rewrite of the Act will likely significantly simplify the process for regulating chemicals and may require EPA to set standards for broad categories of chemicals, such as VOCs.

Surprisingly enough, indoor air pollution has become one of the bigger environmental issues of the 1980s. Dangerous chemicals found in indoor air include asbestos, formaldehyde, lead, combustion by-products, pesticides, and radon. They have produced what is now referred to as the sick building syndrome. One study by the EPA of seven cities found that indoor concentrations of toxic and carcinogenic compounds were 200 to 500 percent higher than outdoor concentrations. Radon, a natural radioactive gas that seeps into houses through their foundations and is often found in water, is an even greater threat. According to the EPA, cancer deaths attributable to radon in the home range from 5,000 to 20,000 per year, making it the most serious environmental health problem in the United States today.

THE JOB MARKET

For the immediate future, the air quality job market is somewhat tight, but it is expected to loosen up as new federal, state, and local programs come on line. Consulting firms and local governments may see the largest increases in hiring of air quality professionals. Opportunities are particularly bright for those with chemistry and engineering backgrounds; also in high demand are those skilled in management and communications and versed in technical environmental issues. Bonus points for those with experience in different environmental media: air, water, solid and hazardous waste.

Gerald Emison, in *Meeting Environmental Workforce Needs*, writes, "While moving into new areas, we must sustain the infrastructure of air pollution control which we have built up over the last 15 years. Keeping the progress we've made to date is real work too! That is why I sometimes find it hard to understand why people talk about air quality as a 'mature' program. It certainly doesn't feel mature to me! I see plenty of exciting new work to keep our solid core of professionals busy for a long time to come."

Clearly, there is still much to be done in the short and long term to ensure air quality that is healthy to humans and the environment. Scientists and policy makers are wrestling with strategies to meet air quality goals set 19 years ago, as well as coping with more recent developments. This translates into important and challenging work in all sectors. Hazardous waste issues, however, are commanding much of the attention and many of the resources that once were directed to air quality programs.

Employment levels in the federal government have declined somewhat; state and local governments have held their own, with hirings or layoffs depending on regional factors; demand for consultants continues to grow as they take over work formerly performed by the government or environmental staffs of corporations.

Many believe air quality staffing, especially at the state and local level, will eventually increase, as new programs come on line and the risk of airborne pollutants is given full consideration. William Becker, executive director of both the State and Territorial Air Pollution Program Administrators and the Association of Local Air Pollution Control Officials, remarks, "Policy is now distinctly skewed in favor of dumping in the air: Acceptable toxic exposure for siting a new hazardous waste facility, for example, might be one part per million, while that same chemical can be burned in an incinerator with a risk of one part per thousand. Ultimately, however, comparative risk assessment will lead to resources and attention going to areas that have the greatest human risk. Therefore, I see a lot of growth in this field in the coming years."

What kinds of professionals are and will be in demand? As in the water quality and solid and hazardous waste fields, the simple, honest answer to this question is that opportunities exist for an extremely wide range of professionals. Those who have the easiest time entering the field are engineers, especially mechanical, environmental, and chemical.

This is becoming an increasingly complicated and technical field: Many more pollutants are being studied, monitored, and regulated; trace toxins and the interaction of these pollutants require more sophisticated monitoring and remediation measures. This creates a need for environmentally oriented scientists and engineers, including chemists, public health professionals, and mathematicians. On the other hand, these complicated programs are creating a demand for the generalist with a technical and environmental orientation: managers who understand a variety of air pollution issues and how they relate to other environmental issues; people who can communicate, verbally and in writing, with professionals and the public, on issues of health risk, economics, and air quality programs; lawyers who understand the web of federal, state, and local regulations.

FEDERAL GOVERNMENT

The rewrite of the Clean Air Act will create new federal programs and some new positions. These will likely be in the areas of basic research, development and oversight of state and local programs, and economic analysis. Areas in which regulation is expected to begin or increase include airborne toxins, indoor air pollution, ozone, and acid rain. Moreover, programs connected to existing regulations will continue to operate. Still, the fact is that federal staffing for air quality programs has decreased in the past ten years. Charles Pratt, of the EPA Manpower and Technical Information Branch, estimates total federal staffing for air quality programs has decreased from 15,000 in the mid-seventies to less than 10,000 in the late eighties. Although some recovery in job prospects is expected, new programs are being discussed in the context of limited budgets and efforts to place much of the staffing burden on consulting firms and state and local government.

Stan Meiburg, director of the planning and management staff for the EPA Office of Air Quality Planning and Standards, envisions a three-part role for the federal government. "First, we will be involved in setting national standards. Second, the federal government will work to provide technical support to state and local air pollution control agencies. This role will be very important as air pollution control regulations become increasingly technical, requiring expertise state and local agencies don't have and can't afford. Finally, we will be responsible for oversight and administration of these programs and standards: Are we making progress? If not, why?"

Jobs at the federal level, therefore, fall into several categories. Basic research and lab work by both engineers and environmental scientists (chemists, biologists, physicists, mathematicians, microbiologists) is a big area. This work will include engineering analysis and developing and designing technologies to meet certain standards; risk assessment, or determination of what regulations are necessary to ensure human health; crop and environmental damage assessment; and mathematical modeling of dispersion of air pollutants and the impact of various control strategies. Professionals with backgrounds in meteorology are examining how pollutants combine and disperse in the atmosphere. Computer science and data management specialists are needed to make sense of the reams of data collected in continuous monitoring across the country.

New regulatory programs will be developed in the areas of airborne toxins, acid rain, and indoor air pollution. In addition to technical personnel, policy analysts, planners, managers, economic analysts, and communications specialists will be required to develop and implement these programs.

Professionals will also be needed to work with state and local air pollution control agencies on their programs. This will include development, review, and oversight of state implementation plans, training of state and local air pollution control personnel, and establishing inspection standards in each of the EPA regions. Increasingly the EPA is using consultants for this work: Seven universities provide training under federal contract; large corporations such as TRW, Inc., and Northrop Corporation are designing air pollution experiment equipment, and consultants are conducting monitoring and lab work. Consequently, federal employees spend a lot of time managing contracts while, as one EPA official jokes, "the contractors do all the fun stuff."

STATE AND LOCAL GOVERNMENT

State and local units of government are called on to implement and enforce a growing and increasingly technical array of air quality programs. This creates a need for more technically competent staff, especially chemical engineers and analytical chemists, and also those who can manage and communicate about these programs—professionals with liberal arts backgrounds who have some degree of technical competence. Because employees in this part of the public sector more often do the hands-on work of ensuring air quality, those who like to see results and finished products might be happier here than in the federal government.

To get federal funding for air pollution control under the Clean Air Act, states must submit to the EPA state implementation plans showing how they intend to comply with NAAQS. The states, in turn, work with local agencies to achieve compliance. State and local agencies also develop regulations and programs that go beyond federal legislation, most notably in the areas of airborne toxins and indoor air pollution.

Since the severity and type of air pollution problems vary by state and region, there is great variety in the local regulations implemented to achieve compliance with Clean Air Act regulations. Some jurisdictions regulate small dischargers such as bakeries, gas stations, and dry cleaners; Portland, Oregon, has worked to limit downtown parking by encouraging the use of mass transit; Los Angeles is considering limiting truck access to freeways during peak pollution periods; Denver has required the use of oxygenated motor fuels to limit hydrocarbon emissions. The types of professionals needed in a given region depend on the local regulatory situation.

The level of state and local air quality employment also depends on the severity of the pollution problem. A state like Montana may have only a handful of air quality professionals in the public sector, whereas more than 500 professionals work for the South Coast Air Quality Management District, which serves Los Angeles. In general, programs are largest in the urban areas, notably on the East and West coasts and to a lesser extent in the Midwest, Florida, and Texas. The number of private sector positions with consulting firms and manufacturers parallels government programs and regulation.

Air pollution control agencies develop and enforce the programs to ensure their area meets NAAQS. Personnel are needed in air quality engineering, modeling, inspections, and compliance monitoring. Chemical, mechanical, and environmental engineers evaluate sources of air pollution, design and set up networks to monitor ambient pollutants and emissions, conduct lab analysis, and analyze computer-generated data.

Environmental scientists, particularly chemists, analyze data and identify the types and sources of pollutants. Some agencies use public health personnel for risk assessment. Inspections are generally conducted by a mix of engineers, scientists, and technicians. Other personnel needs depend on the size of the agency and could include lawyers, metallurgists, microbiologists, meteorologists, toxicologists, and epidemiologists.

Much of the work of local air pollution control agencies, such as inspections, lab work, and maintaining monitoring equipment, is done by graduates of two-year technical schools. However, as William Becker says, this may be changing. "The inspections and equipment did not used to be as sophisticated, and dispersion and health risks could be easily measured; now you need to go to college just to pronounce the names of these toxic pollutants—pollutants that are toxic in minute quantities and require very sophisticated monitoring equipment, pollutants that we also have very little data on.

"Local agencies are still run by engineers, but there is an increasing realization that they need managers, lawyers, public relations people and writers, people who can communicate to the public, mediate, and negotiate. Hence, we are beginning to see an influx of liberal arts majors into the field—people who had not been associated with the field in the past. This is exciting."

PRIVATE SECTOR

Air quality jobs in the private sector are primarily with consulting firms, since all levels of government and industry are increasingly turning to these firms for expertise and experience. Positions range from entry-level field sampling and monitoring to project development and management, and prospects are particularly bright for those with chemistry backgrounds and lab experience.

In the 1970s, when major new environmental regulatory programs were being developed for air, water, and toxic waste, it made sense for companies to have large in-house environmental staffs. This has changed, according to Brian Ketcham of Konheim and Ketcham, an environmental management firm in New York City. "Unless they are continually building and designing projects, it just doesn't pay for companies to have people on staff. An advantage with consultants is you buy instant expertise; they are learning all the time by doing projects with a variety of companies."

Paul Kueser, director of programs and planning for the Air and Waste Management Association, adds, "Take USX Corporation (formerly US Steel) here in Pittsburgh. They used to have an environmental staff of 130. Now they are down to five. The environmental staff that companies now hire are more experienced in project management. They manage the contractors and consultants and ensure the systems are kept working." (There are exceptions to this trend, and many companies still have air pollution professionals on staff.)

Consultants provide a variety of services for a diverse group of clients, including the public sector. Earlier we noted that the EPA is contracting with outside firms for everything from training to monitoring to design and basic research. As the hundreds of trace toxics come under regulation state and local governments are going to need experts in many areas. It is unlikely that the federal government will always be there, so they will turn to consultants.

Dischargers are turning to consulting firms to bring them in compliance with new and tightening regulations. Consultants keep such companies informed about regulations, design, build, install, and maintain systems, and negotiate with regulatory agencies on behalf of their clients.

Anticipated acid rain legislation will require utility companies to cut back dramatically on sulfur emissions, which will create many in-house and consulting positions. Additional new markets include waste-to-energy and hazardous waste disposal facilities. Another area of steady consultant employment is in conducting environmental impact assessments and reviews, which are required whenever development projects may have a long-term impact on the environment. Firms working on environmental impact statements hire urban and environmental planners in addition to engineers and scientists.

Consulting firms are hiring many of the same air quality professionals as is the public sector. The focus again is on engineers, especially chemical engineers knowledgeable about toxins.

One other private sector employer in this field are the companies that manufacture air pollution control equipment. Annual capital expenditure for air pollution abatement in the United States has dropped from $2.2 billion in 1975 to $1 billion in 1984, but it is expected to rise to $8 billion per year by 1995, assuming controls on acid rain are instituted.

GETTING STARTED

Entry-level jobs in the air quality field are most plentiful in state and local government and in the consulting field. Engineering, chemistry, and lab experience will give you the quickest start. Have a specific skill to take to potential employers, along with some related experience, preferably more practical than academic. Plan ahead for government positions, as the process can be quite lengthy. If you are still in school, start your networking now via independent projects and internships. Join local chapters of professional associations.

Chrysler Corporation, Michigan. Paul Kantola checks the regulators on air cylinders used to calibrate Chrysler's emissions testing equipment.

If you are just starting a career as an air quality professional, Roger Westman of the Air Pollution Control Bureau in the Allegheny County Health Department (Pittsburgh) has this advice: "State and local agencies are a good place to start an air quality career. They have the disadvantage of lower pay, but they offer unique experiences and opportunity for growth. Turnover is steady, as people tend to move on after two years to higher-paying jobs in the private sector. It is important to prepare oneself to come to the work force with a marketable skill to fit a slot. I like those who have degrees in the classical fields: chemistry, engineering, and physics. Follow up persistently on leads and interviews, especially since the public sector job process moves slowly."

Having a marketable skill is particularly crucial in landing that first job if you do not have an advanced degree. Many employees in air pollution control at state and local agencies are support personnel with two-year technical degrees. There is a good chance, however, that with a B.A. or B.S. you too will start with a technician-type job: doing fieldwork, operating monitoring equipment, assisting in inspections, collecting data and entering it into computers, and engaging in various lab activities. Then, according to Paul Kueser of the Air and Waste Management Association, "If you are a good writer, you might get promoted, although generally to become a professional in this field you will eventually need to obtain a master's degree."

Corbin Leininger, a CEIP associate with Chrysler Motors Corporation, encourages job seekers not to neglect the private sector. "There is a lot of entry-level work for consulting firms doing fieldwork and air sampling— good entry-level work." One of the best ways to identify these firms is to look in the professional journals such as *JAPCA*, the journal of the Air and Waste Management Association.

Those with environmental science or liberal arts backgrounds such as planning, law, economics, journalism, and political science find starting positions in areas such as technical writing, public relations, economic analysis, research, and state and local planning assistance related to air quality. To get an edge, take some technical courses (like chemistry), know computers, understand air quality regulations and how industries operate, and be able to make sense of technical data and studies.

Stan Meiburg of the EPA offers a particularly useful bit of advice: "Yes, you are going to have to perform a specific task or tasks on your first job, but work to get as broad a preparation early on in your career as possible. Be careful not to get narrow too early in your career or you might wake up one day and find yourself trapped. Think about your career in a holistic way, always thinking about positioning yourself not just for the short term, but for long-term development."

While jobs in the private sector often require a more specific technical background than those in the public sector, they also have more latitude on hiring. Brian Ketcham, founder of a consulting firm, says, "Quite frankly, when I interview I spend more time sizing up the individual, their attitude, and their aptitude than looking at their degree. Are they enthusiastic? Do they appear dedicated? Do they demonstrate attention to detail—a mainstay of success on your first job?" Public sector employers are more bound to job descriptions and requirements. However, they have ways of getting around the personnel process if they want a particular person badly enough.

SALARY

Most of the salary information available for this field applies to engineers and chemists. Entry-level jobs for those with engineering degrees pay in the range of $20,000 to $35,000, depending on schooling and location. Local agencies lie at the low end of that range, state and federal agencies a little higher, and private sector employers in the upper 20s to low 30s. Someone with an M.A. in engineering can expect to start in the low 30s, maybe a bit lower at the state and local level. Those with B.S.s in chemistry start in the $16,000 to $28,000 range. Many other positions, for those with backgrounds ranging from environmental science to communications, start at around $20,000; this does not vary significantly by sector.

CASE STUDY

Allegheny County Air Pollution Control Bureau

Local air pollution control agencies are the pivotal implementers of the nation's clean air policy. There are over 200 of these agencies at the local level and 50 state offices charged with implementing and enforcing national and local clean air programs. Each of these agencies employs between five and 500 people, with most reporting between 10 and 70 employees. (Consult any April issue of *JAPCA* for listings of these different agencies.) These professionals are the front line in carrying out the new programs and initiatives discussed earlier in this chapter.

Despite a decline in manufacturing, Pittsburgh is still known as one of those cities where "they make things." Along with manufacturing jobs and a sense of pride, however, comes an air pollution problem that, according to

Dr. Roger Westman, at one time gave Pittsburgh the nickname Smokey City, much as Los Angeles is known for its smog.

Westman is the division administrator for planning for the Allegheny County Air Pollution Control Bureau, an agency that has spearheaded efforts to clean up Pittsburgh's air. The bureau, part of the County Health Department, exists as a direct result of the 1970 Clean Air Act. Under the provisions of the Clean Air Act, states must devise implementation plans for meeting national ambient air quality standards (NAAQS). The bureau must plan, develop, implement, and enforce the county's portion of the state plan, which requires it to develop source emissions standards that will enable Pittsburgh to meet NAAQS.

According to Westman, "The largest job category at the bureau is engineers: industrial, chemical, mechanical, and environmental. Engineers are about one third of the staff. We also employ chemists, mathematicians, electronics technicians, computer programmers, and meteorologists. Finally, there are opportunities for journalists and attorneys with technical backgrounds."

As the division administrator for planning, Westman is responsible for planning agency programs, establishing management objectives, budgeting, and program review. He does the planning for new or revised state and federal air pollution programs, negotiates with public officials and industry, and is involved in air pollution modeling.

"I use my broad overview of the staff's modeling and technical work to set policy and guide negotiations with the EPA and industry. The staff does the initial work and I come up with the final draft. It is also my job to come up with the funds and resolve any snags."

It usually gets complicated when you get down to the nitty-gritty of complying with air quality standards. For example, Westman says, "Sulfur dioxide levels are very high in Pennsylvania. The state, using computer modeling, developed a sulfur dioxide standard and reduction strategy. Unfortunately, the model was developed under rather simplistic assumptions, such as a flat terrain. The Pittsburgh area is notorious for its rugged terrain and for industrial sources set among hills and valleys. So, we had to develop sophisticated technology and computer analysis to incorporate these factors into a viable plan for attaining the standard. This was a real challenge in monitoring, data analysis, modeling, and planning."

The Air Pollution Control Bureau encompasses the following divisions:

- Planning, which employs engineers and a meteorologist to guide the bureau's activities.
- Enforcement, which has the first contact with generators of pollution. This division inspects plants, negotiates agreements on emissions, and

investigates complaints. Attorneys, industrial hygienists, engineers, and inspectors staff the division.

- Air Monitoring, which is responsible for ambient air sampling and primarily hires electronics technicians with advanced training, chemists, engineers, and non-college-educated technicians.
- Source Testing, which tests emissions sources such as factories and incinerators and monitors mandated self-testing of these sources. Most personnel in this division are engineers and top-notch technicians.
- Quality Assurance, which tests instruments, inspects test sites, and runs its own tests to verify results. Almost everyone in this division is a chemist or chemical engineer.
- Computer Services and Data Analysis, which employs engineers and mathematicians to prepare air quality reports and maintain permit files.

To give a better sense of how federal regulations are implemented at the local level, Westman traces the involvement of the bureau in carrying out Section 112 of the Clean Air Act, which sets national emission standards for hazardous air pollutants. "The EPA was unable to come up with specific standards for airborne toxins and instead published an incomplete list of air pollutants it felt should be regulated. It asked states to implement the regulation and provided the funding to do so. We then began the process of training staff members, acquiring equipment, and researching and interpreting our powers under the federal regulations.

"Establishing regulations to meet ambient air quality standards starts with modeling, air monitoring, and data analysis. If, for example, we need a 15 percent reduction in a particular pollutant I go to Engineering, which proposes where the reductions could come from. This information is turned over to the Legal Section, which helps write the regulations. Once regulations are established, Enforcement must devise the appropriate application, engineering review, and implementation systems. Control and monitoring devices also have to be developed. If a regulation were passed today in Congress it would be approximately four years before actual enforcement monitoring could begin.

"As my title might suggest, I do a lot of administrative work. I usually have at least one meeting a day, am always on the phone, and spend most of the rest of my time reviewing air quality data, drafting papers, and resolving problems in the office. Most of my interaction is with county agencies, but I am still involved at the state and federal level and do a lot of traveling. Like everyone else, I also sometimes get stuck with surprises from the boss, such as drafting a position paper for the Health Department on the Clean Air Act, which I found on my desk this morning.

"I earned a B.S. in chemical engineering from Northeastern University and a Ph.D. in chemical engineering, specializing in air and water quality control, from the University of Kentucky. My first job at the bureau was as an air pollution engineer and I gradually climbed to handling administrative functions."

George Manown, supervisor of the Inspection Section of the bureau's Enforcement Division, sheds some light on how regulations, once formulated, are enforced by the agency. "In this particular unit of Enforcement, we focus on responding to complaints. Working for me are four field personnel, two engineers, and two air pollution inspectors, whose main job is to answer complaints submitted by residents throughout the county— there may be a malodor in an area, or the steel mill may smell particularly strong on a given day. The inspectors wear beepers and respond to calls by heading out into the field and, where appropriate, taking air samples and setting up equipment to determine if there are any unusually high concentrations of chemicals in the air.

"If a problem exists, they determine the source and turn any violations over to the legal staff, who take action to notify and possibly fine the source as well as see that appropriate pollution control measures are taken. In 1987 we responded to approximately 1,600 such complaints. To ensure the competence of our staff, we require them to attend a training session every six months on how to read smoke for capacity and content. We also review permits for open burning. All in all, enforcement is a public, people-oriented job.

"My entry into the air quality field was rather unexpected. I obtained my undergraduate degree in education from Point Park College here in Pittsburgh and have been previously employed in various industries— insurance, real estate, and so on.

I was unemployed when I found out about an opening here from the deputy director. They were looking for an engineering process technician, something I knew nothing about. So I went to the library, did research on the area, and took the test. I got the job and started here on a coke oven inspection team. I worked on the team for three years and was then hired by a coke plant I had been overseeing. I stayed there for ten years and worked in the Environmental Control Division, which was a great learning experience. I was in charge of the air program and because I was within a small company I didn't have the luxury of specialization. I had to learn every aspect of air quality from emissions inventory and air monitoring to source testing. I also dealt extensively with the bureau from a private sector perspective, attended seminars, was a member of the trade association, and presented papers at their meetings as well as for local organizations.

"In 1986 I returned to the bureau as an engineer 2, which wasn't easy to do: Although I had gained all the necessary knowledge through practical experience, I didn't have an engineering degree. Consequently, as part of the civil service requirements, I had to prove to the state I was qualified. I submitted a ten-page summary of my qualifications, which convinced the state to approve my civil service application.

"Quick changes in employment within pollution control are not uncommon around here. It's like one big fraternity; you see your colleagues at professional association meetings, and one year they will be working in industry, the next they'll be in government. That is why it helps to have a varied background. I competed with other engineers for this position and gained an edge through my background in computers and my varied experiences."

At the entry level, Darlene Stringos, an air pollution engineer 1, is in charge of the abrasive blasting program. "The first step in overseeing the abrasive blasting project is the review of the permit to make sure that adequate compliance measures are proposed. I do an initial site observation to make sure blasting will not present health problems for nearby residents.

"Once a construction site is established, I consult with our meteorologist to determine an appropriate site for monitoring. I assist the contractor in

PROFILES

Corbin Leininger, CEIP Associate, Chrysler Motors Corporation, Highland Park, Michigan

This profile will give you more information about air quality jobs in the private sector and give you a closer look at an entry-level job. Since this interview Leininger has taken a position as an environmental coordinator with PPG Industries' Coatings and Resins Division in Normal, Illinois.

"I work in the Plant Engineering and Environmental Planning Department, which is a small group within the Quality and Productivity Office of Chrysler Motors Corporation. We provide air quality compliance overviews for all Chrysler assembly plants, focusing mainly on monitoring stationary sources for compliance with the EPA's standards for volatile organic compounds (VOCs) and particulates.

"I work as part of a sampling team of three people: one specializes in chemistry and VOCs, the second in sampling techniques and particulate matter. My work includes operating and maintaining various sampling equipment, lab and field analysis, re-

the location of equipment in the field from which I collect data to be entered into my computer and later analyzed. I also collect samples of water and soil to check for contaminants. Site inspections are a never-ending process because there are always new sites being established and I must constantly move the equipment according to the project's progression. Working in the field takes up about six hours of each day.

"In addition to the fieldwork, I generate reports for my superiors, meet with officials concerning any interruptions in the project, handle citizens' complaints, and hand out pamphlets informing residents of potential hazards and means of identifying them. If ambient air monitoring reveals that the project is not in compliance, the site must be shut down temporarily until better compliance measures are taken.

"I like the personal contact with the public in this job, but I realize that the position is limited, so I'm constantly looking for ways to further my education and broaden my background. I have a B.S. in mining engineering and am working on my M.S. in environmental engineering at the University of Pittsburgh. Previously, I worked for U.S. Steel, where I got extensive environmental experience. There I met people from the Air Pollution Control Bureau."

If you like the idea of being on the ground floor in carrying out the next generation of air quality programs, then a local agency might be for you.

---

port writing, and interpreting regulations. Chrysler has a mobile lab that travels to Chrysler sites from Delaware to St. Louis to Canada. Much of our work revolves around meeting emissions standards at the company's automotive painting operations.

"Let me give you an example of a current project. EPA regulations require a 90 percent destruction efficiency of VOCs from paint oven incinerators. Typically, we travel to a plant site with our lab and survey the site, noting such factors as the flow volumes and the location of inflow and outflow ducts. Our team then develops a sampling strategy. Much of the team's sampling techniques are witnessed by regulatory officials. After the samples are taken, they are shuttled to the mobile lab for hydrocarbon analysis. Finally, we write up the report and give it to the appropriate people. In addition to the intellectual challenge, this is physical, dirty, hard work—hauling around equipment and climbing around hot incinerators and assembly line machinery.

"Diversity makes this job. Chrysler is a big company, yet the environmental group is small. I have been able to get involved in many different projects and have learned a lot about manufacturing processes. The pace is a little more laid back than in consulting firms. I have also enjoyed the travel. One downside is that I would like to work with a more diverse group of people. But that is the nature of our work; it is technical, unlike environmental marketing and sales or permitting, which are more people oriented.

"One has to realize that this is a big corporation. The main goal is to produce quality cars as cheaply as possible. Environmental regulation is an add-on cost, so in a way, environmental issues are a nuisance to the manufacturing groups. At the same time the corporate office sees our importance and the group has a fair amount of clout. All in all, we get along fairly well in what is a bit of a love-hate relationship.

"I received a B.S. in environmental affairs and environmental science in 1984 from Indiana University, with a concentration in hazardous waste management. The program was 60 percent science, 40 percent policy. The science helped me get started; the policy hasn't proved very useful yet, but I anticipate it will come in handy later in my career. After graduating, I interned at the Indiana Division of Land Pollution Control, where I tracked down leads on possible abandoned hazardous waste sites. In 1985 I started an internship at Chrysler through The CEIP Fund.

"When I was in school there was information available about public sector jobs, but very little about work in the private sector, even though that is where a large percentage of the jobs are. It was hard to get an idea of what kind of work was being done and what opportunities were available. One of the best ways to get this information I have found is to look in the professional journals.

"The bottom line, of course, is that everyone wants quality experience. What I didn't know then is that there are many consultants doing fieldwork and air sampling. They are looking for qualified people with little experience to do good entry-level work. The pay is low, but everyone has to pay their dues."

Jane Armstrong, Senior Project Manager, EPA National Motor Vehicle Emission Lab, Ann Arbor, Michigan

This profile will acquaint you with air quality work at the federal level, focusing on mobile source emissions. It also discusses some of the frustrations and satisfactions of managing environmental programs.

"The Clean Air Act, specifically the parts that pertain to mobile sources, *is* our work here at the EPA's National Motor Vehicle Emission Lab. The Clean Air Act was fairly general in setting goals, establishing responsibilities, and delegating the planning process to the states; the EPA puts the meat on the Act by developing regulations. We do the technical investigations and studies needed to come up with a plan and program for complying with a particular requirement of the Act.

"For each regulatory burp from the EPA, there will be significant economic impact on the individual, so our research in part is used to determine the economic impact per car or per individual when we are developing a project or regulation. We break this out by a number of factors: what the materials cost, engineering, labor, maintenance, and so on. This helps the EPA and congressional policy makers weigh the cost and benefit of proposed regulations.

"Being a *manager* implies that I don't *do* anything. This is not a production-oriented position; rather, I review what other people do, develop project goals, and delegate the work. The products we produce are the results from our testing programs. An example is our program that tests catalytic converters to see if they are effective.

"How do we plan our projects? Once a year I meet with my boss to establish priorities and plan projects for the year. Other projects come along as the year progresses; a state, for example, may request assistance on a certain issue, so I delegate the project work throughout the department. I consult with the staff on how best to get their projects accomplished within the resources of the agency, but most of my staff are very self-driven and work well without a lot of supervision.

"Other work that I am involved with includes serving as liaison with the local, state, and federal governments, giving briefings for politicians and policy makers, and writing economic impact statements for upcoming legislation.

"Working as a senior project manager at the national level takes on a completely different focus than it does in industry. Whereas industry is geared toward good service and good products, we have more national regulatory concerns and also have sovereignty over federal, state, and local government. It has been satisfying to really be a part of the mission by working for the EPA, but one must have respect for the dangerous amount of power one wields. Generally the compensation for an overworked, underpaid federal employee is the job security and pleasurable atmosphere. But we still play political football every four years.

"The optimal background for a position with the EPA here at the emission lab would be an engineering degree with an additional concentration in planning, biology, or natural resources. We also hire lab technicians for vehicle emissions testing, mechanics, electronics repair personnel, and program analysts. One interesting position at the EPA, as an environmental protection specialist, requires a renaissance person of sorts because you must be able to combine the technical, legal, and liberal arts aspects of the work.

"I climbed the ladder the hard way. My bachelor's degree is in literature and my master's was in library science. I started here in the library. Eventually, I found that my background was often a conceptual hindrance. People have a tendency to judge you by the degree you hold, so I went to the University of Michigan to get an MBA.

"After I got an M.B.A., my next promotion was to a technical job in the Engineering Division as a state liaison. In this position I often repre-

sented the EPA before state legislatures, and while everyone likes to
roast a fed in those situations, I quickly
gained respect when they realized that
this pregnant woman knew more about
carburetors than they did."

Patricia Vopelak, Supervisor of Engineering Feasibility, Planning Department, Illinois Power Company, Decatur, Illinois

Since joining Illinois Power in 1980 Patricia Vopelak has had a variety of different responsibilities in the environmental side of the company. Her experiences are chronicled here as a way of explaining how environmental issues are handled at a utility.

"In my present position I supervise technical and economic analyses to solve problems relating to generating unit performance, electric production costs, environmental regulatory compliance, and customers' energy alternatives. One of our jobs in Planning is to investigate the economic impact of air quality regulations on Illinois Power. Depending on how legislation is structured, the company will have to devise new ways of attaining emission standards, which is where we come in. What the legislature decides directly affects the measures we take to comply. Part of our job is to provide information to our Public Affairs Department so they can communicate to policy makers. We keep abreast of the

impact of current legislation as well as current emission control technologies. Because acid rain legislation could have a significant impact on the company, Illinois Power is frequently called on by our members of Congress for information.

"Here in Planning we see our role, in a sense, as providing a service to the Environmental Affairs Department and many other areas of the company. Typically, Environmental Affairs will collect the environmental information and it will be our job to do the technological and economic analysis and produce a report that is used in decision making.

"For example, one of our facilities is running out of space at its ash pond

IN SUMMARY

Although there are new programs coming on line, getting that first job in the air quality field may require more persistence than in some other environmental protection fields. Careers in air quality are as varied and interesting as the professional chooses to make them. Many upper-level air quality professionals are reaching retirement age or are making parallel moves into hazardous waste management, ensuring that one need not

and the company must come up with a method of disposal for the fly ash and bottom ash. I am managing this project along with a chemical engineer who will be doing all the economic analysis. Environmental Affairs is providing us with the data on the requirements for building a new ash disposal facility. They must ultimately get the construction permits. The Engineering Department will design this facility and give us cost figures. Power Production is analyzing the effects of burning some of the residue.

"You can see how very quickly it gets very complicated. My job is to coordinate everything and make sure we get our end product on schedule: a report to get our construction permit. I get a lot of satisfaction from this but get frustrated by people who can't stick to a schedule—it comes back to me. The biggest challenge is communication, then sticking to schedule . . . and juggling. Last week, for example, I was working with Environmental Affairs to put their pieces together, Power Production wanted to know where things were, and one of the vice presidents was asking how much this project was going to cost.

"When I first started at Illinois Power I had a hard time guessing which way my career was going to go, because I was not an engineer. Well, I was the first nonengineer to be a supervisor in the Planning Department, and I believe the engineering mindset is changing; it doesn't hurt to be an engineer, but it doesn't seem as essential. Take Environmental Affairs: Of the 23 staff members only five are engineers; the rest are either biologists or support staff.

"I would encourage students to consider the possibility of working in private industry or more specifically for a power company. There has been a dramatic increase in employees in this department since 1980, predominantly as a direct result of solid and hazardous waste regulations.

"I received a B.S. in biology and environmental studies from the State University of New York at Stony Brook and my M.S. in environmental science from Miami University in Oxford, Ohio. This was an excellent program that required either a senior thesis or an internship during the final year. I chose to do the internship and worked for the U.S. Geological Survey, where I helped produce an annotated bibliography of New York lakes. Though most of my work has been on air quality issues, oddly enough, my graduate focus was on water resources and land use."

remain on the bottom rung for long. In short, don't let the prospect of a little more preparation and work up front scare you off if you are interested in the field.

RESOURCES

See also the Resources sections of other chapters for publications on environmental advocacy, education, and business, which cover air quality among other environmental issues.

Air and Waste Management Association. See Resources, chapter 8, for description.

State and Territorial Air Pollution Program Administrators and the Association of Local Air Pollution Control Officials. 444 N. Capitol St., N.W., Washington, D.C. 20001.

California Air Resources Board. Publishes *Employment Opportunities*, which does an excellent job of laying out employment opportunities at state and local air pollution control agencies, from the perspective of the state with the most significant air pollution challenge. State of California Air Resources Board, 1234 U St., Sacramento, Calif. 95818.

Meeting Environmental Workforce Needs: Education and Training to Assure a Qualified Workforce. See Resources, chapter 2, for description.

10 Water Quality

We have entered a new era in the water quality industry. The challenges facing us in hazardous wastes, groundwater, and other water quality areas are enormous. To meet these challenges, there will have to be another revolution.

Beth Turner, President, Water Pollution
Control Federation

DEAD FISH and oil slicks provided much of the stimulus for the first Earth Day in 1970 and the subsequent environmental push of the early seventies. The issue of declining water quality was relatively simple, visual, and very emotional—our waters were dying. Congress responded to the public outcry by passing legislation that set a broad goal to "restore and maintain the chemical, physical, and biological integrity of the nation's waters." Major amendments to the Clean Water Act in 1972 set a goal of fishable, swimmable waters throughout the nation.

In some respects progress has been remarkable. Our waterways certainly appear cleaner, and many are cleaner. Lake Erie, for example, pronounced biologically dead in 1972, now has thriving populations of perch, walleye, and largemouth bass. However, we are now faced with additional pollution problems, less visible but no less serious. The most prominent among these include toxins in the waters, nonpoint pollution from runoff, and contamination of our groundwater supplies.

There is a wider range of opportunities for water quality professionals than could have been imagined in the seventies or even early eighties. Given the complexity of the issues, these opportunities are going to hold steady for some time, and could expand. Amendments to the Clean Water Act in 1987 and varied and ambitious state legislation have combined to send a whole new set of water quality initiatives out of the blocks, even as professionals work to implement and improve on the first round. This is creating increased demand for water quality professionals in the field— although many argue that funding for personnel has not kept pace.

Activity is shifting to state and local efforts, and this is where much of the hiring will occur. New regulatory initiatives will also create more jobs in the private sector, primarily in the consulting field.

How does this translate into demand for specific disciplines? First, there will be a continued need for traditional water quality professionals: civil, environmental, and chemical engineers. Increasing concern about toxins is going to create greater demand for people with chemistry background (chemical engineers and organic and analytical chemists), and also for toxicologists, environmental engineers, and public health and risk assess-

East Bay Municipal Utility District, Jackson, California. Jonathon Strobel examines EBMUD maps of the Camanche Recreation Area to analyze use patterns of the watershed around the reservoir.

ment specialists. There will be much work for industrial engineers knowledgeable in process modification and chemistry.

Groundwater scientists—hydrologists, geologists, and geological engineers—can't be trained quickly enough to fill demand, which will be six to seven times greater in the 1990s than in the 1980s. Finally, all sectors need qualified managers who know the field and the issues and especially managers who understand the interrelations among environmental problems in the media of air, water, and land.

ISSUES AND TRENDS

Federal involvement in water quality issues goes back to 1948, when Congress began to provide minimal funding to states to construct wastewater treatment facilities. It wasn't until 1972, however, that the federal government took charge of regulating the quality of the nation's water supplies.

There are two major strategies embodied in the Clean Water Act. The first is federal assistance to finance the construction of local sewage treatment systems so that wastewater is treated before it is released into waterways. The second is a requirement that all industrial and municipal wastewater discharged directly into waterways meet various pollution limitations.

Implementation of the Act has been extremely controversial. Industries charge that regulations change constantly and compliance is cumbersome and expensive; environmentalists have successfully sued the U.S. Environmental Protection Agency (EPA) for foot dragging on issuing standards for specific industries and pollutants and also on enforcing existing regulations.

Bottom line: Has the Clean Water Act achieved its goals? In some areas yes, in others no. A survey of state environmental officials found that overall water quality remained roughly stable between 1972 and 1982, with water quality improving in 13 percent of stream miles, staying the same in 84 percent, and deteriorating in 3 percent. While enforcement enthusiasm may be questioned and fine-tuning is definitely needed, it is generally accepted that at the very least a regulatory structure is in place to control conventional pollutants.

In 1987, a major congressional rewrite of the Clean Water Act strengthened existing regulations and addressed several new concerns. A key element is a shift of attention to toxic contaminants. These are substances such as heavy metals and organic chemicals that may have a severe, possibly irreversible effect on human health or the environment in low concentrations.

Toxins enter water systems through a host of mechanisms, including industrial discharge, urban and rural runoff, and airborne deposition (acid rain also increases the leaching of certain toxic elements in the soil). A 1984 National Water Quality Inventory, for example, lists 37 states as having elevated levels of toxins in their waters.

Nonpoint sources of water pollution, as opposed to point sources, such as factories, are another area of significant concern. This includes runoff from farmland, construction sites, mining areas, and city streets. The Conservation Foundation in 1984 estimated that over half of the nation's water pollutants come from nonpoint sources that are essentially nonregulated. Such pollutants include heavy metals, damaging nutrients, sediments, and pesticides. Remedies for nonpoint-source pollution are more complicated than for point-source pollution and present a formidable challenge to policy makers.

Whereas initial water quality efforts concentrated on surface water—lakes, rivers, and streams—groundwater, the invisible 98 percent of the nation's water supply, until recently received scant attention. Yet more than 50 percent of the nation depends on groundwater for its drinking supply. The lack of attention to groundwater arose partly from the assumption that surface contaminants would not permeate groundwater as readily as they would surface water. But groundwater, once contaminated, is difficult and expensive to purify. This problem has been made worse by land disposal of hazardous waste and increased pesticide use—both of which lead to percolation of toxins into groundwater.

These three interrelated issues—toxins, nonpoint-source pollution, and groundwater contamination—form the focus of new activities in the arena of water quality, discussed later in this chapter.

Another area of increasing concern is the environmental degradation of estuaries and coastal waters in the United States. This is related to environmental problems mentioned earlier—industrial, urban, and agricultural waste—and also sheer population overload. In 1984, the U.S. Bureau of the Census reported that 40 percent of the U.S. population lived within 50 miles of the Atlantic and Pacific coasts. This figure will rise to 75 percent by 1990, exacerbating pressures on coastal waters.

Finally, the environmental quality and survival of wetlands is of major concern. Wetlands, which exist on the coast and inland, play an important role in moderating the effects of floods and drought and serving as a natural water treatment process by removing silt and chemical pollutants, among other things. Wetlands are also an important habitat for fish and wildlife. Unfortunately, because of drainage and development, the nation is losing wetlands at a rate of 500,000 acres a year, so fast that you can watch the recession in some Louisiana parishes. Increased federal, state, and local emphasis on wetlands acquisition, study, and protection is likely—though some say it is too little and, in some areas of the country, may be too late.

THE JOB MARKET

FEDERAL GOVERNMENT

Responding to renewed public concern for water quality issues, Congress was unusually united in overriding a presidential veto and passing the Clean Water Act amendments in 1987 (formally known as the Water Quality Act of 1987). This Act, the backbone of U.S. water quality regulation, contains significant changes from earlier versions. If you are considering making a career in this field, examine this legislation and the subsequent regulations. What follows is only a summary.

The biggest change in the Act is a shift of requirements and responsibilities to the states. The bill requires states to identify bodies of water that do not meet water quality standards, come up with programs to control nonpoint sources of pollution, and identify and regulate sources of toxic contaminants. This is known as a water quality–based approach because it focuses on specific bodies of water and supplements existing industry-by-industry discharge regulations.

The bill also phases out federal assistance for municipal wastewater treatment plant construction by providing seed money to set up state revolving loan funds. New responsibilities for the EPA include a five-year program for improving water quality in estuaries, aid for lakes damaged by acid rain, tightening of implementation procedures for industrial discharge regulations, and an increased commitment to comply with the 1978 Great Lakes Water Quality Agreement.

Notably absent were programs relating to groundwater monitoring, protection, and remediation—even though the EPA gives this issue high priority. Nevertheless, water quality professionals speculate that major groundwater regulations of some form are likely to appear in the next several years. (As we shall see later, states are not waiting for Congress to act.)

Whereas the Clean Water Act focuses on the quality of waterways, the Safe Drinking Water Act regulates the water we consume. The 1986 amendments to the latter provided for control of at least 83 trace substances, many of which were unknown when the Act initially was passed in 1974. These include inorganic, synthetic organic, and volatile organic chemicals, microbiological parameters, and radionuclides. Congress also inserted provisions to establish a groundwater protection program, particularly in areas around drinking water wells. Federal appropriations for implementation of this act will be increased by 80 percent by 1991. However, this Act regulates municipal wastewater treatment facilities; that is where the bill will be paid and the jobs will be. More on this later.

These are the two major federal water quality acts, but there are several others worth mentioning. The Marine Protection, Research, and Sanctuaries Act, or the Ocean Dumping Act, passed in 1972, regulates ocean disposal of sludge and industrial waste. Regulations are being tightened for ocean sludge disposal and are being promulgated for offshore hazardous waste incineration. However, as coastal waters and estuaries continue to deteriorate, many policy makers are calling for a comprehensive federal legislative package.

The EPA has made development of a wetlands policy by 1990 a top priority and is currently focusing on a dredge and fill permit program, identifying wetlands requiring immediate corrective actions, and strengthening permits and compliance actions. Finally, there is the Federal Insecticide, Fungicide, and Rodenticide Act, which focuses on protecting groundwater from pesticide contamination.

The EPA is the federal agency responsible for administering all of these water quality programs and so is the major federal employer in this field. But don't rule out other federal agencies. The U.S. Fish and Wildlife Service (Department of the Interior), the Army Corps of Engineers (Army), the National Oceanic and Atmospheric Administration (Commerce), and the Soil Conservation Service (Agriculture) are just a few examples of federal agencies that hire water quality professionals. All of these agencies, and many others, have research facilities and specific responsibilities in the areas of water quality and supply. Fish and Wildlife, for example, conducts research on the impact of water quality on fish populations. All agencies are involved in environmental impact statements and assessments for construction projects. Even the U.S. Forest Service and the Bureau of Land Management, although not considered environmental protection agencies per se, hire water quality professionals to assist in planning and managing their land holdings. Researching these opportunities at the federal level will require some digging. But it will be time well spent. A good resource to start with is the annual *Conservation Directory* (National Wildlife Federation) or the *Directory of Environmental Information Sources* (Government Institutes, Inc., 1988). Federal agencies can also provide career information and lists of job titles of professionals they employ.

In summing up water quality personnel needs at the federal level, Henry

L. Longest 2nd of the EPA notes in *Meeting Environmental Workforce Needs* (Information Dynamics, 1985), "As we focus on groundwater, estuaries and oceans, and sludge management, we will need to improve our technical base in these areas. We will need to increase our toxins management and risk analysis capability. We will need to improve our monitoring and laboratory capabilities. We will continue to need high levels of technical skills in environmental engineering and sciences. As we delegate more responsibilities to states and local governments, we will need to have the skills to help them solve complex problems, skills that they may not be able to obtain, maintain, or afford. We will need technical and nontechnical people who are also good managers and program evaluators. Many of us will spend more time overseeing and evaluating than we have been. We will need more financial management skills to help local and state governments figure out what they can afford and how they can pay."

STATE GOVERNMENT

The 1987 Clean Water Act amendments, while retaining a federal regulatory prerogative, significantly shift responsibility to the states. Peter Piecuch, editor of the *Journal of the Water Pollution Control Federation*, says, "In environmental regulation the federal government goes through cycles; it takes authority, then it gives it back to the states. Right now there is an emphasis on state regulation, with the federal government setting the broad regulatory outline through the Clean Water Act and having the states fill it out with their own programs."

Under the Act, states are required to develop programs for controlling nonpoint-source and toxic contaminants. In addition, states are required to use water quality–based standards, meaning state and local governments must look more closely at specific bodies of water and specific dischargers. This shift of responsibility is going to require states to (1) beef up in-house personnel and expertise for program planning, development, and research in the areas of toxic, nonpoint-source, and groundwater pollution and (2) increase inspection and laboratory personnel to implement and enforce these acts. This is above and beyond the role states play in overseeing and enforcing all current Clean Water Act regulations.

States have also initiated water quality legislation and programs that go well beyond the federal scope, as is the case with so many other environmental issues. Groundwater is an issue on which states are now carrying the ball. Groundwater management strategies exist or are under development in 46 states. The emphasis of these programs is on prevention and developing information on land use and groundwater characteristics (mapping aquifers, developing state classification systems, and monitoring groundwater quality). As a consequence, with the exception of consulting firms, states are the biggest public employer of groundwater scientists, followed by the federal government and, last, local bodies. (See Resources for information on groundwater science careers.)

As for nonpoint-source pollution control programs, which states must develop with assistance from the EPA, a more interdisciplinary professional will be needed. According to Robbi Savage, executive director of the Association of State and Interstate Water Pollution Control Administrators, "Nonpoint control is a new, integrated discipline. We need people with a management and scientific background who understand the regulatory and legislative process and also how surface water and groundwater move and interface. Keep in mind we are moving beyond the planning phase of this issue and into implementation. Environmental studies might be a useful degree for tackling this problem."

States are also responding to water quality problems unique to their region and thus have staffs with corresponding specialties. Midwestern states are concerned with the water quality of the Great Lakes; the West and Southwest are working on issues of water supply; many East Coast and Gulf states are focusing on wetlands acquisition and protection; some of the mountainous states are working on river protection; and coastal states have developed or are developing legislation in response to the degradation of coastal waters and estuaries. In the last example, one specialty in demand would be marine resource management. Then there are major cleanup efforts under way in certain bodies of water—Puget Sound, Chesapeake Bay, and Boston Harbor, to name three with which water quality professionals are concerned. If you are interested in employment in a particular region, look closely at the water quality programs of state and local governments in that area; directories of agencies and organizations are a good place to start identifying possible employers.

LOCAL AND REGIONAL GOVERNMENT

Ensuring adequate water quality is a local and regional endeavor. Local units of government are the ones that (1) treat all commercial, industrial, and residential wastewater that goes into the sewer system before being released into local bodies of water and (2) purify water for human use and consumption. Efficient performance of these two functions at the local level is a goal that the federal government has both promoted and required, through wastewater treatment construction grants and setting drinking water and wastewater standards.

The system is far from perfect. A survey by states and the EPA esti-

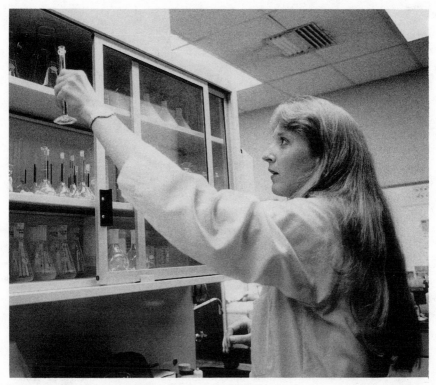

City of Hayward Waste Water Department, Hayward, California. Debora Ander-
son worked in both the lab and the field while helping the city of Hayward's
wastewater treatment plant conduct tests on wastewater content and the efficiency
of the treatment.

mates it would cost $76 billion to construct or improve wastewater treat-
ment facilities identified as having water quality problems—a far cry from
the $18 billion authorized in the Clean Water Act. Nonetheless, improve-
ments under the program have been dramatic. For example, in 1982 142
million Americans were served by secondary water treatment, an increase
of 57 million since 1972.

Local water treatment authorities also serve as the front line for much
Clean Water Act enforcement and implementation, specifically the pretreatment provisions that set discharge standards for industry. The chain
of command works as follows: The Clean Water Act authorizes the EPA to
promulgate a variety of standards for industry and wastewater treatment
facilities. States are required to pass identical legislation to get federal
funding and authority to implement and enforce the provisions of the Act.

City of Hayward's wastewater treatment plant, Hayward, California. Settling ponds are one of the steps taken in wastewater treatment.

States concentrate their efforts on areas not served by wastewater treatment authorities and on enforcing standards for industries that discharge into surface waters. Local water treatment facilities, often called publicly owned treatment works (POTWs), apply to the EPA and receive authority to enforce Clean Water Act standards for industries that discharge into their sewer systems. Thus, inspectors who knock at the doors of industry to measure their effluent are likely to be POTW officials.

The reauthorization and expansion of the Clean Water Act and Safe Drinking Water Act directly affect POTWs and will increase staffing and expertise requirements. According to Gary Logsdon, chief of the Microbiological Treatment Branch of the EPA's Drinking Water Research Division, "The focus of these two acts on toxic trace chemicals is going to increase the need at the local level for technically oriented people to monitor and analyze water quality more thoroughly. The need for expertise will also definitely increase the use of consultants."

POTWs are going to be responsible for designing and installing new systems to remove and detect toxic contaminants. This creates a need for chemical engineers, industrial engineers, toxicologists, risk assessment specialists, analytical chemists, and organic chemists, as well as continued demand for civil and environmental engineers, the backbone of the waste-water treatment business. These same professionals will be in demand for private industry, which must implement pretreatment standards at their facilities. Finally, more complicated standards mean more enforcement and inspection personnel.

Nonpoint runoff is being tackled by a federal-state partnership that will no doubt eventually involve local units of government in implementation, if not enforcement. These programs require staff with a wide variety of backgrounds.

The public sector especially needs professionals with strong management and broad environmental skills. According to Robbi Savage, "These managers, in addition to being able to communicate to the media and interest groups, must better understand the integration of various environmental issues. For example, the practice of making decisions on air issues without evaluating the impact on water quality has got to stop." A hard science or environmental studies background with an MBA or M.A. in public administration from a top-notch school would be one way to prepare for such a role.

PRIVATE SECTOR

Since 1972 the EPA has been promulgating regulations for specific industries and for a variety of pollutants. As a result, most companies have had to install pretreatment systems to treat wastewater before it is discharged into local sewer systems or waterways. Reauthorization of the Clean Water Act creates new standards, especially for toxic pollutants, and has toughened enforcement against companies not in compliance with current standards. These systems must be maintained and updated.

This is creating in-house staff positions, but as the EPA's Logsdon observes, "It's the consulting firms that are multiplying like jackrabbits—experts are most often brought in from the outside." Consulting firms do everything from analysis of specific problems, to design and installation of new systems, to maintenance and regulatory paperwork for operating systems. Chemical engineers, industrial engineers, lab specialists, analytical and organic chemists, and toxicologists will be in demand to comply with the new toxin-oriented discharge standards.

Consulting firms come in all shapes and sizes, from the one-person firm that handles only wastewater problems for electroplating firms in Chicago to the international firm that handles everything from engineering to economics to environmental remediation and has offices in New York, London, Tokyo, Paris, and Washington, D.C. Often a large firm will get a federal contract and hire local firms or specialty firms as subcontractors. Entry-level positions are more common at the larger firms, as the smaller companies often don't have the resources to train people.

NONPROFIT SECTOR AND ACADEMIA

Opportunities in water quality work are unusually abundant in the nonprofit sector, at least relative to the number of positions normally found in the environmental nonprofit sector. National groups such as the Natural Resources Defense Council, Inc., have spent enormous amounts of time over the past 15 to 20 years on legal, legislative, educational, and research activities aimed at bringing about effective national water quality legislation. Thus, a network of organizations exists in this area at the local, state, and national levels. Further, as Shari Schaftlein of the West Michigan Environmental Action Council says, "Foundations are funding water quality work, especially for nonpoint-source pollution and groundwater activities." Foundations have a lot to do with the issues and organizations that receive funding, so keeping attuned to the environmental priorities of foundations can be one measure of where jobs are going to be. This is not the easiest research to do. Start with annual reports of foundations and talk to veterans of the fund-raising scene.

In addition to advocacy and policy projects, organizations such as the National Audubon Society and various foundations fund water quality research and habitat restoration at nonprofit organizations and universities. This includes monitoring, lab analysis, pilot projects, and full-blown wetlands restoration and remediation initiatives. Generally, this is scientific research that deals with practical water quality problems and solutions as opposed to academic research. Good preparation for this field includes field and lab skills, a diversified scientific background, and experience in designing and implementing projects. Academia is also a major force in water quality research; jobs are found at universities with substantial graduate programs in water quality. Check with the trade associations for information on such programs.

GETTING STARTED

Opportunities in the water quality field are being driven by reauthorization of major water quality legislation, concern over toxic and nonpoint-source pollutants, groundwater and coastal contamination, and wetlands destruction.

Demand for environmental and civil engineers will remain stable. Concern over toxic materials in effluent, runoff, and groundwater is creating positions in all sectors for people with the scientific and technical background to detect these trace toxins, analyze the public health and environmental impacts, and design methods of removing these contaminants from the water. Good backgrounds for this work include analytical and organic chemistry, toxicology, chemical, industrial, and environmental engineering, mathematics, and risk assessment.

Groundwater scientists will be in extremely high demand over the next decade. These professionals monitor groundwater quantity and quality, develop computer modeling of groundwater flow, and engage in treatment of polluted groundwater. The most common undergraduate degrees in this field are geology, civil engineering, and chemistry. Most of those with undergraduate degrees find jobs doing on-site sampling and measurement. Most consultants, however, indicate they prefer candidates with an M.S. in hydrology. Undergraduate course work should include geology, groundwater engineering, water chemistry, inorganic chemistry, engineering hydrology, and calculus.

These are some of the emerging issues and backgrounds in high demand. Almost without exception, however, water quality professionals cite other ways to enter the field. Statisticians and computer specialists are working on risk assessment; those with financial backgrounds are working on financing public and private wastewater treatment facilities; microbiologists and biologists are working in labs and in the field.

As in most environmental fields, if you have a B.A. or B.S., entry-level jobs are easiest to find if you possess specific, technical field and lab skills. "Employers don't know what to do with an entry-level generalist," one professional offers. Those with master's degrees have broader options. Many consulting firms need research, lab, and field technicians and hire entry-level personnel. Local (and to a lesser degree state) governments hire many entry-level workers, especially inspectors and lab technicians at municipal wastewater treatment facilities, water purification plants, and health departments.

Keep in mind that you may have to take some form of candidate ranking examination for government jobs. There are, however, two ways to land an entry-level job in a local bureaucracy. The slow way is to follow the civil service process. The fast way, and the way to avoid competing with 90 applicants with master's degrees, is to make sure employers know you and are aware of your skills and availability. This can get you hired for short-term projects and give you an inside line on permanent positions. The local level has a high turnover rate, and promotions often come from within the ranks.

SALARY

With the exception of particularly hot disciplines, such as hydrology and chemical engineering, salaries vary less by specialty than by sector and region of the country. Entry-level positions at the local level pay around $15,000 for candidates with B.A.s and B.S.s. Engineers start at around $20,000. State and federal government are a little better, with entry-level salaries for those with bachelor's degrees about $20,000 for most disciplines.

Pay for private sector jobs in this field is roughly comparable to that in the hazardous waste management field, with starting salaries ranging from $20,000 to $25,000, groundwater scientists and engineers being at the top end of that scale.

CASE STUDY

Cleaning Up Puget Sound

What kinds of professionals are involved in an effort like the long-term cleanup and management of Washington's Puget Sound? And how do they translate regulation and policy into the reality of taking a polluted body of water and making it clean? This Case Study, by focusing on three professionals involved in protecting the health of Puget Sound, will give some answers to these questions.

In 1985 the Washington state legislature, in response to political pressure and press coverage on the deteriorating condition of Puget Sound, authorized the creation of the Puget Sound Water Quality Authority (PSWQA), charging it with developing and implementing a comprehensive plan for the protection and enhancement of water quality in Puget Sound. The authority has jurisdiction over the Puget Sound basin, which extends from the crest of the Cascade Range to the crest of the Olympic Mountains.

The key areas targeted by the legislature for inclusion in the authority's plan are (1) contamination of bottom sediments by organic and inorganic chemicals, (2) bacterial pollution, and (3) the loss of wetlands. Kirvil Skinnarland, director of planning and compliance for the agency, comments on the planning process and structure of the effort: "The authority is a somewhat unusual organization in that it was assigned by the legislature to develop the Puget Sound management plan by working through existing agencies rather than by creating new agencies, which is more often the case in the legislative process. We have been successful also to a great degree because of the cooperation we have obtained from state and local agencies.

"Another key, of course, has been funding. We were successful in obtaining an initial $12 million in general funds for state activities. Further, the state of Washington's tax on tobacco products is put into a fund for local water quality activities and the conversion of primary municipal treatment plants into secondary treatment plants. These funds are also used for nonpoint storm water runoff programs and lake- and stream-oriented projects.

"The staff of the PSWQA are top-notch, well-trained, and highly motivated professionals who work collaboratively. Within the organization, there are technical experts who work on scientific issues related to developing, carrying out, and monitoring the plan; a Public Outreach Division, which coordinates with citizens, city and local governments, the state legislature, Congress, and the media; and a Planning Division, which carries out the technical aspect of developing a coherent long-term plan on paper as well as creating documents that report on conditions in Puget Sound. This area also requires a lot of cooperation with many different state and federal agencies.

"Our comprehensive plan, completed in January of 1987, establishes programs for control of point-source and nonpoint-source pollution, prevention of loss of wetlands, protection of shellfish beds (both commercial and recreational), public education, and reduction of storm water runoff. Our strategy for preventing the loss of wetlands includes efforts to acquire them and strengthen existing regulations and protection programs. The authority's plans will be reviewed and updated regularly."

One of the primary agencies assigned to implement the measures of the plan is the Washington Department of Ecology. Jim Krull, chief of environmental regulation and planning, talks about the role of the department in the management of Puget Sound. "The PSWQA plan crosses many program and agency boundaries. Therefore, the Coordinating Section of our Water Quality Division is closely involved in developing and implementing these programs. Whereas the PSWQA has worked on the development of a feasible plan, we utilize our staff of environmental engineers, scientists, and planners; sanitary and chemical engineers; hydrogeologists; chemists; lab analysts; and urban and land-use planners to implement the plan with corresponding programs.

"For example, we implement the nonpoint-source aspects of the plan through grants to local governments, providing technical assistance and guidance on watershed and nonpoint programs at the local level. The plan emphasizes municipal and industrial waste dischargers and includes guidance and procedures to control toxic pollutant discharges. In addition, a bill has been passed that enables us to increase discharge permit fees and to use these funds to employ permit writers and inspectors and monitor company facilities.

"Our project on contaminated sediments from dredging sites encompasses inventorying disposal sites, setting up criteria and controls, and developing remedial action plans. We maintain a storm water control program, which designs and implements programs as well as authorizes permits and supplies local governments with guidance and technical manuals. Our participation in the wetlands protection program includes assessment of standards for government protection of wetlands, examination of local protection measures, and making recommendations on state regulations on such issues as shoreline management.

"As part of these new responsibilities, we recently enhanced the quality control and capacity of our own labs, certifying us as a lab resource for the EPA. This necessitated hiring lab personnel, mainly chemists and biologists. We conduct ambient monitoring of water quality and sediments in Puget Sound every summer and have an oil spill contingency plan. We also allocate grant money to local governments to develop and implement projects for the management of household hazardous wastes. More conventional studies we have done revolve around identifying local areas of algae and oxygen concentration, which indicate sources of nutrients, such as nearby sewage treatment plants, and help us plan the optimal location of these plants."

Lea Mitchell learned about the PSWQA while following the proposed cleanup efforts in the newspaper and felt it would be a unique opportunity for her to use her natural science background. Although the authority was not actively looking for entry-level people, Mitchell persistently called and sent letters expressing her interest, and after four months was hired as an intern. While working for the PSWQA, Mitchell was engaged in technical research, literature searches, gathering data from various agencies, writing, and public relations work.

She is now working as an environmentalist 1 for the Shellfish Protection Section of the Washington Department of Social and Health Services. She describes the relation of her work to the overall Puget Sound remediation effort: "One of my responsibilities is to periodically go out on the sound in a boat and collect water samples to measure fecal coliform levels. I also do shoreline surveys, which are like reconnaissance missions—I walk the beaches and streams along the sound looking for potential contamination sources such as open sewers, spills, and failing on-site sewage systems. When I find a hazard I investigate it and include it as an area of concern in my report. I've learned a lot about how the watershed works just by doing these surveys. They also give me a chance to work with the public and educate them on our work, since I am frequently approached by people who are curious about what I'm doing.

"For the past several years commercial shellfish beds have been closing because of federal regulations pertaining to contamination levels. This is fine as a method of preventing human consumption of the contaminants, but it does little to ameliorate the problem. As a result of the authority's plan, there has been a recent attempt to take on more responsibility for correcting the problem and reopening areas to shellfish harvesting. We've divided the Puget Sound into regions to facilitate our monitoring efforts. I cover one region, the Hood Canal area. In monitoring the shellfish beds, I do on-site inspections of shellfish operations to ensure that they are meeting sanitation standards and marketing their product legally.

"Another project I'm working on is developing an inventory describing the status of commercial beds in the area. The final product will include tables, classifications, maps, and color lifts. This has been a real challenge for me because the work is very detailed and production oriented, and I have had to learn graphics skills.

"My work for the Department of Social and Health Services has been a welcome diversion. I took the job because I wanted to do more fieldwork and to get away from the congestion of Seattle. Here my challenges are of a more physical nature—the weather, boats, and dogs—whereas while working for PSWQA the challenge was more intellectual."

Based on Mitchell's experience, her advice for those interested in breaking into the field is to "go beyond the newspapers and bulletin boards. Look inside of yourself, learn your real potential, and then brainstorm—pretend there are no barriers. If you know enough about yourself and what you want, you will find you can do a lot more than fill a slot in an advertisement. Once you figure out what you want to do, be resourceful and you can create your own job."

PROFILES

Shari Schaftlein, Water Quality Program Director, West Michigan Environmental Action Council, Grand Rapids, Michigan

This profile communicates three major elements of work in the nonprofit sector: day-to-day projects can be incredibly diverse; education is a major objective; and one's thoughts are never far from fund-raising.

"The West Michigan Environmental Action Council is a nonprofit citizens' organization dedicated to the protection and enhancement of the Michigan environment. Our goals are achieved through public education, encouraging research on environmental issues, and advocating environmentally sound public policies. We work to secure passage of environmental legislation and also to protect specific resources such as the Nordhouse Dunes in west Michigan. Water quality, land use, pesticides, natural areas preservation, and hazardous waste are the major environmental issues we work on.

"My primary responsibility is to administer all water quality projects and grants. As part of my work I also must keep informed on water issues, oversee the interns and volunteers, write grant requests, and provide advice to the executive director and board members on policy issues. I also write position papers recommending specific actions, follow these up with appropriate letters, and finally spend time on public relations and education.

"One of our projects was the Plaster Creek Watershed Study, which outlined programs and recommendations concerning urban and rural land use as it affected this watershed. We took samples and evaluated water quality, researched issues and problems, wrote up the study and recommendations, and promoted the results of the study, for both advocacy and educational purposes.

"A good portion of my time is devoted to developing and administering projects funded by foundations. In the nonprofit sector virtually all funding comes from grants. We are constantly working to build up an endowment so that we will eventually be able to maintain our organization on the interest from the endowment.

"I also consult individuals with questions on water quality issues as well as answer questions from citizens who need general information or have run into specific environmental problems and need assistance in working through the system. I usually get a few information requests per day. Connecting with the public is a major role of a nonprofit and one we do not take lightly.

"Our organization publishes a newsletter, so I spend quite a bit of time writing articles for this and other publications. I also participate in conferences, workshops, and brainstorming sessions. One frustration of my job is that most of my time is spent reacting to incidents of environmental degradation after the fact, and not enough on preventive measures.

"I received a B.S. in public affairs in 1983 and an M.S. in environmental sciences, both from Indiana University. These programs offered a wide variety of water-related science courses needed for work within the nonprofit environmental sector. There are few paid professional environmental advocates, so you are called on frequently to comment on a wide variety of environmental issues.

"An advantage of the program at Indiana University was the exposure to engineering, econometric, and legal aspects of environmental science. These courses alert you to the real-world constraints in developing solutions to environmental problems. I would not have been as effective in the environmental field if I had specialized in one very technical aspect of environmental studies; that kind of background is geared to consulting and government work, where there are pigeon-hole job opportunities. I'm not a research scientist, but I have a diverse enough knowledge of the basics to be able to speak the language of scientists and translate their findings to politicians and the public.

"A challenge to those of us working in the Great Lakes region will be the interrelation between air quality and water quality: 80 percent of PCB (polychorinated biphenyls) contamination in Lake Superior, for example, comes from air deposition. We will be working to deal with this in the rewrite of the Clean Air Act."

David Piposzar, Environmental Health Administrator, Allegheny County Health Department, Pittsburgh

The attention of public health officials has shifted from infectious diseases to toxins and pollution as the major issues in the field. This Profile shows how local health departments are involved.

"The Health Department is responsible for promoting individual and community wellness, as opposed to health, which can be an ambiguous term. We attempt to achieve this goal by preventing illness, disease, or premature death resulting from exposure to biological, chemical, or physical hazards in the environment. Our tools are regulation, health codes, and legislation. Communication and education also aid us in our ultimate goal of prevention.

"We serve a population of 1.4 million in 129 municipalities ranging from Pittsburgh to very rural areas. Consequently, we must deal with a mixed bag of rural and urban concerns— some areas depend on wells and individual sewage systems, whereas cities like Pittsburgh have highly developed water treatment facilities. Our agency must spend a lot of time communicating with officials of different localities to identify their needs and to factor them into our program development. County and regional agencies often face the challenge of serving large and diverse populations. This makes the work tough but interesting.

"The Health Department employs 450 professional and technical staff in the Bureaus of Air Pollution Control, Environmental Health, and Medical Services. They are aided by 100 support staff.

"My role is to be the liaison between the director's office and the Bureaus of Air Pollution Control and Environmental Health. As assistant to the director, I'm responsible for bringing significant problems to his attention, analyzing proposed solutions, and offering suggestions to improve department services or procedures. I also routinely review environmental legislation with our staff and legal counsel to establish the department's position on important issues. Much of my time is spent in internal and external meetings and telephone conversations.

"One example of a special project I work on is the Emergency Response Program, which coordinates services in the event of contamination of the air, soil, or water. This proved to be quite useful in the January 1988 Ashland Oil, Inc., spill, in which nearly a million gallons of diesel fuel spilled into our rivers and threatened drinking water supplies for 2.7 million residents in Allegheny County and downstream communities. We played a major role in the emergency response and related health issues.

"Our department worked closely with other county, state, and federal officials involved in the cleanup and restoration of drinking water supplies. We provided 24-hour in-plant technical assistance for water plant operators, sampled raw and finished water, and gave final approval to reopen plant intakes. We worked closely with schools, hospitals, and community officials to furnish alternate water supplies and establish sanitation procedures.

"I graduated from Pennsylvania State University with an undergraduate degree in zoology and started with the Health Department in 1974 as a field inspector for lead poisoning prevention programs. I just started at the bottom and worked my way up. That is a way to progress at a local agency which works very well for some people.

"In this field there is a great need for management capabilities. I would encourage students to get an advanced degree in public health, with course work in business or public administration. Most people who have a technical background without any management background tend to have problems as they become promoted.

"A constant concern in local government is budget constraints. As issues change, the question of whether to retrain old employees or hire new ones often arises. I think there is a tendency to just transfer individuals within the agency with the expectation that they will retrain themselves to be successful in their new positions. This works only to a point.

"My concern is whether the schools of public health are actually preparing students well for the environmental emphasis of jobs in health administration. We are in stiff competition with industry, and students tend to gravitate to corporations and consulting firms because of higher salaries."

Richard L. Taylor, Environmental Engineer, Research and Development Center, BP America, Inc., Warrensville, Ohio

Richard Taylor's job is a good example of an entry-level position in engineering. Of particular note is the significant responsibility he is given on his first engineering job. Taylor is now a corporate environmental engineer with Parker Hannifin Corporation in Cleveland.

"As an environmental engineer for the Environmental Technology Group of BP America, I provide technical support to all divisions of the company. Research and Development is a project-oriented division with work that falls into two categories: technical support and research. With technical support projects, a business unit within BP America may ask us to design or modify a treatment system or conduct pilot scale studies of an alternative treatment system. Research projects, on the other hand, more often come from the corporate level and are often developed in anticipation of regulatory changes.

"The engineers in our group collaborate on projects; on one project I may be the project manager, and on another I will be called on for fieldwork or support work. This allows entry-level people to practice coordinating projects while adding diversion to the work of upper-level engineers. This was a surprise to me. My vision before I entered the working world was that entry-level jobs consisted of having a boss who came in every morning with a list of things to do. I expected to be pushed from behind; to the contrary, you have to push yourself. When working on a project there are no limits or guidelines. It's a lot different from solving textbook problems—you have to set your own goals and figure out ways to achieve them.

"Your education provides a theoretical background; work gives you the practical application—sampling, audits, and so on. This is why getting work experience while in school is important—if a position is open in a company and the applicants include someone just out of school with no work experience and another just out of school with experience, hands down the person with experience will get the job.

"I have a B.S. in chemical engineering with a concentration in environmental engineering from Case Western Reserve University in Cleveland. During my senior year I began looking for a job and found that most positions in the environmental field required three to five years' experience. I quickly realized that I was going nowhere in my job search, so I began applying to graduate schools. First, though, I took a summer internship through CEIP at BP America in the area of hazardous waste.

"Now I'm pursuing a master's degree at the University of Akron. I think I've found my niche in the environmental field. When I was initially taking courses in straight chemical engineering, I thought the application was extremely boring and couldn't picture myself mapping out pipes for some refinery all my life. This, coupled with an interest in environmental issues, inspired me to pursue a concentration in environmental engineering in addition to my chemical engineering major. The environmental engineering program at Case had been discontinued, so I had to develop the course sequence myself. I would encourage others to do the same.

"I'll admit sometimes it is difficult to be working in a corporate environment when you have strong environmental interests. I am asked to develop processes to attain certain environmental standards required by law, but in my own mind I know that lower levels are feasible. I think that this moral dilemma wouldn't be as big a problem if you worked for the EPA because you would have more freedom in setting standards, but at the same time I feel I'm making a more direct impact as far as environmental improvement is concerned. Given my interests and priorities, I am very pleased with where I am in my career."

IN SUMMARY

Of all the environmental fields covered in this book, water quality is among the most wide open as far as range and number of opportunities is concerned. Scientists and policy makers are still working to implement early water quality efforts, and a second generation of programs focused on toxins, groundwater, and nonpoint sources will quickly be upon them. Issues that are proving to be more severe than originally imagined, such as groundwater contamination, are making more evident the interrelated nature of environmental pollution—a landfill today may create a contaminated aquifer tomorrow. Professionals who have good technical backgrounds and can see beyond their particular disciplines are greatly needed in this field, at all levels of government and in the private sector.

RESOURCES

American Water Resources Association. A multidisciplinary organization dedicated to the advancement of research, planning, management, development, and education in water resources. Publishes *Water Resources Bulletin*, annual membership directory, and many special publications, including *1988 Survey of Employment Opportunities in Water Resources*. Has annual meeting and student chapters. 5410 Grosvenor Lane, Suite 220, Bethesda, Md. 20814.

Association of State and Interstate Water Pollution Control Administrators. The national professional organization of state water quality program administrators. Has many special publications on water quality issues in the United States. Holds membership meetings twice annually, seminars. Hall of the States, 444 N. Capitol St., N.W., Suite 330, Washington, D.C. 20001.

American Water Works Association. Organization for water works professionals. Publishes *American Water Works Association Journal* (monthly), which includes regulatory summaries, conference information, and job listings. Has state chapters, annual meetings, special publications. 6666 W. Quincy Ave., Denver, Colo. 80235.

Water Pollution Control Federation. Professional organization. Publishes monthly journal. 601 Wythe St., Alexandria, Va. 22314.

National Water Well Association. Professional association for those involved in groundwater protection. Publishes *Groundwater Science Careers Backgrounder, Well Log* newsletter (monthly), and *Water Well Journal* (monthly). Runs Job Mart, a job placement service. 6375 Riverside Dr., Dublin, Ohio 43017.

Association of Ground Water Scientists and Engineers. A division of the National Water Well Association. Publishes *Journal of Ground Water* (bimonthly).

Freshwater Foundation. Publishes *U.S. Water News* (monthly), *Journal of Freshwater* (annual), *Facets of Freshwater* (quarterly). 2500 Shadywood Rd., Box 90, Navarre, Minn. 55392.

Cousteau Society, Inc. In addition to carrying on the many research projects and explorations made famous by Jacques-Yves Cousteau, the society publishes educational materials and numerous technical publications, as well as *Calypso Log* (bimonthly) and *Dolphin Log* (bimonthly children's publication). 930 W. 21st St., Norfolk, Va. 23517.

Pollution Engineering: The Magazine of Environmental Control. See Resources, chapter 8, for a description.

The Great Lakes Directory of Natural Resource Agencies and Organizations. Produced by the Freshwater Foundation in 1984 for the Center for the Great Lakes. Profiles hundreds of organizations working on natural resource management around the Great Lakes. Center for the Great Lakes, 435 N. Michigan Ave., Suite 1408, Chicago, Ill. 60611.

Part IV

NATURAL RESOURCE MANAGEMENT

11 Land and Water Conservation

Susan Witt works for the Community Land Trust in the Southern Berkshires, Inc., in Massachusetts, in an area under heavy development pressure. The land trust acquires land and plans for its use so as to preserve the rural landscape of Berkshire County and strengthen the local economy.

Tom Stanley is a natural resource manager for Cleveland Metroparks, where he works with a staff of ten to maximize and manage the ecological diversity of a 19,000-acre system.

Sue Alexander is director of the Alaska office of the Wilderness Society and is working to build support for congressional protection of the Arctic National Wildlife Refuge in northeast Alaska.

Steve Starland directs the Wild and Scenic Rivers Program for the Washington State Parks and Recreation Commission. He is heading up an assessment of rivers in the state and is developing plans to manage recreational access to the rivers to maintain their pristine quality.

A WIDE range of professionals, agencies, and organizations are involved in the conservation and preservation of land and water resources. These people include natural resource managers, environmental planners, environmental advocates, lawyers, ecologists, and land acquisition professionals, to name a few. They work for a variety of employers, including local park systems, conservation districts, state agencies, private land trusts, consulting firms, the federal government, and nonprofit organizations. The field of land and water conservation encompasses environmental protection, resource management, and many other areas. Preservation of land and water resources requires the spectrum of environmental professionals; from those keeping the land and water free of pollutants to planners and educators to those managing natural resources and recreation.

Land and water conservation often appeals to those interested in environmental careers, and competition in this field can be keen. However, this is one of the more active environmental fields, in part because the public is increasingly concerned about development pressures and recreational access. As Ed Becker of the Essex County (Massachusetts) Greenbelt Association points out, "There has been an economic boom over the past five years which has increased development pressures and caused people to sit up and take notice. Beyond a reaction to development, however, I sense that the public, and not just those of us working in the field, is taking a more holistic view of environmental and resource protection and demanding appropriate action. It's as if the education and work of the past 20 years is coming to fruition. This is quite encouraging and bodes well for professionals who want to get involved in this field." As one planner puts it, "There are not necessarily a lot of jobs, but since there is a lot of demand, clever people are finding work."

Public support for land and water conservation efforts is arguably at an all-time high. An additional factor driving employment is the creation of whole new subfields in what many had viewed as a mature field. Assessing and maintaining biological diversity and natural heritage, creative land preservation vehicles, and integrated resource management are just a few of the current trends.

A systematic listing of all professionals involved in land and water conservation would include every occupation described in this book. Listed here, then, are the major types of work to be done in this field.

- *Planning.* A whole spectrum of planners are involved in local, regional, and national conservation efforts. These include environmental, land-use, water quality, and natural resource planners. If the profession is taking a more holistic view of land and water conservation, as many assert, planners with a natural resource background are going to be increasingly in demand. (See chapter 5 for a thorough discussion of this work.)
- *Natural Resource Assessment and Management.* Professionals in this area are involved in identifying natural resources, flora, fauna, ecosystems, and watersheds, and setting up data bases and geographical information systems. They are also managing these resources, trying

State Coastal Conservancy, Oakland, California. Richard Retecki analyzes development along California's coast with Mark Wheetley of the State Coastal Conservancy.

to maintain and, in many cases, restore ecological diversity and to balance recreational pressures with the conservation of ecosystems and natural resources.

- *Maintenance and Restoration of Environmental Quality.* An essential part of conserving a particular watershed or ecosystem entails limiting environmental contaminants, including acid rain, agricultural pesticide runoff into rivers, and hazardous waste dumping. This is where the field of land and water conservation becomes especially integrated with other fields.
- *Preserving Open Spaces and Natural Habitats.* Some professional work to ensure that land, water, and ecosystems are saved from development or other detrimental human intervention. They work in all sectors: Nonprofit land trusts work locally and nationally, as do advocates like Kent Olson of American Rivers, Inc., or Sue Alexander of the Wilderness Society; professionals at the state, and to a much lesser extent federal, level implement land acquisition programs and programs that designate wilderness areas for protection. Working in all sectors are those with legal, real estate, and financial expertise.

ISSUES AND TRENDS

Increased development pressures are driving stepped-up land acquisition and preservation efforts. Peg Elmer of the Vermont Agency of Natural Resources comments, "Land-use control efforts are cyclical. There was a lot of concern in the early seventies. Then it died out as the economy slumped. Now we have had a five-year economic boom with a lot of development. People don't like to see change happen quickly and are driven to action when the field next to them is developed. There is a groundswell now."

As a result, there are efforts at all levels to acquire and preserve open spaces. Land trusts, which will be discussed later, are growing in number and acquiring land for preservation. State legislatures are passing comprehensive growth management legislation that mandates planning and inventorying, land acquisition, and often stringent curbs on development seen as detrimental to an area's character or a particular natural resource. Voters and legislatures are also approving state bond issues to acquire land. In 1988, for example, the Massachusetts legislature approved $500 million for land purchases—a tremendous amount of money for a state government.

At the federal level, the Land and Water Conservation Fund, started in 1965, has spent billions of dollars in matching grant programs, but it has been criticized because funds are often used for capital projects rather than land acquisition. Some in Congress are working to establish a new fund, structured like an endowment, to acquire land and make grants to state and local governments for land acquisition efforts.

There is an increasing amount of cooperation among sectors on land acquisition and preservation efforts. The Nature Conservancy, for example, often buys the development rights on a piece of land and holds it until a government agency can work through the red tape to acquire the property.

Much of the current land acquisition push has been spurred by a feeling that with skyrocketing land costs and a growing population, time is quickly running out on opportunities to set aside land and water resources for future generations.

Development pressures have also brought water supply and quality issues to the forefront in many regions. This has been an issue of increasing importance in California and the Southwest, but it is also cropping up in areas not normally thought to be prone to water shortages, such as parts of New England. This is partly because of the inextricable link between water quality and quantity. In other words, if a significant aquifer becomes contaminated and can no longer be used, an area is more prone to water shortages. Professionals involved in water supply issues include hydrologists, soil scientists, agricultural scientists, engineers, geologists, and lawyers. (See chapter 10 for more details on water quality.)

The process of managing natural areas is becoming more technical, holistic, and complicated. The public sector has more natural areas to manage. Much more significant, however, is a slow but fundamental change in the manner in which these resources are being managed. There are a couple of reasons for this. As Jim Burns, a botanist with the Ohio Department of Natural Resources, says, "It used to be you would acquire a piece of land and say, 'All right, we have a natural area.' Now we are realizing you can't just let that area sit and expect it to be the same 20 years from now; that area has to be managed. There are few areas not altered by humans. So we in the field are now saying, 'What did this area used to be like? Was it a prairie or old-growth forest?' and then setting out to re-create that original ecosystem."

A second factor requiring more active management of natural areas is the ever increasing demand for recreation. As the number of people who want to use an area increases, natural resource managers have a smaller margin of error and must work harder to balance the recreational demands with the objective of preserving the land for future generations.

There appears to be a movement toward more holistic management of natural areas—management that integrates short- and long-term planning and is preventive and ecological in intent. Steve Starland, manager of the state of Washington's Wild and Scenic Rivers Program, comments on this new orientation of natural resource management: "One would think the conservation field is all settled by now; surprisingly, a lot of disciplines are just getting started or combinations of disciplines are being used for the first time. For example, coordinated river management—that has never been done before out West. It used to be we managed separately the trees, the fish, and the wildlife—if that. Now, we need people to figure out how to put it all together. In a way, there are whole new fields developing."

State and local governments are leading the way in land and water preservation efforts, with assistance (and a lot of pushing) from nonprofit organizations. Many of the new and expanding initiatives in the land and water conservation arena appear at the state and local level. This is true for land acquisition and growth management as well as for planning and natural resource management. This decentralization is a trend that is expected to continue, regardless of a changing national political climate.

Decentralization has both positive and negative aspects. Many feel it is very positive that states and localities are developing the technical competence and commitment to be involved in conservation efforts and that, because of their close proximity, they are best equipped to decide what should be preserved. On the downside, some professionals expressed dissatisfaction with the role of the federal government, describing it as often antagonistic to land conservation efforts. Finally, there is great variance of activity among states, and some wonder whether states will maintain this level of commitment to land conservation in less healthy economic times. If you are considering entering the public sector in this field, you should follow these issues closely.

Nonprofit organizations play a significant role in this field. Part of their growth can be attributed to public concern about the conservation stands of national politicians, but the evidence indicates the growth of this sector and the very useful role it plays in conservation will continue.

ACTIVITIES AND JOBS

LOCAL, STATE, AND REGIONAL AGENCIES AND ORGANIZATIONS

Responding to a number of forces—development and decentralization of government responsibility, to name two—agencies and citizens are becoming more involved in the conservation and management of natural resources at a local level. Expect significant variation in the level of activity from region to region and even among neighboring municipalities.

This activity takes place on a number of fronts. Towns and regions are expending resources to plan where they want to be in the future—developing master plans and working to implement them through zoning and development regulation, as well as land acquisition and conservation strategies.

Nonprofit land trusts are a major force behind land acquisition efforts, working to acquire land outright or purchase easement or development rights on properties. According to Susan Witt of the Community Land Trust in the Southern Berkshires, the function and strategy of a land trust vary considerably: "In the Northeast, land trusts are being used to keep the scale of development in proportion to a community; in a Midwestern community they might work to save family farms; in the Ozarks to better manage the forest land, economically and environmentally. The key is preservation and economic development through local ownership and control. Community-based land trusts are going to have a big future in land preservation in America. Their strength is that they are community based and focus on land in an integrated way, not from a single-issue orientation."

According to the Land Trust Exchange, a national service center for local and regional nonprofit land conservation organizations, half of the 740 land trusts were formed within the last ten years, one third of them within the last five years. Increasingly, these land trusts are hiring staff knowledgeable in law, real estate, planning, and local politics.

Assisting these local efforts are lawyers with experience in real estate and conservation issues, real estate professionals, planners, and natural resource staff to manage land owned by these trusts and local units of government. Positions are also being created by local units of government and conservation districts to enforce environmental and natural resource regulations.

Another local presence are soil and water conservation districts. There are 3,000 of these districts nationwide and they are staffed by a combination of local and state personnel as well as federal employees of the Department of Agriculture's Soil Conservation Service. They work with individual landowners and units of government to reduce soil erosion, preserve long-term viability of the land, and limit nonpoint-source water pollution. Although these agencies may be more visible in rural communities, urban conservation districts work on such issues as storm water management and nonpoint erosion and toxic pollution from development and redevelopment activities.

Natural resource management professionals are employed by numerous federal agencies; however, if employment is growing in this field it is at the state and local levels. Also at this level, new disciplines and issues are being explored.

Natural resource management is becoming a less reactive and more proactive field; there is recognition that natural areas will not manage themselves. Tom Stanley of the Cleveland Metroparks System says, "We have eight to ten staff who implement our natural resource management plans. When I first started in the seventies we used to try and borrow maintenance crews for our various projects, but you had to send people out with them to tell them what to cut or plow under, what was part of a grassland meadow and what wasn't. Eventually, we put together our own crew, people with a natural resource management background. I've been noticing lately that organizations and agencies with relatively smaller parcels of land under their jurisdiction are hiring people to plan and implement natural resource management; places like arboretums and nature centers are no longer viewed as collections of plants, but as ecosystems. This may be just one person and their responsibilities might include fixing the chain saw, but it is a position where one previously did not exist."

An increasing number of natural resource management jobs are with private nonprofit organizations such as nature centers, arboretums, community land trusts, and national organizations such as the Trust for Public Land, the Nature Conservancy, the National Audubon Society, and the National Wildlife Federation.

Closely tied to natural resource management is the subfield of habitat restoration, sometimes referred to as ecosystem restoration. This might entail re-creating a destroyed ecosystem, such as a prairie, or altering or creating outright a new ecosystem. One example of the latter is rerouting waterways to use wetlands as natural water purification systems. Other projects include a prairie restoration project at the corporate headquarters of Steelcase, Inc., in Grand Rapids, Michigan; the planting of local flora along highways; reintroducing wildlife to an area; or getting rid of non-native wildlife and vegetation. Traditional natural resource managers and specialists, ecologists, and landscape architects are involved in such projects.

At the state level the issues get more complicated because of bigger parcels of land and the involvement of more units of government. Nevertheless, some of the same issues apply. Steve Starland of the state of Washington says, "Take rivers. We are beginning to look at a river as an integrated corridor that includes the land bordering the river and its ecosystem, not simply a body of water. We try to balance different interests on the river, with varying degrees of success. Some want to dam up the river for hydropower; others want powerboating. Then there are the canoeists and hikers, commercial fishermen, and those who want the river kept in as natural a state as possible. We must decide the priorities since you can't satisfy everyone. In the past, there was more of a tendency to react to the demand for facilities such as boat ramps. Complicating this whole planning and implementing task is the involvement of many different units of government and organizations."

Commenting on some of the professionals who get involved in this process, Starland continues, "There are planners (natural resource, urban, land-use, and recreational), general resource managers, resource specialists (water, hazardous waste, fisheries and wildlife biologists) who offer data and help clarify specific problems, educators, and public involvement specialists. Another type of professional is a facilitator. This person, not necessarily trained in formal mediation skills, must have independent knowledge and background on the subject, and must be able to bring together different groups and agencies at the table. The top-down meeting and hearing structure doesn't seem to work in these matters." The professionals mentioned by Starland could work in a variety of state agencies from traditional departments of natural resources to state environmental protection agencies and departments of parks and recreation and agriculture, or special bodies such as coastal commissions or watershed districts.

Another area seeing a lot of activity at the state and regional levels is water resources management. This work includes various watershed studies that focus on water quality, supply, and recreational needs.

Finally, as states become more active and professional in managing their resources, they need to survey and otherwise gather and process data on the resources within their borders. Two of the major vehicles here are natural heritage programs and geographical information systems.

Natural heritage programs are aimed at identification and preservation of biological diversity within a state. This is achieved by tracking the status and distribution of rare and natural elements and making this information available to policy makers and the public. The impetus and staffing for natural heritage programs originally came from the Nature Conservancy, a nonprofit organization that worked with state natural resource departments, which later assumed responsibility for staffing these projects. Forty-eight states now have such programs. Susan Crispin coordinates five full-time staff and two to six seasonal interns for the Michigan Natural Features Inventory. "We conduct county-by-county surveys to find rare natural plants and maintain a data base that is used by local, state, and federal agencies as well as developers and environmental activists. A typical information request might be something like 'What is the most important wetland community in the state?' We employ field biologists and ecologists who can understand the ecology of communities and ecosystems. This is an emerging field, which is being called conservation biology."

Geographical information systems are computerized data bases that allow users to locate many different types of information on parcels of land in the state: location of underground storage tanks, aquifers, and wells; type of vegetation and soil; hazardous waste sites; and current uses of particular parcels of land. These systems are likely to change dramatically the professions of environmental planning and natural resource management. A variety of professionals are working to develop, maintain, and use these systems, including field biologists, cartographers, geologists, geographers, natural resource specialists, and computer personnel. Computer-assisted mapping is a related field that is also growing.

FEDERAL GOVERNMENT

Many of the natural resource management programs just described employ a large percentage of federal land and water conservation personnel. Because of budgetary constraints and a philosophical swing toward development interests among appointed administrators, however, there has been less innovation and fewer new opportunities at the federal level during most of the 1980s. Consequently, federal jobs in land and water conservation are very difficult to find these days. Still, the U.S. Forest Service, for one, is a major federal employer of natural resource personnel, with 36,000 full-time and 8,000 temporary employees.

Federal landholding agencies own 700 million acres of land, roughly one third of all land in the United States. These lands are managed primarily by five agencies within the U.S. Department of the Interior: the Bureau of Land Management, the U.S. Fish and Wildlife Service, the National Park Service, the Bureau of Indian Affairs, and the Bureau of Reclamation. Major holdings are also managed by the U.S. Forest Service, the Tennessee Valley Authority, and the Departments of Defense and Energy.

Robert Chandler, superintendent of Olympic National Park, in discussing natural resource management by the National Park Service, sheds some light on the status of these activities in the federal government: "Each national park has a resource management division that does planning, environmental compliance, project design, and monitoring of resource management activities. At Olympic there are four resource management specialists making sure projects are completed as designed. There is also a natural science studies group that includes wildlife biologists, fisheries biologists, botanists, and general biologists who conduct research activities. Over the last several years the National Park Service, at the administration as well as congressional levels, has realized the importance of resource management activities and has put more money into addressing these problems. Unfortunately, this has not translated into many new positions to accomplish the goal. This has direct bearing on people who are already in the system. The competition is tough for resource management or scientist jobs. Most come into the park as park rangers or naturalists or biologists at the entry level, and once in, they try to compete for some of the resource management positions."

According to Judith Frazier, a wilderness coordinator with the U.S. Forest Service, recreational demands could boost federal hiring in the near future. "There is an ever growing need for recreation in this country. Since we aren't acquiring new acreage to expand into, we intensify our efforts in managing what we have. This is eventually going to create new federal natural resource opportunities."

The Soil Conservation Service of the U.S. Department of Agriculture is one of the few federal agencies with a presence in virtually every county in the United States. The 14,000 employees of the service work in partnership with local soil conservation districts to reduce soil erosion and pollution from soil runoff and to manage storm water. Other responsibilities include administering federal programs such as the Small Watershed Protection Program, the Rural Abandoned Mine Program, and the Resource Conservation and Development Program and to enforce erosion requirements pursuant to the Food Security Act of 1985, or the Farm Bill. The service primarily hires soil scientists, engineers (agricultural and civil), and biologists.

INDIAN NATIONS

Indian nations own and manage significant parcels of land in the West and hire the gamut of land and water conservation professionals, especially natural resource managers and specialists. Contact these tribes separately, as each has its own hiring procedures. See the *Native American Directory* (National Native American Co-op, 1982; P.O. Box 500, San Carlos, Ariz. 85550) for information.

CONSULTING FIRMS

Consulting work in the land and water conservation field is less common than in the environmental protection fields. Nevertheless, use of consulting firms is increasing in all areas as corporations and government agencies look to consultants for expertise not found on staff. These firms work primarily with government agencies but also with corporations and utilities that have large parcels of land to manage. Much of the work done by consulting firms in land and water conservation will revolve around specialties covered in other chapters: water quality, hazardous waste, forestry, and planning. Watershed management studies, for example, might require a consultant to measure and assess nonpoint runoff. Other areas where consultants are getting involved include habitat and ecosystem restoration. One factor limiting consulting work in this field is that government agencies often contract work to universities which might otherwise go to consultants. Entry-level consulting jobs are difficult to find in this area. It is far more common for experienced professionals to leave a public sector career to start or join a consulting business.

NONPROFIT SECTOR

We have already discussed the growth in nonprofit land trusts and expansion of their efforts both locally and nationally to preserve and manage land, natural areas, and ecosystems. Nonprofit organizations also have an active and growing presence in advocacy and public education efforts related to land conservation. This is true nationally, statewide, and locally. All have benefited from the public's concern that not enough was being done to preserve natural resources. For example, Sue Alexander of the Wilderness Society notes that the society's national staff has more than doubled since 1980, a trend not out of line with that in other organizations. This increase has allowed the Wilderness Society to staff ten field offices around the country.

A more significant development is the flourishing of statewide and grass roots organizations. This is a trend R. Montgomery Fischer, executive director of the Vermont Natural Resources Council, believes will not be short-lived. "There is quite a future in local nonprofits. People are giving, foundation grants are up, and I'm not alone in thinking nonprofits are better at spending money. It's something of a fluke, but we have six openings right now and are opening a second office in the state. One reason nonprofits are so important at the local level is their work to ensure implementation of a tremendous flood of state legislation related to growth management, planning, and land preservation. In Vermont we have had 35 to 40 major pieces of state environmental legislation enacted in the past several years."

Eric Partee, executive director of Little Miami, Inc., which is working to preserve the Little Miami River near Cincinnati, comments, "Besides riding herd on government agencies to live up to their legally mandated responsibilities, it is a responsibility of nonprofits to be creative, to come up with the new initiatives. We must also educate, communicate, and sell our ideas. I try to think of what we do as a product. I try to market this product so that people are so enthralled by it that they can't do without it and will pay for the work of Little Miami, Inc."

Nonprofit jobs in this field tend to be for those with a wide range of skills: education, policy formulation, management, fund-raising, and communications.

GETTING STARTED

> *Getting started in this field requires a building process. It's not like other fields, say hazardous waste, where if you have the right degree you just waltz into a great job. First off, I recommend an interdisciplinary education with an emphasis on the hard sciences. Get up to speed on the regulatory structure—local, state, and federal. Then do some real work. This opens doors and gives you a leg up on someone with a purely academic résumé. You have to structure yourself financially to pay some dues. If you care enough about the field to do this it ultimately pays off.*
>
> Ed Becker, Executive Director, Essex County (Massachusetts) Greenbelt Association

There are many ways to get involved in land and water conservation with a variety of backgrounds not specifically related to natural resource management; planning, environmental education, recreation, and the environmental protection fields are a few. If you want to combine those skills with work in land and water conservation, you should take natural resource management and ecology courses and look for volunteer opportunities to combine your skills.

If the area of natural resource management is your major focus, there are many specialties within this discipline. Although technician-type jobs exist for those with two-year degrees or those with bachelor's degrees, because of tight competition most professional jobs go to those with master's degrees. There are exceptions, such as people who have unique experiences and skills. For your undergraduate degree, the basic sciences are recommended: biology, botany, zoology, or natural resource management. Double majors involving hard sciences and liberal arts will put job hunters one up on the competition.

Although graduate school is the time to specialize, professionals repeatedly stress that they are looking for applicants who also understand relationships. Steve Starland of the Washington State Parks and Recreation Commission advises, "We are not looking for someone who just understands the trees or the fish or the streams or the timber industry, but people who can put it all together." Good preparation would include course work in biology, the ecology of ecosystems and communities, and possibly even population biology courses. Course work on public policy as it relates to resource management is also useful, but it should not be pursued at the expense of a hard scientific grounding. Master's degrees that encompass this type of work include natural resource management, ecology, botany, and forestry.

PUBLIC SECTOR

In speaking about getting that first job in the public sector, Steve Starland says, "The easiest way is to get started before you get out of school by taking internships or work-study assignments. Although you need a graduate degree to compete for many permanent positions, there are some basic, technically oriented positions that you can get with an undergraduate degree; many will be seasonal jobs. Try to get yourself known within the agency you want to work for; contribute to a report that the agency prepares so you can have your name in print. Most people don't want to be surprised—if they know you, you're that much ahead of the game. Plus, even as a seasonal employee, you have an instant network. People are keeping their eyes open for you." Some state and federal agencies, such as the U.S. Forest Service and Soil Conservation Service, have cooperative education programs with universities. This is an excellent way to get your first position.

Entry-level positions can involve anything from trail maintenance to research projects. According to Susan Crispin of the Michigan Natural Features Inventory, "One good source of entry-level positions is in field surveys for all the various surveys and assessments that state and federal governments are conducting. We recently had a problem finding entry-level field biologists." Local conservation districts are also increasingly hiring entry-level personnel to enforce land-use and other environmental regulations.

Take stock of some of the realities before you enter this field. Jim Burns of the Ohio Department of Natural Resources counsels, "Very rarely will you get out of school with your master's and land a permanent position right away. I was doing contract work for two years. You are also probably going to have to relocate a lot. Some people give up and go back to school and become a teacher. I'm glad I stuck it out."

NONPROFIT SECTOR

Although the nonprofit sector is flourishing, tight budgets mean nonprofits don't like to take chances with staff. Consequently, hiring is still largely an insider's game. It would be very rare for you to be hired right after graduation without some internships or work experience. As Sue Alexander puts it, "I have no problem with people having to pay their dues. I did, and so did just about everyone else I know."

Employers like applicants with a broad-based education—it might be a double major in politics and biology, or business and natural resource management. Eric Partee of Little Miami, Inc., adds, "We also like to see someone who has experience working with nonprofit organizations. Become an officer in a local nonprofit, learn what it takes to get things done, to coordinate volunteers, run meetings, deal with the Army Corps of Engineers and local members of Congress. If you want to work for a local organization or land trust, understand the local politics and issues."

Entry-level jobs might include assistant to the director or researcher, or in the case of natural resource management, conservation assistant. You will be doing research and literature searches, writing policy papers, staffing subcommittees, and helping to coordinate volunteers.

TIPS FOR JOB HUNTERS

- Land and water conservation is a very popular field; demand for jobs exceeds the supply. However, there is an upsurge in work in this area, making employment prospects better than at any point since the mid-seventies. Go beyond the departments and agencies traditionally associated with land and water conservation; there are a lot of conservation jobs tucked away in the most unlikely government offices.

• Your particular skill can probably be packaged creatively to help you get started in this field, whether it is in law, planning, real estate, journalism, environmental protection, or some other field. Because of the tight competition, however, if you are entering that part of the field for which a scientific background is required, you will likely need a master's degree or some very impressive experience.

• When employers discuss optimal education and experience, the key term is *broad based:* In scientific fields, like natural resource management, employers want to see applicants who understand ecosystems and how the various components of a natural area fit together. In nonprofits and policy-oriented settings, employers want to see people with a combination of science and liberal arts background, people who understand the technical *and* political aspects of their work.

• Try to get on the state and federal job registers while still in graduate school. It may take several years for a test or opening to come up, and you can be getting your master's degree in the meantime.

SALARY

It is difficult to come up with useful salary figures because of the wide variety of careers included in this field. Starting salaries for land- and water-related positions at the state level are below $1,500 per month for seasonal work and between $15,000 and $22,000 annually for permanent positions. Those with law degrees start between the mid-20s and low 30s. Salaries at local park districts and agencies are generally lower and spread across a wider range than at the state level. The nonprofit sector offers even more variety; starting salaries would likely range from a low of $14,000 to the low to mid-20s if you have a graduate degree and some relevant experience. There are smaller nonprofit organizations where the executive director is still making only $20,000. Generally, however, nonprofits are attempting to be competitive with the public sector.

CASE STUDY

California Tahoe Conservancy

Professionals in the land and water conservation field are involved in land acquisition, natural resource management, planning, and preventing environmental degradation of natural areas. The California Tahoe Conservancy performs all these roles as it attempts to balance numerous demands on the Lake Tahoe region. An agency like this depends on creative and cooperative working arrangements with other departments and levels of governments and with individuals in achieving its objectives.

Lake Tahoe, on the California-Nevada border, is one of the largest freshwater lakes in the West and is known for its pristine waters and beautiful surroundings. Because of its scenic beauty, the area has significant economic value. Over the years there has been a steady increase in activity and development related to tourism. As a result of the development, increased sedimentation has been reducing visibility in the lake at the rate of one to one and a half feet per year; previously, the visibility range was 80 to 100 feet. The Tahoe area has become one of the most highly regulated areas in the country, primarily under the direction of the Tahoe Regional Planning Agency (TRPA), an interstate agency responsible for regional and long-range planning, permitting, and regulation.

Whereas the job of TRPA is reactive, in that it either approves or disapproves permits for proposed development projects, the role envisioned for the California Tahoe Conservancy is more affirmative. The conservancy is an independent state agency within the Resources Agency of the state of California. Established by state law in 1984, the conservancy has jurisdiction over only the California side of the Lake Tahoe basin.

Dave Gregorich has been involved with the conservancy from the beginning. "I was working for the California Coastal Conservancy as a program analyst doing wetlands and waterfront restoration. After the voters passed the $85 million Lake Tahoe Acquisitions Bond Act in 1982, I was one of the staff of an advisory commission whose job it was to recommend how to spend the money and who would have the authority to implement the Act. We recommended the activation of the Tahoe Conservancy."

Gregorich ended up on the staff of the conservancy and was involved in setting up its programmatic and administrative activities. The conservancy has a staff of 20, including a program staff of ten, an executive officer, and legal, administrative, and clerical personnel. Gregorich is administrative officer, charged with managing day-to-day operations of the agency.

"The conservancy is not a regulatory agency. Rather, it was established to develop and implement programs through land acquisitions and site improvements to preserve water quality in Lake Tahoe, maintain the scenic beauty and recreational opportunities of the region, provide public access, preserve wildlife habitat areas, restore lands to protect the natural environment, and ensure, at the same time, equitable treatment of landowners.

"Thirty to forty years ago the Tahoe basin was heavily subdivided with disregard for the landscape or environment. Development led to erosion and sedimentation. The main program of the conservancy has been land acquisition, centered on what we call environmentally sensitive lands, which include high hazard lands and stream environment zones. Within these categories are lands with steep slopes or highly erodible soils; riparian, marsh, and meadow areas; sensitive shore zones; human-modified land; and substandard lots. We have estimated that there are 6,500 to 7,100 environmentally sensitive lots and parcels on the California side of the basin and have acquired 2,700 parcels at a cost of $30 million.

"To complement the acquisition program, we place a great deal of emphasis on our second major program, erosion control, which addresses the effects of existing development with the goal of reducing the amount of sediment flowing into the lake. In this program our focus is on cut slopes that can be revegetated or reduced to a better angle. We stabilize retaining walls, line roadside drainage and dirt channels with rocks, and contribute funds for paving dirt roads. We also create sediment basins in low drainage areas so that sediment can fall out, and we work to restore marsh, meadow, and wetland areas.

"As my title may suggest, my work on acquisition and other projects is primarily administrative. I prepare staff reports describing the various projects our people are working on and generally make a case for the project. My recommendations and reviews are submitted to the board and are also subject to public review. This requires that I attend almost all of the biweekly staff meetings of departments. My fieldwork includes project work and meetings with city and county agencies and public utilities."

Sandy Triphan is a program analyst involved in the legwork of land acquisition and in the conservancy's wildlife programs. She describes the land acquisition process as follows: "A letter to the owner of property we have classified as environmentally sensitive initiates the land acquisition process. This letter describes the conservancy's objectives and reasons we wish to protect this property through acquisition. If a favorable response is received, the land must be inspected and the soil sampled. Appraisals of the land are contracted for and reviewed by our staff, title reports are completed, and once the landowner accepts our offer based on this preacquisition work, we are ready to approach our board for approval. On approval, we can close on escrow and authorize payment. Throughout the process we are in contact with many agencies and individuals, particularly the owner.

"To give you an idea of what that entails, today I prepared a document for a landowner to sign, drove out to inspect a building, and took measurements for a fence we wish to install to protect the property we are acquiring. I finished four other permits and prepared a categorical document for the state. Later today I plan to come up with a design for the fencing, which I will submit and, when it is approved in about three weeks, I will obtain the materials and hire the labor for construction."

Triphan had a double major in social sciences and science, parks, and recreation at California State University at Sacramento and also did graduate work in anthropology and education there. She credits her experience as a park ranger for 12 years as giving her the management background needed for this position. "I really enjoyed my work as a park ranger, but quite frankly, the demands of the profession just were not worth the low salary. Given this experience, my advice to others is to get a wide variety of work experience and be careful not to get 'over-degreed,' which will better enable them to keep their options open."

Land acquisition is critical to the work of the conservancy. Equally important, however, are management and restoration efforts. This work is handled by the wildlife enhancement, public access, special acquisition, and erosion control programs. Tamara McCandless, a program analyst, describes the wildlife enhancement program and some of the other programs she coordinates at the conservancy. "When I first interviewed for the job they couldn't give me a definite job description, so what I'm doing now is a lot different from what I was doing during my first year here. At the outset most of our efforts were put into acquisition, covering everything from writing initial letters, doing fieldwork, reviewing appraisals, reviewing applications, inspecting the land, and so on—I started to feel more like a real estate agent than an environmental professional! Fortunately, after we started to fulfill that mandate we diversified into other programs.

"To a certain extent we all run around fighting fires and have never really been assigned to one department. This system has allowed us the freedom to take on areas of special interest to us. My primary responsibility is still acquisition and the preparation of our biweekly reports on acquisitions, closures, and the status of other properties. I have also taken a special interest in the wildlife habitat enhancement program. This program gives grants to other organizations to do wildlife habitat enhancement projects and also uses grant funds to develop programs on our own acquired lands.

"To initiate this program, we took a look at the basin as a whole to determine what was needed. One of the projects that had long been suggested by TRPA was the creation of an artificial reef in the lake to increase the number of offshore fish. Up until that time no one had offered to take on the task because of all the hoops one would have to jump through. I suggested to our board that we develop the project. The first thing I had to do was call together the chief executive officer of the Forest Service, representatives of the regional office of the California Water Quality Control Board, and representatives of the Department of Fish and Game to discuss the best methods of construction and structure of the reef.

"I took these ideas, drew up a proposal, and identified sites for the reef, which I submitted to our board. With their comments I reworked the plan into the final draft, which was approved. The next step was getting all the permits for development of the reef—quite a task: I had to get a stream or lake alteration permit from the California Department of Fish and Game; I went to the State Lands Commission, which owns the bottom of the lake, and got a 50-year, no-fee lease of the site; the regional office of the Water Quality Control Board had to be contacted for an exemption to dump the reef boulders in the lake (they are classified as waste); the Army Corps of Engineers had to approve any obstructions to navigation in the lake; and, finally, I obtained approval of the plan from the TRPA.

"The next steps were to write and manage bids for barge owners to place the boulders in the lake and coordinate the logistics of obtaining the boulders from the California Transportation Department. Finally, I went out during the project start to direct the placement of the boulders on a very cold and stormy November day. Since that time I've worked with the Department of Fish and Game in monitoring the program and have contracted with them for services. So far the reef is doing what we had expected—it has created a habitat for crayfish, which nongame fish prey on, and as a result the nongame fish population has increased.

"Other projects we promote are grants to state parks for meadow restoration (the goal of this being to halt the normal successional stages of forest takeover of meadowlands because species in Tahoe need that habitat), grants for endangered plant species restoration, and assistance with osprey nesting platforms and bald eagle perching sites established by the Forest Service. In these instances I work with the agency developing the project to help them iron out their proposals, making sure they address all the concerns of wildlife and will accomplish the desired task, advise them on the permit process, and go out to oversee the start-up of the project.

"All in all, I've been very pleased at the progress we are making here at the conservancy. Before accepting this position I was doing research work at Indiana University on acid rain. I was really fed up with doing a lot of research that wasn't being utilized because of politics, so I submitted my internship application to CEIP. I had hoped for a position that would enable me to make an impact and I think I found it."

Dave Gregorich talked about the challenges facing an agency charged with the dual role of preservation and providing access to the public. "Lake Tahoe's reputation as a pristine and environmentally sound area attracts thousands of recreationists, which raises the question of how to accommodate them while preserving the area's beauty. One project that our staff is always working on is the public access program. While doing fieldwork and acquiring lands, we constantly add our plots to the map of existing parks and facilities—always on the lookout for ways to connect facilities and reduce congestion. We conduct projects ourselves as well as award grants to other agencies. We currently have ten ongoing projects running a tab of around $3 million. The projects include bike trails (in an effort to create a path around the entire rim of the basin), enhancements and improvements of beachfront parks, and improvement of public parking near beaches."

The Tahoe Conservancy is a relatively new model—an attempt to combine in one agency the elements of land acquisition, planning, and manage-

PROFILES

Jan Henderson, Area Ecologist, U.S. Forest Service, Olympic National Forest, Washington

This profile gives you a sense of the field research and lab analysis that go into natural resource management decisions.

"In the Pacific Northwest region of the U.S. Forest Service, Oregon and Washington, there are seven area ecologists, each of whom covers two to four national forests; my forests are the Mt. Baker–Snoqualmie and Olympic. My project is to classify and inventory plant communities on national forest land and to help the Forest Service use that information in its land management practices. I see my role as trying to help the Forest Service put forestry and land management on an ecological basis rather than a production basis. As such, I try to get people to look at management practices that will best fit the ecosystem by presenting detailed research of specific communities in the national forests. Before I started at the Forest Service I envisioned myself approaching my conservation work from a strong emotional, advocacy point of view. I have since discovered that I can better achieve my goals by taking a more scientific point of view.

"The administrative work alone for the two national forests could be a full-time job if I let it be, but I try to confine all of that work to the winter months, as we spend most of the summer in the field. We begin in mid-June and go until mid-September, during which time I'm only in the office long enough to pick up my gear, fill out my time slips, and look at the mail. I usually take five or six crew members with me who are also ecologists to do plot surveys, which become our data base. The sites are usually two to six

ment. Many parts of the country, however, are facing the same challenge as is the Lake Tahoe region: how to be involved in seemingly inevitable development in a manner that retains the natural beauty and ecosystem of an area. Florida, New England, the Southwest, and the West Coast are only the most visible of these areas. These are highly controversial, emotionally charged issues, involving huge sums of money. We are already seeing a variety of governmental and private responses to these issues, creating new agencies and professions. As the country continues to grow and the public demands conservation of our natural resources, this activity can only increase.

---

hours away from home and require that we backpack to the area. We sleep in tents and work long days, usually 10 to 12 hours for up to eight days at a time.

"I first locate a site that supports the particular community we want to study and we lay out the plot, which usually covers an area of about a fifth of an acre. We count the number of trees, measure their height and diameter, identify their species, take increment cores for total age and the last ten years of growth, identify all vascular plants, estimate the cover or canopy in terms of percent, identify all mosses, lichens, and liverworts, which are important animal food, record all bird songs, animals, and animal signs, do soil analysis, record any dead trees, make note of the temperature, and then mark the site on a photo using a road as a reference point so that it can be found again. We do about 150 to 200 of these a summer. During the winter we analyze the core and

soil samples, plot our sample sites on maps, enter the data on a computer, and run various statistical analyses. A lot of decisions about preservation and conservation have been made as a result of our work.

"I work directly for the supervisors of the two forests, but I see them only one or two times a year, when we meet to discuss the objectives for the coming year. I also have one or two administrative advisers, but otherwise my work is pretty much left for me to conduct. This is one aspect of my job I really like—I'm given the freedom to do the kind of research I like to do; I work in areas that others recreate in, it's challenging, and it makes an impact. But you must also be able to tolerate the bureaucracy and not let it get you down.

"Entry into these fields, especially into the U.S. Forest Service, is *very* competitive, but I'd say applied ecology and rare plant study are two areas with slightly more room for entry. I received my B.A. in forestry from Washington State University, and my M.S. in forest ecology and Ph.D. in botany and plant ecology from Oregon State University. When I went into graduate school I didn't know where I was going to end up or what I'd be doing. After I received my Ph.D. I went into teaching at the college level and after years of doing research and teaching became recognized in the field. I moved into this area of study in the Forest Service as the ecology program was expanding. The way most people enter the program is by working on a seasonal or part-time basis until an opening comes up. This functions a little like an internship: grooming people for future positions but still allowing them the option of taking the experience and being hired elsewhere. Two things are needed to do well in this field and those are a good scientific, ecological background and a wildland resource background. A major in plant or forest ecology is usually a prerequisite."

Stephen Small, Tax and Environmental Lawyer, Powers and Hall, P.C., Boston

"All of what I do on a regular basis is tax work—individual income tax, audits, representing developers, partnership planning—the whole gamut, but my particular interest is in the intersection of tax law and land preservation. One area where it does cross is in restrictions and easements on parcels of land.

"I received a B.A. in English from Yale University and a master's in journalism from Northwestern University. After working at a newspaper and in Congress for several years, I became interested in law and went to night law school, specializing in tax law, and received my degree from Georgetown University. While at Georgetown, three of us students convinced the school to offer a course on historic preservation law—a relatively new legal discipline at the time. I wrote a paper on the tax benefits of donating historic preservation easements and land conservation easements, which was published in two law journals. I enjoyed the intellectual challenge of mixing property law and tax issues. Following law school, I went to work for the Internal Revenue Service because I wanted to make a career of tax law. I was assigned to write the regulations on income tax deductions for the donation of conservation easements. I spent a couple of years on it and got to know the area and people in the field well. At that time there were very few land trust professionals.

"I left the IRS in 1982 to join this law firm and initially didn't spend a lot of time on land conservation projects because there simply weren't that many cases. That has changed. Over the past year or so I have been approached by more and more people who have problems in this area. A typical case would be a client who has a very valuable piece of land in a desirable location and knows that if he doesn't plan appropriately will be subject to a large estate tax. One client had enough money to pay the estate tax but wanted to avoid having to. He eventually decided to put a conservation easement on the land to generate an income tax deduction and to lower the value of the land. In the second step, he simply gave the land to his children and paid the gift tax, which was lower because of the easement.

"Most of my clients would like to protect their land and leave it to children or other relatives. They realize that if they do so without proper planning, their heirs will not be able to come up with the estate tax and the land will have to be sold to developers, defeating the purpose of willing it to the heirs and not fulfilling the owner's desire to protect the property from development. Conservation and preservation easements are often a viable solution.

"Environmental law, like all areas of law, has a great number of specialties. It would be impossible to find one person who could handle every kind of environmental case—a smart and honest lawyer knows his boundaries and will refer you to another lawyer if he is unable to handle a case. The catchall phrase *environmental law* includes areas such as land acquisition projects, land-use law, toxic torts, municipal zoning work requiring approvals of subdivisions, work with officials to get building projects off the ground, and state and federal regulation. When many people think of 'environmental law' they think of land preservation, land-use, and wetland regulations. Unfortunately, these regulations often become mere requirements you must meet *before* you can rape and pillage the land. Environmental and land-use law is thriving, but a lot of its aim is not to *protect* the environment. More often than not you end up working for developers if you're an environmental lawyer, and if you do that kind of work you are not achieving your conservation goals. Unfortunately, the good guy conservationists don't have much representation.

"If someone wants to work in the area I'm involved in he or she must be a good tax lawyer and be knowledgeable about real estate law. It is a wide-open field, but there still isn't enough demand on the regional level to make it a full-time practice.

"It is very hard as a new practitioner to become established in large and competitive fields of law like corporate reorganizations and partnerships; it takes somewhat less time in new, evolving areas of law, such as conservation easement law. Nevertheless, there is a very long learning curve of about seven or eight years before anyone learns enough about a particular field or specialty to begin to be an expert. I don't urge anyone to specialize too early. Get a good overall knowledge of law and learn to think like a lawyer first."

Dale Allen, Southeast Regional Manager, Trust for Public Land, Tallahassee, Florida

"The Trust for Public Land (TPL) is a land conservation organization specializing in open space and community land conservation in urban and metropolitan areas. Our projects range from abandoned railroads, parks, and gardens to urban nature preserves. In addition, we act as an intermediary between government agencies and landowners to facilitate the public acquisition of land. We also provide technical assistance to land trusts that help train local groups in nonprofit land acquisition. Increasingly, we have become involved in joint venture land acquisition with other nonprofits, whereby we secure a parcel of land while the community raises the money to repurchase it from us.

"For example, the mayor of the city of Winter Haven, Florida, recently called me with a desperate situation. They had been informed that 2.4 miles of railroad right-of-way through the middle of downtown and adjacent to the city hall and police station were being abandoned and would be sold by the railroad. Even more critical to the community, however, was that the land to be sold included a two-block area (the site of the original station depot) in the heart of the city, which for many years had been leased by the city and managed as Winter Haven's Central Park.

"The city obviously had not anticipated this expense and could not directly pursue a purchase, so they called on us to help. I went out to inspect the land and to meet with the mayor in order to understand the circumstances and assess available city resources. I also met with representatives of the railroad, who were willing to negotiate because they would much rather sell to one buyer than go through the hassle of subdividing the land. I negotiated a transaction whereby TPL would purchase an option for a predetermined price; the option also gave TPL six months of precious time. The next step was to return to city officials and establish a time frame in which the city could finance the purchase. Numerous other details had to be addressed, such as title work and surveying the right-of-way. Eventually TPL solved the public financing dilemma by selling all the nonessential portions of the corridor to a consortium of businessmen, to cover our costs, then donating the critical park and community land to the city.

"At TPL each project is overseen by a project manager whose work is sup-

IN SUMMARY

Hooper Brooks, director of the Regional Open Space Program of the Regional Plan Association in New York, says of the land and water conservation field, "There are not necessarily a lot of jobs in this field, but there is a tremendous amount of demand. Consequently, clever people are going to find work." Indeed, the field will probably always be relatively tight, as funds for agencies involved in this field are usually scarce and many want to fill the jobs that do exist. The good news is that your work is strongly supported by the public, and that support is growing. Those who succeed in this field as we enter the 21st century will possess strong scientific, *integrated* backgrounds, relevant experience, and, above all, persistence and commitment.

plemented by surveyors, appraisers, lawyers, planners, biologists, accountants, and real estate brokers. We do not maintain a staff of these professionals because our regional office negotiates in 11 states, and it would be impossible for anyone to be knowledgeable about each county and city government's regulations. We also deal extensively with elected officials and public employees at the local, state, and federal levels.

"TPL itself employs generalists with a strong commitment to land conservation. Project managers must be people oriented, capable of working with professionals in law and real estate and conducting negotiations with sophisticated individual and corporate landowners, and knowledgeable about the political process. We have five such individuals in our office and everyone does a lot of everything. A great deal of my time is spent on the telephone, drafting and negotiating contracts and proposals, making presentations, and traveling, which takes up as much as 30 percent of my time but is un-avoidable. Some administrative functions particular to my position include preparing expense and revenue budgets, overseeing the other project managers, structuring projects, organizing staff meetings, evaluating staff members, and thinking of new ways to achieve TPL's open space land conservation goals.

"I earned my M.S. in geography and land-use management from Florida State University and worked for the Florida House of Representatives and the Florida Department of Natural Resources before coming to TPL. I started at the bottom eight years ago and have been a regional manager for little over a year. When I applied for the job, I felt it was a good use of my generalist background and the subject area hit home with my environmental interests. Ever since I was young and growing up in Florida I have spent time outdoors hiking and camping and I have done a lot of volunteer work with the Florida Audubon Society and the Sierra Club."

RESOURCES

Listed here are only some of the trade and professional organizations active in the land and water conservation field. The annual Conservation Directory *(National Wildlife Federation) is an excellent source of information on additional organizations as well as state and federal agencies and departments active in the conservation field.*

The Job Seekers Guide to Opportunities in Natural Resource Management for the Developing World. See Resources, chapter 4, for description.

The Nature Conservancy. Publishes bimonthly magazine. Has many land and water conservation programs operated by professionally staffed field offices in 46 states. Also has an international program. 1800 N. Kent St., Arlington, Va. 22209.

The Wilderness Society. Publishes *Wilderness* (quarterly). 1400 Eye St., N.W., Washington, D.C. 20005.

Ecological Society of America. Publishes *Ecology* (bimonthly). Center for Environmental Studies, Arizona State University, Tempe, Ariz. 85287.

Soil and Water Conservation Society. Publishes *Journal of Soil and Water Conservation* (bimonthly). 7515 N.E. Ankeny Rd., Ankeny, Iowa 50021.

National Association of Conservation Districts. Publishes *Tuesday Letter* (weekly); "Guide to Conservation Careers" (1984), pamphlet with bibliography of publications on careers in conservation. 509 Capitol Court, N.E., Washington, D.C. 20002.

American Land Resources Association. Citizens' organization working to promote wise management of forests, soil, water, wildlife, and other natural resources. Has internship program. Publishes *American Land Forum* (bimonthly). 1516 P St., N.W., Washington, D.C. 20033.

Land Trust Exchange. Provides technical assistance to land trusts. Publishes *Exchange Journal* (quarterly), *National Directory of Local and Regional Land Conservation Organizations*. 1017 Duke St., Alexandria, Va. 22314.

Natural Resources Council of America. Federation of national and regional conservation organizations and scientific societies interested in conservation of natural resources. Publishes *NRCA News* (monthly). 1015 31st St., N.W., Washington, D.C. 20007.

Trust for Public Land. Works to acquire and preserve land in urban and rural areas. Provides technical assistance in land acquisition. Publishes *Update* (quarterly). Has six regional offices. 116 New Montgomery St., Fourth Floor, San Francisco, Calif. 94105.

North American Lake Management Society. Publishes *Lake Line* (bimonthly), proceedings of annual conference, and other publications. 1000 Connecticut Ave., N.W., Washington, D.C. 20036.

12 Fishery and Wildlife Management

SOMETHING ABOUT the field of fisheries and wildlife attracts a lot of people, people with fire in their eyes that tells you this is their passion. They seem to be the people who take the greatest pleasure in being outdoors and feeling connected with the environment. This connectedness has assumed another meaning in recent years as calls have increased for taking fisheries and wildlife management beyond the game-oriented approach and integrating it into broader natural resource management and into all of our experiences in the outdoors. This gradual shift may be more evident in some areas than others, but it is going to require an influx of dedicated, highly trained professionals to build on the excellent work of the past and take the field into a promising future.

The popularity of this profession is both a blessing and a curse for the field and those who enter it. Each year there are many more highly qualified applicants than there are jobs. The caliber of professionals who make it is almost staggering, as is the frustration of some who struggle to find permanent employment. Another side of this passion for fish and wildlife work is that people may be drawn to a career because of a love for fish and wildlife, without thinking carefully about what the work entails; such people are prone to be frustrated when they don't get out into the field as often as they would like.

Reports by the two major professional associations, the American Fisheries Society and the Wildlife Society, show where professionals are working. In a survey of 80 percent of the schools offering wildlife degrees, of the 601 wildlife graduates *hired* in 1986 for wildlife-related positions (out of

1,376 graduates), 28 percent were hired by the federal government, 41 percent by state and provincial governments, 12 percent by colleges and universities (34 percent of all Ph.D.s), 17 percent by the private sector, and 2 percent by other sectors. Those not hired took nonwildlife-related employment, went on to graduate school, or kept on searching.

In a survey of 56 schools offering fisheries degrees, of the 310 fisheries graduates *hired* in 1985 for fishery-related positions (out of 595 graduates), 26 percent were hired by the federal government, 35 percent by state and provincial governments, 13 percent by colleges and universities (20 percent of all Ph.D.s), 21 percent by the private sector (58 percent of whom were hired by aquaculture firms), and 5 percent by other sectors.

All told, there are approximately 21,000 wildlife professionals and 16,000 fisheries professionals currently working in North America. There has been a decrease in the number of employees hired by the federal government and a relative if not numeric increase in fish and wildlife professionals hired at the state level. The private sector is also hiring an increasing percentage of professionals, as are local units of government, although the latter is not categorized in the surveys just mentioned.

At the federal level, the two largest employers are the Department of the Interior's U.S. Fish and Wildlife Service and the Department of Agriculture's Forest Service. Other federal agencies employing fish and wildlife professionals include the Bureau of Land Management, National Marine Fisheries Service, Army Corps of Engineers, Environmental Protection Agency, National Park Service, the military services, and the Peace Corps. Important state agencies in this area include departments of fish and wildlife, forestry, conservation, environmental protection, and parks and recreation.

Colleges and universities hire a significant percentage of graduates, not only to teach but also for various research projects. Many of these are temporary positions. Private sector employers include utility companies, timber firms, oil companies, and private fisheries and aquaculture industries. There are many employers with one-of-a-kind jobs to offer, such as wildlife ranges, scientific foundations, zoological parks, and hunting and fishing clubs. Finally, consulting firms hire fishery and wildlife professionals, usually with experience, to work on contracts with the public and private sector as well as universities.

The U.S. Fish and Wildlife Service defines the work of wildlife and fishery biologists as follows:

> *Wildlife biologists* study the distribution, abundance, habits, life histories, ecology, mortality factors, and economic values of birds, mammals, and other wildlife. They plan and carry out wildlife management programs, determine

conditions affecting wildlife, apply research findings to the management of wildlife, restore or develop wildlife habitats, regulate wildlife populations, and control wildlife diseases.

Fishery biologists study the life history, habits, classification, and economic relations of aquatic organisms. They manage fish hatcheries and fishery resources, and gather data on interrelations between various species of fish and the effects of natural and human changes in the environment on the survival and growth of fish. Fishery biologists determine rearing and stocking methods best adapted for maximum success in fish hatchery operations and devise methods to regulate fishing to secure an optimum sustained yield.

These descriptions serve to outline the range of *tasks* you will handle in this profession, but they don't give you much of a sense of what *jobs* are actually like. They also have a tendency to emphasize the glamorous parts of the jobs, as if you will spend all of your time out in the field observing wildlife. As a refuge biologist for the U.S. Fish and Wildlife Service says, "There is a notion that we spend all of our time working outside. In fact, because of paperwork, many of us spend most of our time in the office. People should be aware of this before they get started in this profession."

Fishery and wildlife professionals work as lab scientists, technical writers, journalists, and educators. Field biologists and technicians do research in the field or carry out wildlife management directives. Law enforcement personnel also work more in the field. Management personnel spend a lot of time developing and implementing programs and negotiating with other agencies and sectors of government.

Finally, many fishery and wildlife professionals find employment not directly related to their fields. They might be field biologists for a state natural resources department or work on natural resource management for the U.S. Forest Service. Such positions can serve as back-door strategies to gain employment in the fish and wildlife field, through a lateral move or departmental transfer.

JUST HOW TIGHT IS THE JOB MARKET?

Tight. But then, this is nothing particularly new. The job market has always been tough in this field, and yet, every year new graduates find entry-level jobs. In *A Survey of Compensation in the Fields of Fish and Wildlife Management* (see Resources), Carl Sullivan, executive director of the American Fisheries Society, speculates that there are possibly twice as many fisheries graduates each year (approximately 1,000) as there are job openings arising solely from attrition (500).

On the wildlife side, Harry Hodgdon, executive director of the Wildlife

Society, concluded in his study of 1986 wildlife graduates that overall only 44 percent of the graduates had obtained full-time employment one year after graduating (34 percent of those with B.A.s, 66 percent of those with master's, and 87 percent of Ph.D.s).

There is no secret behind these numbers. There are just more people who want to enter this field than there are jobs, and the universities are willing to accommodate them. It has been this way since at least the early seventies, and federal budget cuts and tight state budgets have only made it worse. On the bright side, most in the field believe these cuts were to the bone and employment can only go up. Further, many employees are approaching retirement age, particularly at the federal level (50 percent of employees in the U.S. Forest Service, for example, are expected to retire in the next five to ten years).

Although the job market is tough, you would be doing yourself—and the field—a disservice if you made your career decision solely based on how many jobs are available. Sylvia Taylor, a district supervisor for the Wildlife Division of the Michigan Department of Natural Resources, says, "Yes, the field is tight and if you have only a casual interest there is not a high probability you will get a job. However, the country needs as many people trained in fisheries and wildlife as we can get. I am also of the opinion that 90 percent of the jobs that will exist five years from now haven't been invented yet. If you really want it, go for it and pull out all the stops."

ISSUES AND TRENDS

The fishery and wildlife fields have broadened and become more integrated, working with a wider variety of species, moving toward issues of habitat depletion, ecosystem study, and toxic contamination of species and their habitat. This is creating the need for a new type of fish and wildlife professional, different from the professional of the past, who was often an expert in the biology of a particular species, more often than not a game species. Dr. Rupert Cutler, president of Defenders of Wildlife, conducted a survey in 1979 when he was an assistant secretary in the Department of Agriculture. He asked regional foresters and state conservationists, "What kind of biologist is needed in the 1980s?" One regional forester answered, "The biologist is well versed in the biological details of animals, and usually in depth about one species of animals, or one class of animals. However, his knowledge of habitat and habitat requirements related to populations of wildlife in total is sadly lacking."

Cutler says conservation professionals "stressed that the interdisciplinary team approach needed in the field must begin in the academic environment. One respondent said, 'To be an effective team member, a biologist or wildlife specialist should have a good working knowledge in other fields such as outdoor recreation, plant materials, forestry, agronomy, limnology, and landscape architecture. The effective wildlife specialist recognizes that natural resource technology is becoming increasingly complex. Each specialist need not be an expert in these fields, but should be able to recognize opportunities and potentials as well as problems. Few schools have directed their curricula toward total ecosystem management.' I believe that these sentiments apply to the field of fisheries as well." (Cutler summarized this survey during his keynote address at a 1985 conference sponsored by the CEIP Fund and the University of Michigan School of Natural Resources.)

A generalist is a valuable person in the field of fish and wildlife management. This does not imply the era of the specialist is over. Far from it. And it may sound like a Catch-22: you've got to know everything and also have a specialty. Given the competitive nature of the field, this is the reality. To put it a little less harshly: You need a niche to make yourself unique and to be able to perform a specific function for an agency. However, that is not enough. You also need to be able to understand not only how to make your work relevant to the rest of the fish and wildlife circle, but also the gamut of resource management professionals—foresters, ecologists, biologists, and planners—and the public and policy makers. The ideal mix of expertise and whole-picture approach varies from agency to agency and sector to sector. You should begin to make yourself aware of what types of professionals agencies are looking for. The U.S. Fish and Wildlife Service and U.S. Forest Service, for example, still focus heavily on specialization; on the other hand, jobs with Indian tribes often require you to be involved in a wide range of activities.

Fish and wildlife professionals increasingly work with other environmental professionals and agencies to plan, develop, and implement fishery and wildlife programs in conjunction with overall natural resource management plans. This is part of a further-reaching trend of environmental agencies at many levels of government working together on integrated natural resource planning and management. The 1974 Forest and Rangeland Renewable Resources Planning Act, for example, requires that ten-year plans of the U.S. Forest Service provide for maintaining viable wildlife populations. This integrated planning requirement has increased the relative importance of the Forest Service as an employer in the area of fisheries and wildlife. In addition, fishery and wildlife professionals have been extensively involved in the flurry of watershed planning efforts, which cross state boundaries and involve many sectors of government and interest groups (see chapters 10 and 11).

Interaction with other professionals and agencies is necessary because the issues related to protecting fish and wildlife populations have broadened considerably. Development is rapidly destroying fish and wildlife habitats. Open spaces important to wildlife, particularly larger species, are decreasing, as are wetlands that support varied fish and wildlife populations. Sylvia Taylor, the wildlife supervisor from Michigan, acknowledges, "Every time you alter the land someone or something loses. That's why we, as fishery and wildlife professionals, have to be involved in all matters relating to the land." Christine Drivdahl, Habitat Management Division chief with the Washington Department of Wildlife, adds, "The high priority of habitat depletion issues is starting to be recognized. At the same time we as professionals cannot just look at the fish and wildlife. There are the hunters, hikers, developers, and tribal Indian nations whose interests must be taken into consideration. The recent negotiations among the Indian nations, timber companies, and wildlife and fishery interests in the Pacific Northwest exemplify the negotiating process which I believe is going to become the norm in the future."

Habitat once destroyed may be gone forever. A relatively new effort, however, aims at mitigation of damage by requiring the party that is reducing habitat at one location to create or restore appropriate habitat at another location. Ron Klein, a wildlife biologist for Portland General Electric in Oregon, discusses how this process works: "Regulatory agencies used to let development happen as long as losses of habitat were minimized. A lot of small losses add up. Now there is more of a determination to hold the line. In other words, if your development leads to destruction of habitat, you may be required to compensate by finding a chunk of land in poor condition and restoring it to increase its habitat-carrying capacity or, if you destroy a fish habitat, you may be required to help construct a fishery. This is not just true for rare plants, animals, and fish, but for common species as well.

"I tend to think that this is part of a larger trend of natural resource management going beyond the walls of government. Part of this is because government is so strapped for resources. Don't kid yourself, though; it happens because government requires that it happen. The end result is that mitigation projects are popping up around the country, carried out by utility companies, developers, timber companies, and other businesses with large landholdings. Some are doing these projects with in-house staff, and others are using consultants. In effect, these companies are becoming natural resource management agencies, owners and managers of wildlife preserves."

Toxic contamination of the habitat and food supply of fish and wildlife further broadens the range of issues and the types of professionals involved in this field. More and more, environmental degradation and toxins in the air, land, and water are recognized as harmful to fish and animal populations. This means more research scientists are involved in the fishery and wildlife field. The Profile of John Gannon in this chapter shows one such scientist at work.

State and local governments are becoming more involved in fish and wildlife issues, as in most other environmental issues. Harry Hodgdon of the Wildlife Society observes, "The demographics of the United States are rapidly changing, with the population becoming more urbanized. We are looking for open space and wildlife enjoyment closer to home. This is creating positions in and around urban areas ranging from habitat enhancement to wildlife education to professionals controlling wildlife damage and also human damage to wildlife."

Rupert Cutler of the Defenders of Wildlife adds, "It is encouraging to see more comprehensive fish and wildlife management at the state level. Part of this is made possible by enlarged data bases such as the information collected by natural heritage programs and geographical information systems. We are also witnessing a shift toward paying attention to nongame species and their habitat, not just the white-tailed deer or largemouth bass. This is aided by the nongame income tax checkoffs available in many states. In addition, some states have passed their own endangered species acts and are playing a lead role in protecting endangered species." (A federal Endangered Species Act does exist, as does a Nongame Act, formally called the Fish and Wildlife Conservation Act of 1980. Those interviewed expressed dissatisfaction with implementation of the former and said implementation of the latter was never funded.) "Finally," Cutler continues, "a direct result of this activity is that states are getting more involved in fish and wildlife education and are also taking these educational efforts to major urban areas."

Another reason for the increasing focus on state and local fish and wildlife programs is the decreasing role of the federal government. The U.S. Fish and Wildlife Service, the U.S. Forest Service, and the National Oceanic and Atmospheric Administration are among the agencies that had been more involved. Employment levels for these agencies have decreased in absolute numbers in the 1980s, and, although many think an increase in hiring will be necessary to fill vacancies, almost no one projects that employment will increase to pre-1980 levels.

ESPECIALLY FOR FISHERY PROFESSIONALS

With regard to the fishery profession, Will Sandoval, a harvest management biologist with the Muckleshoot Indian tribe's fishery program, says, "Over the past ten years the job market in fisheries has been quite cyclical, with the highest proportion of openings, in a relative sense, dependent on what is trendy. For example, when the United States and Canada were working on fishing treaties in the early to mid-1980s there was a lot of money to implement the treaty. This meant a lot of modeling, tagging, computer work, and basic research. The focus has now shifted more toward habitat and water quality issues, especially nonpoint sources of pollution. These trends can move fast, and the astute professional or student works hard to stay on top of the field and factor such shifts into career plans." A fishery biologist for a utility adds, "Right now there is a lot of fishery activity related to the utility industry, at least where hydropower is significant: mitigation projects and pollution studies. However, if we hit another energy crisis, smart money would say concern over the fishery implications of energy production would become less of a priority."

Two other areas are receiving increased attention in the fishery profession and should be noted here (see also Getting Started). The first is a dramatic increase in aquaculture, or fish farming, in the United States and a shift away from open-access fisheries to conditions in which ownership of or proprietary right to fish stocks is controlled by corporations, states, and individuals. Catfish is a prime example. In 1976 the annual harvest of wild catfish exceeded cultured production by more than 10 million live-weight pounds. Twelve years later, however, more than 90 percent of catfish marketed in the United States comes from aquaculture. This trend has created and will continue to create fishery positions, predominantly in the private sector, but also public sector technical assistance and regulatory jobs.

Marine fishery issues are also coming into prominence, primarily because of a broader concern over environmental degradation of coastal waters and estuaries. Declining water quality and habitat have significantly affected commercial fishing stocks, especially shellfish. This has led to calls for stepped-up research on water quality and fishery issues, increased enforcement and education activities, and creation of new regulations and possibly legislation regarding coastal waters, wetlands, and estuaries. Should this concern be translated into programs and regulations, the result would be increased staffing at the federal, state, and possibly local levels.

GETTING STARTED

One of the best ways to break into this field and survive is to have diverse education and experience. We look for someone who has, say, a degree in wildlife and experience in forestry or vice versa. Continu-

ally we hear, "Our fishery biologists can't understand what our foresters are saying." The field is becoming more and more integrated; it is hard to get by being a one-faceted person. Besides the reality that we are becoming more interrelated, there are heavy demands on agencies, which requires the professionals that we hire to be able to play many roles and understand the whole ecosystem. We can't send 15 people from our agency to the bargaining table during a negotiating session critical to resources we manage.

Christine Drivdahl, Chief, Habitat
Management Division, Washington
Department of Wildlife

Of all the fields discussed in this book, fisheries and wildlife may be the hardest to break into. Even so, consider the flip side of some grim statistics discussed earlier in the chapter: In one survey, 44 percent of wildlife graduates *did* obtain employment in their field within a year of graduation, as did 66 percent of those with master's degrees. Fifty-two percent of fisheries graduates found employment in their field within a year. Considering that the average job hunt for all fields takes six months to a year, this is not so grim. In short, *a lot of people are finding jobs in the field.*

Whether you are headed in the direction of fisheries or wildlife, you are advised to read this entire section, as there is much overlap between the advice for the two fields.

Since competition is so tight, a master's degree is advisable. However, it is not just *that* you have a master's that impresses employers, but *why* you got a master's, *how* you structured your graduate degree, and *what* you learned. Sylvia Taylor of the Michigan Department of Natural Resources says, "Employers like to see candidates who approached their graduate degrees with some sense of purpose and direction, rather than just going immediately on to graduate school right after obtaining their undergraduate degrees. What did you set out to learn? What skills did you pick up? Wildlife and fisheries fields are so tight and there is the Catch-22 of 'We want a generalist who has the desired specialty.' Therefore, I recommend getting one or more internships during or after college, determining opportunities and niches, and *then*, armed with this information, specializing in graduate school."

And what about the range and content of your undergraduate and graduate study? Most professionals recommend an integrated course of study stressing ecosystems as well as fish or wildlife biology. Besides preparing you to be a better professional, there is a practical reason for this: You broaden your job options. The University of Minnesota, for example, has begun to offer a combined fisheries and wildlife undergraduate degree for that very reason. Other schools are following suit, offering combinations including fisheries, wildlife, forestry, ecology, and biology.

A side or back door approach is often used by fishery and wildlife professionals to get a job in the field. This strategy entails starting at an agency in an unrelated position that is easier to get, then transferring to a fishery or wildlife job. Such positions include natural resource specialists and managers, employees of natural heritage programs, and water quality personnel. Take this route with some caution, since there is no guarantee of later transfer and you may become a specialist in another area, limiting your ability to move back to fisheries and wildlife. Obviously, you must also be qualified for your interim position—another argument for a broad-based education.

Rupert Cutler of Defenders of Wildlife says, "Fishery and wildlife biologists are lacking in administrative, management, and communications skills. I recommend taking some courses in business administration, office management, planning, programming, budgeting, finance, and public relations. This will make you a better professional and will give you an edge in the job search. The bottom line in your education is that you should be attempting not to take the cookie cutter approach and be like everyone else, but through a diversity of study, to make yourself uniquely qualified for a niche."

Formal education alone is unlikely to get you a job in the fish and wildlife field. Seasonal and part-time work, internships, and special projects are almost essential for obtaining full-time employment. Not only are there numerous field skills you must acquire, but, given the competition and scarcity of openings, it's useful to be a known commodity. Christine Drivdahl offers an inside look at how public agencies operate beyond official policy: "Many of us at the state, local, and federal level operate under protracted hiring freezes and can rarely create new staff positions. However, there is often latitude to move money around for specific projects. Employers usually do this when there is an individual they know *and* want. In short, if you're willing to hang around and make yourself known you can sometimes work your way into your own job. A lot of hiring occurs in this manner."

It is also in your interest to join and become involved in the professional associations: the Wildlife Society and the American Fisheries Society. Both have student chapters at universities. Go beyond these chapters to meet active professionals. Both associations offer accreditation for fishery and wildlife professionals and have combined to establish JOBSource, an up-to-date, detailed bank of national and international job vacancies, summer jobs, and internships (see Resources).

Even though the field is tight, try to resist the temptation to take whatever is available just because it is available. Initially, you can't be too picky in this field, but keep in mind your longer-term career goals. Is the position in a specialty you enjoy? Is there too much structure, or not enough? How often will you get out in the field? Will Sandoval offers some insight on this subject: "My job is unpredictable, requiring me to juggle a number of projects at a time. I like that. Some prefer more structure, finishing one project before they move on to another. If, for example, I worked for the U.S. Fish and Wildlife Service, I would likely have a particular specialty, say chinook salmon or coho, or maybe harvest statistics. Think about these types of issues when you consider your career."

Finally, look at the federal, state, and even local employment procedures and get on their job registers as soon as possible, either for job openings or just to be informed of the next test for the position you desire (some are held several years apart). Do this while you are still in school.

WILDLIFE

Graduates with the best chances of successful careers in wildlife are those who have stressed a broad ecologically based approach in both their formal education and their work experiences. Increasingly, wildlife professionals are called on to work on issues of habitat destruction, contamination, and restoration; comprehensive natural resource management planning, involving numerous types of professionals and agencies; and multispecies wildlife issues. This requires not only a broad scientific education but also the skills mentioned earlier, such as planning, administration, communications, and negotiation.

Sylvia Taylor, who has a B.S. in chemistry and an M.S. and a Ph.D. in botany, takes this call for a broad-based education one step further: "Rather than a straight wildlife degree, consider getting a solid biology degree with a lot of field experience; take courses in everything from limnology and forest ecology to ornithology and organism biology; go to a school with a biological station and stay there one summer. If you get a fisheries or wildlife degree, narrowly defined, where do you go if there is no job? With a more general natural resources or science degree you also have the option of entering the field through the side door—getting a job with a state department of natural resources and being transferred to the fish and game department, which is much easier than getting a job there outright."

Taylor suggests another career option some may overlook. "I think students should step back and look again at technicians' jobs. Technicians do the work most students seem to want to do when they originally go into fishery and wildlife programs. They are the ones who get to wrestle with the animals and catch the fish while we biologists are looking at aerial maps and arguing with foresters. In the past, these technicians' jobs, which in many states pay well, went to graduates of two-year technical schools. Because of increasing competition, many are now going to those with four-year degrees *who have the field skills.* These skills include forestry work, trapping, knowledge of the fieldwork behind timber sales, duck banding, and handling of basic machinery. I'm sure the same applies in the fishery field."

Entry-level positions in the wildlife field are often as an assistant or part of a team. Tasks include doing wildlife counts and census work, inventorying resources, patrolling, talking to hunters and the general public, conducting literature searches, or any of a variety of special short-term projects.

FISHERIES

Everything said earlier about the importance of a broad ecologically based education applies to the fisheries field. However, there may be more areas of specialization in fisheries which students should consider, although not at the expense of a general fishery and science education. The following chart, taken from Ira Adelman's article *Placement of 1985 Fisheries Graduates* (*Fisheries*, July–August 1987), gives an overview of which spe-

Specialization	Relative Response
Management	100
Culture (aquaculture)	90
Computers/biometrics	50
Population dynamics	40
Water quality/toxicology	25
Genetics	15
Marine biology*	15
Early life history	8
Pathology	8
Physiology	5
Socioeconomics	5
Urban fisheries	3
Education/writing	3

*The relative response for this specialization is skewed because many respondents live in states with no coastline.

cialties will be in demand with state agencies in the immediate future. Agencies were asked to check those specializations in which they expected to fill positions in the next five years. A relative response of 100 signifies the most frequent response.

Will Sandoval lends some perspective to these responses: "The field moves fast and the trends often change rapidly. This underscores the importance of figuring out ways to keep abreast of the field while you are looking for a job and even while you are in school."

One safe bet is that experience and skills in computers, statistics, and modeling will prove to be useful as harvest management and population dynamics grow in importance. Another growing area in which these skills are needed is aquaculture. Aquaculture is probably the largest private sector employer of fishery professionals and has been steadily expanding. In general, a prerequisite for private sector employment is a stint with a public agency, ideally at a fishery.

Entry-level fishery positions include much fieldwork: conducting surveys, measurements, and other research, assisting a fisheries biologist, overseeing the work of seasonal or part-time employees, or interacting with the public on fishing regulations. Other entry-level work includes computer data entry, report drafting, paperwork, statistical analysis, and equipment construction and repair.

Another way to get started in the fishery field is with the Peace Corps. Helping increase food production in developing countries through growing and harvesting fish is one of the Peace Corps' objectives, and volunteers work in aquaculture, inland fisheries, and marine fisheries. Besides the hands-on experience, volunteers also receive one-year noncompetitive eligibility for positions with the federal government. Many have used this edge to gain positions in fisheries and natural resource management with the federal government.

Despite a rough job market, Penn Esterbrook of the Maine Department of Marine Resources says of the future of the fisheries field: "There has been a tremendous increase in per capita consumption of fish in the United States in the past ten years. Far overshadowing this trend, however, is a growing worldwide population and need for protein, a need that is going to increase the importance of many sectors of this field, nationally and internationally."

SALARY

Periodically, the National Wildlife Federation publishes a survey of compensation in the fields of fish and wildlife management. The latest survey was published in 1985 (see Resources). Adding 16 percent to adjust for increases, the following are average salaries in 1989 dollars for positions in state government:

Game or fishery technician	$16,200–$23,200
Junior fishery biologist	$19,700–$27,800
Senior wildlife biologist	$20,900–$30,200
Senior fishery biologist	$22,000–$32,500

Interviews revealed that starting salaries in the public sector of the fishery and wildlife field for candidates with B.S.s and M.S.s ranged from about $16,000 to $24,000, with the higher salaries going to those with master's degrees. Federal employment starts at GS-5 or GS-7 for fishery and wildlife biologists with bachelor's degrees, GS-7 to GS-9 for those with master's degrees, and GS-11 or GS-12 for those with Ph.D.s. Pay scales as of January 1988 for these grade classifications were as follows: GS-5, $15,118–$19,654; GS-7, $18,726–$24,342; GS-9, $22,907–$29,783; GS-11, $27,716–$36,032; and GS-12, $33,218–$43,181. Private sector employers (utility and timber companies, for instance) offer starting salaries of about $23,000, and entry-level consultants' salaries are comparable to state government salaries.

CASE STUDY

Inland Fisheries Division, New Hampshire Fish and Game Department

Duncan McInnes is the chief of inland fisheries for the New Hampshire Fish and Game Department. "When most people think of the fish component of a state fish and game department they think of our most visible function: hatcheries and stocking fish. This is only one program; we are also involved in a wide variety of other programs and issues. These include public education, enforcement of fishing regulations, providing access to recreational fishing, studying environmental degradation, improving habitat, conducting research, doing natural resource planning within our agency and with other agencies, and inventorying fish resources in the state. In addition, the state has a Marine Fisheries Division involved in coastal and estuarine issues.

"The Inland Fisheries Division is divided into two sections: Hatcheries and Management and Research. The Hatcheries Section has a staff of 31, distributed among five hatcheries. These hatcheries raise mostly brook, brown, and rainbow trout, but also Pacific and Atlantic salmon. The emphasis is on improving our hatchery techniques so as to raise larger and healthier fish in a shorter period of time.

"Our Management and Research Section is involved with many programs. One is the anadromous fish restoration program, which is designed to restore self-sustaining runs of American shad and river herring and to establish a run of Atlantic salmon."

Jonathan Greenwood, a fisheries biologist 2 in the department, works on the anadromous fish program on the Merrimack and Connecticut rivers. "The anadromous fish program is a cooperative project of federal and state agencies such as several fish and game departments that border the area of restoration, the National Marine Fisheries Service, U.S. Fish and Wildlife Service, and the Forest Service," says Greenwood. "*Anadromous* refers to fish that spawn in freshwater but spend a large portion of their lives in the oceans. The program began in 1969 as part of an effort to reestablish Atlantic salmon and herring in the rivers. These species had once abundantly inhabited 28 New England rivers. However, a variety of factors, principally the construction of dams, overfishing, and water pollution, created an obstacle to their spawning cycle and the Atlantic salmon population was eliminated or dramatically reduced in many rivers.

"This project is a cooperative effort on the part of several federal and state agencies. The directors of each agency, a technical support committee, staff biologists, and representatives from each agency meet once a month to assess the program's various projects. My role as representative of the Fish and Game Department includes coordinating the transfer of American shad and Atlantic salmon from fisheries and hatcheries to various rivers, conducting surveys relating to habitat and population dynamics, formulating management and assessment plans, and working with policy and technical committees to develop agency reports on the project.

"My work load depends on the season. I usually do heavy fieldwork in the spring and summer, stocking adult shad and young Atlantic salmon, conducting stream habitat surveys, and collecting biological information. The growth, survival, and population densities of the young fish observed during the fall sampling assist the biologists in predicting how well these fish are performing in various streams. When the waterways start to tighten up in the winter, I'm back inside writing more reports and attending meetings.

"I just spent the last six weeks in the field coordinating fish stock transfers in the hatcheries and stocking the fish throughout the Merrimack and Connecticut river basins. The work involved a combination of ten field staff from the U.S. Fish and Wildlife Service, the Forest Service, the state Fish and Game Department, and volunteers from Trout Unlimited, a nonprofit sporting organization. We often have to pack the fish in to the tributaries, carrying them in water jugs in backpacks, by canoe, or by car—quite a logistical problem because I have to coordinate days with hatchery supervisors to obtain the fish (which are sometimes out of state), drive out to pick up the fish, meet with staff at various locations to distribute the fish, as well as make sure the right amounts of fish are stocked in the proper areas.

"Today I'm reviewing the federal program we administer—assessing staffing requirements, developing a work plan for the next five years, and preparing annual performance reports of our work. The paperwork element of these jobs is largely underestimated. Nevertheless, I like the work and in this business when you're lucky enough to get in, you stay."

Duncan McInnes says, "Another area of major emphasis within the Inland Fisheries Division is the Statewide Inventory and Classification of Public Waters of New Hampshire. These surveys attempt to determine water quality, fish habitat, fish populations, and the health of these populations. These surveys have been conducted on a county-by-county basis and are scheduled to be completed in 1990. Most of our biological staff is involved in inventory work—usually, two biologists inventory a pond or stream with the assistance of biologist aides."

Larry Miller is the regional fisheries biologist for northern New Hampshire. He talks about his role with the department: "My duties and activities include talking to children's groups about the way fish breathe, developing water resource management plans for entire river systems, and collecting biological information in the field. I do fish kill and pollution investigations, and I review plans for development along water bodies. Necessity teaches you skills like outboard motor repair in a snowstorm using a Swiss army knife.

"Our current emphasis is on an inventory of public waters. The survey area in northern New Hampshire includes 120 ponds and large lakes plus a couple of hundred miles of stock streams. A typical day of pond inventorying starts with making sure all the equipment is in working order, packing it all into the truck, and proceeding to the study area. On arrival, we unpack all our gear and launch the boat, making sure to double-check the oxygen meter, netting, and water sampling devices. The actual surveying includes taking water samples, temperature and oxygen profiles, and phytoplankton and zooplankton samples, and doing a basic water chemistry analysis. Then we set our nets. The next day we return and pull the nets. We measure the fish for length, determine sex and condition, and take scale samples. Then we get ready to do it all again the next day.

"What most people don't realize about natural resource positions is the seasonal nature of our work. We don't do the same thing every day or during every season. We do most of the survey work and sample collection in the summer, the field season. The winter months are spent summarizing our information into reports, computer coding data, doing statistical analysis, and collecting information from the preserved samples taken during the summer.

"Although the biological work is the main emphasis of my job, I spend time on public relations, business management and budgeting, personnel management, and planning. Unfortunately, my formal training did not prepare me for these roles. Therefore, I would suggest that those considering this field take business and communication training. Biologists deal more with people than with the critters they study.

"One more thing: This is a popular field and hence very difficult to get into. It has also been glamorized a lot, usually by sports and outdoor enthusiasts. I got into this field because I really enjoyed biology and the scientific, technical aspects of the work. I was originally going to be a medical research technician, but realized I would have to work in a big city in a big complex. I looked at my past and realized I wouldn't like to work behind fancy electrical equipment all day. It seemed fisheries biology would be a good balance. It's one of many areas in which you can apply scientific techniques and interest."

Other projects of the Inland Fisheries Division include assessing lake trout and landlocked salmon populations, collecting salmon eggs, monitoring smelt populations (a prime food source for salmon), maintaining and building new boat launches, protecting the environment of the state from development and chemical contamination, stocking trout, and educating the public.

"As you may have guessed," says Chief McInnes, "I oversee and supervise the hatchery and biological staff, making sure production and stocking schedules are conducted properly. I also handle the administrative duties such as overseeing the budget, making sure the money is spent properly, answering correspondence, reviewing fishery laws and regulations, and updating them when necessary.

"Our department is small when compared to departments in other states like Pennsylvania and New York. I would say that there are more opportunities in those states. In a small state like ours you may eventually have to move to another state in order to advance.

"As far as education is concerned, entry-level biologists must have a four-year degree, although a graduate degree is preferred. The four-year degree should focus on science (biological and physical), English (both oral and written skills are very important), knowledge of computers, mathematics, and statistics. On top of this should come a strong social science background."

PROFILES

John Gannon, Section Chief, Habitat and Contaminant Research, National Fisheries Center—Great Lakes, U.S. Fish and Wildlife Service, Ann Arbor, Michigan

In addition to law enforcement, maintaining wildlife refuges, operating fish hatcheries, and a variety of other activities, the U.S. Fish and Wildlife Service has five major fishery laboratories and 30 research field facilities throughout the country, one of which is profiled here. You can draw many parallels between this fishery research center and similar facilities in the wildlife field.

"There are two main components to our work here at the U.S. Fish and Wildlife Service National Fisheries Center for the Great Lakes: long-term assessment of fishing resources and population dynamics, and habitat and contaminant assessment. The first is a cooperative effort among the federal government and several states focusing on research on fish population characteristics and the forage base necessary to maintain a self-sustaining stock of game fish species in the Great Lakes. Our research helps determine allocation of fishery resources and the direction of research and management projects, and influences stocking rates, harvest projections and quotas, and efforts to boost natural reproduction. Biologists in this section spend a considerable amount of time doing traditional net and technically advanced hydroacoustics surveys to determine population dynamics. Field research is usually done from April to November and in the winter they process and analyze the data collected, which gives a good mix of fieldwork and desk work.

"The second major focus here is habitat and contaminant assessment, of which I am section chief. Our work does not involve as much fieldwork but is more lab oriented in that we examine the effects of toxic contaminants on fish and other organisms. This area of research borders on fish health, since we often check for tumors and other diseases.

"Our laboratory contributed to the knowledge of adverse effects of nutrient pollution on water quality in the Great Lakes. There have been great improvements in this area, but the target was also very specific: phosphorus released from waste treatment plants, which are point sources and relatively easily controlled. Now we are dealing with low-level and multisource contaminants, of which there are thousands produced and hundreds with known or suspected toxic effects on biota. You can't take them on a one-by-one basis; you have to understand their structure, activity, and relationships and focus your research efforts on the potentially most toxic groups of chemicals. We have also come to realize that you can increase the water quality, but without habitat improvement we will not realize the full extent of ecosystem restoration and integrity. This area is pretty much in its infancy, so we are still doing a lot of classification, inventory, and research work.

"I am heavily involved in personnel supervision as well as in research program development, and in order to do this I am on a lot of interagency and international committees. I attend meetings and conferences, relate information gathered at them to our staff, and then assist in the development of new projects. Whereas the staff does the fieldwork, I synthesize information to bridge the gap between the research results and policy decisions. I get a lot of professional satisfaction out of leading a staff of research scientists into productive research that will have an influence on legislative and management decisions.

"I received a B.S. in biology from Wayne State University, an M.S. in science and fisheries from the University of Michigan, and my Ph.D. in zoology from the University of Wisconsin at a time when environmentalism was at its peak and Earth Day was still a big event. I became active in environmental matters and eventually my career developed into a dual focus on aquatic ecology with an emphasis

on pollution biology and environmental education and communication.

"I worked in academia for most of my career, in research positions at the University of Michigan and the State University of New York, until I joined the International Joint Commission and then moved to this position. I enjoyed teaching, but I had always been interested in research, so I took positions that were not on the tenure track. I grew tired of short-term grants and contracts and gave up academic life for government positions, which offer a long-term research and monitoring mission closer to the decision-making process. Concurrent with my academic positions, I was involved in scientific professional societies, which gave me experience in management and enabled me to make a reasonably smooth transition into my present work.

"I worked as a research assistant during college, which simultaneously helped me to focus my research interests and broaden my knowledge of scientific problems. I believe the variety of hands-on work helped prepare me for the multidisciplinary approaches necessary for solving complex research and management problems."

Al Solonsky, Aquatic Biologist, Hosey & Associates Engineering Company, Seattle

Although consulting firms are not a major employer in the fish and wildlife field, the use of consultants is growing, and this sector should not be overlooked in career planning.

"Hosey & Associates Engineering Company is an environmental, engineering, and hydrology consulting firm that works primarily with hydroelectric power and water resource companies. It is easiest to describe my work by placing it in the context of what has been going on in the utility industry since the early 1900s. A lot of the private power companies and public utilities in the Pacific Northwest developed hydroelectric projects between 1905 and 1940. Initially, licensing requirements for operation of hydro facilities were relatively simple. In the past 15 years, however, more stringent licensing has been required by the Federal Energy Regulatory Commission (FERC). The regulatory requirements have become more sophisticated, not only in terms of operation, maintenance, and dam safety, but also in the need to provide more environmental mitigation.

"Hydroelectric project licenses are granted for a 50-year period, and many are now expiring. Those facilities which are reapplying for licenses must meet these new elevated standards of FERC. This is where we come in. Our firm conducts the necessary environmental and engineering research and works with federal and state environmental agencies, Indian tribes, and the client to satisfy all licensing concerns. Because of treaties with the various Indian tribes, they are party to the process and participate with the federal and state agencies in reviewing any projects or programs that may affect the fisheries resource.

"The licensing process consists of three stages: In the first stage you apply for a permit and submit a preliminary permit (description of the project and existing environment) with a list of relevant studies that are needed to address resource issues. In the second stage application is made and all relevant agencies and tribes

comment on the studies that have been completed. Negotiation often takes place during the third stage to finalize details and work out an acceptable mitigation plan. The whole process can take any number of years to complete.

"I grew up in Eugene, Oregon, and always knew I liked science but wondered how I was going to turn that into a career. I ended up at the University of Oregon studying biology but only stayed a year. I decided to take a year off to travel instead of going through college just for the sake of getting a degree. I went to Israel and worked in a kibbutz for six months and then heard of a position at an aquaculture research station funded by the Israeli government in the Sinai desert on the Red Sea. The job sounded exciting, so I applied and was accepted. The facilities were in a remote location and we were doing research on the best methods of growing fish in floating sea pens, ponds, and cages.

"I spent about a year and a half there and decided to return to school in the States. I returned and spent another year at the University of Oregon, at the end of which I transferred to the University of Hawaii. During the summers I worked on coral reef ecology studies with my professors. I graduated with a degree in fisheries and continued my studies at San Francisco State University's Moss Landing Marine Laboratory, where I wrote a thesis on artificial reefs and received my M.S. After getting married and moving to Seattle, I did some part-time work inspecting salmon and crab in storage facilities until a CEIP internship with Puget Power and Light Company came my way. One problem for me was that most of my experience was in the tropics, but they gave me a chance and things worked out well. I later found out about my present job through my business contacts, applied, and made the switch.

"I would encourage people to look into universities that have natural resource programs and not to narrow their evaluation of universities to just academic programs—find out if they have good practical application programs like cooperative fisheries units, Sea Grant Programs for marine resource research, and other summer internship programs. Also try to find universities that are close to public research institutes like those at the University of Washington, University of Hawaii, some California state colleges and universities, University of Miami, and Oregon State University."

Gustav Bekker, Wildlife Biologist, U.S. Forest Service, Olympia, Washington

Seasonal work is practically a prerequisite to finding permanent entry-level positions in fish and wildlife management, and both types of jobs are likely to involve fieldwork and research, along with some exposure to computers.

"I started working full time for the U.S. Forest Service right after I graduated from the University of Idaho with a double major in forestry and wildlife in 1987. This was not my first experience with the Forest Service— I had several seasonal positions during school. I'm working at the Olympia Forestry Sciences Lab conducting research on northern spotted owls, which inhabit the old-growth forests of the West Coast. Our project is a prey-base study to determine why the spotted owls live in old-growth forests, what they eat, and what their habits are. This multiyear project was initiated in 1985 and is funded through congressional appropriations. The project started with only three or four people and now has a staff of 60 or 70.

"There is an intense controversy stemming from the lumber industry's desire to log 200- to 300-year-old forests on the West Coast. Environmentalists argue preservation of old-growth forests is necessary for the survival of certain species such as the spotted owl. The U.S. Fish and Wildlife Service, responsible for listing endangered and threatened species, has been deliberating over the case of the spotted owl and in January 1988 decided not to list it as an endangered species. The Fish and Wildlife Service was taken to court on the national and local levels by environmental groups such as the National Audubon Society, which claim that the decision was political and not made in light of biological and ecological data. I guess I didn't expect to find myself in such a controversial position on my first job!

"This study is one of the outcomes of this debate. We are looking at the food supply of the spotted owl, which is mainly flying squirrels, and trying to determine if these squirrels inhabit only old-growth forests in sufficient quantities to maintain populations of the spotted owl.

"Summer is the most enjoyable time for me, since that is when we do most of our fieldwork. This revolves around selecting representative sites from which to study the spotted owl and their prey. We select stands and then spend several days walking and looking at the prospective sites to see if they meet our specifications. Sometimes the area has been recently altered—maybe a road was built through it—so we have to start all over. Once we have found a stand on which to conduct our research, we survey a trapping grid, which must be very precise in order to meet our statistical model requirements. After we survey the grid, it takes another one or two days for four or five people to carry in the traps on backpacks and set them up, one trap on the ground for each one in a tree. We also do vegetation surveys of our trapping stations in which we note the various types of vegetation.

"Trapping squirrels gives us an idea of their density and abundance in different types of stands—young stands, mature stands, and old-growth stands. On a typical day during this time I am at the office by 7:00 A.M. I mix the bait on Monday morning and spend all day in the field setting traps—a lot of walking. The next day I tag, weigh, and note the sex of all the squirrels that were caught. We

RESOURCES

JOBSource. The same job listing service noted in Resources, chapter 4. There is a special program for the American Fisheries Society and the Wildlife Society. Computerized, up-to-date listing of positions. 418 S. Howes, Suite D, Fort Collins, Colo. 80521. 800-727-JOBS.

American Fisheries Society. Holds annual meeting, symposia, and workshops. Has regional chapters. Publishes annual membership directory, the *Directory of North American Fisheries and Aquatic Scientists*, *Fisheries* (bimonthly), and the *Journal of North American Fisheries Management* (quarterly). 5410 Grosvenor Lane, Bethesda, Md. 20814.

Wildlife Society. Conducts annual and various special meetings. Has regional chapters. Publications include the *Journal of Wildlife Management* (quarterly), *Wildlife Society Bulletin* (quarterly), the *Wildlifer* (bimonthly). 5410 Grosvenor Lane, Bethesda, Md. 20814.

Defenders of Wildlife. Promotes the preservation and protection of wildlife and wildlife habitat through education, litigation, research, and advocacy. Maintains speakers' bureau, provides statistics and research, conducts public education, and maintains data bases on endangered species, wildlife, and refuges. Publishes *Defenders* (bimonthly). 1244 19th St., N.W., Washington, D.C. 20036.

release them and start the process over again the following week. Over a period of years, using statistical models, we can determine the density and abundance of various mammals that inhabit the stand. Recently we've also been working on a pilot study using radio telemetry on tagged flying squirrels to study their movements and feeding patterns. The squirrels are nocturnal, so I've also been working nights to monitor them.

"I guess I didn't expect to be working so hard. These are not typical eight-hour days or 40-hour weeks. When five o'clock rolls around, I still have more work to do. There are a lot of expectations and challenges, which require flexibility and extra hours.

"There are basically two ways of entering the U.S. Forest Service. The first is to follow federal hiring procedures, which include completing Standard Form 171 (the federal application), taking any exams, getting rated, and being put on a waiting list, a process that can take *years*. The second method is to determine an area you would like to work in, apply for a summer, seasonal, or any position, then do the best job you can. Plan on being there several years so the supervisors get to know you and your work. It is more than likely that they will eventually create a position for you. This is the method that worked for me."

National Wildlife Federation. Largest conservation organization in the world. Has state chapters, annual meeting. Awards fellowships for graduate study in conservation. Sponsors paid internships. Publishes annual *Conservation Directory, National Wildlife Magazine* (bimonthly), and numerous other publications. 1412 16th St., N.W., Washington, D.C. 20036.

International Association of Fish and Wildlife Agencies. Publishes newsletter (bimonthly). 444 N. Capitol St., N.W., Suite 534, Washington, D.C. 20001.

Trout Unlimited. Publishes *Lines to Leaders* (monthly). 501 Church St., N.E., Vienna, Va. 22180.

National Audubon Society. Publishes *Audubon* magazine, *American Birds* (both bimonthly). 950 Third Ave., New York, N.Y. 10022.

The Conservation Foundation and World Wildlife Fund. Publishes *FOCUS* (bimonthly). 1250 24th St., N.W., Washington, D.C. 20037.

Fish and Wildlife Reference Service. A computerized information retrieval system and repository that provides state research information to biologists, management personnel, and other interested persons. Publishes quarterly newsletter, hard copy of technical reports. Operated by Sterling Software under contract with the federal government. Most services cost; waivers or reduced fees can be obtained through universities. Sterling Software, P.O. Box 6044, Rockville, Md. 20850.

Peace Corps. Recruitment Office, 806 Connecticut Ave., N.W., Washington, D.C. 20526.

A Survey of Compensation in the Fields of Fish and Wildlife Management. Published periodically by the National Wildlife Federation, 1412 16th St., N.W., Washington, D.C. 20036.

Wildlife and Fisheries: Career Opportunities (1986). West Wind Productions, Inc.

13 Parks and Outdoor Recreation

Americans have always loved outdoor recreation. However, I think we are now seeing a change in attitude. People view leisure time not as a privilege but as an earned right. The result is going to be an increased use of outdoor areas and a demand for more recreational opportunities, especially close to home. By the year 2000, not so far away, it is estimated that 1 in 10 persons will be employed in the hospitality industry, up from around 1 in 20 today. This field might not grow along the traditional paths, but rest assured, it is going to grow. There are major problems that must be confronted by professionals in this field, but I also see great opportunities ahead.

Jim Peterson, President, National
Recreation and Park Association

MANY WHO are reading this book and considering a career in the environmental field would trace their decision to outdoor experiences as a youth. It might have been a particular family outdoor vacation or perhaps a favorite local park. Our parks—local, state, and national—are great environmental socializers and as such serve a function well beyond making a particular parcel of land available to the public.

Perhaps that is why many people first look to the parks when they think about an environmental career. These individuals invariably make several discoveries. First, there are many career possibilities besides being a ranger or a forest firefighter. Second, natural resources management is only one of many tasks handled by park personnel. There is planning, public relations, business management, education, research, and a host of other activities associated with running any large agency that interacts with the public. Finally, competition for that first full-time job, especially at the federal level, gives the word *intense* new meaning.

Aspiring environmental professionals researching a career in the field of parks and outdoor recreation might scratch their heads at what appear to be many contradictions. Everyone you talk to will tell you about how the field is expanding exponentially, but it is quite a task to find an employer who has the resources to hire you. Some types of jobs seem as if you almost have to be born into them, and others go begging for qualified applicants. Finally, in some areas, the field is undergoing a revolution, whereas other aspects have remained virtually unchanged for decades.

There are a couple of reasons for some of these seeming contradictions in professed demand and actual hiring trends. First, the field of recreation can be very broadly defined to include everything from restaurants to health clubs to national parks. More specific definitions depend on whom you are talking to. Second, despite the growing demand for recreational opportunities, recreation is often the first line item cut from the budget. Dean Tice, executive director of the National Recreation and Park Association, observes, "We still haven't got over that characterization of recreation funding as something of a luxury, something nice to have but not essential. So we often find ourselves in this funny situation where people are demanding more recreation at the same time as our elected officials are cutting funding in budgets. I hope this is just a matter of lag time."

WHERE WOULD YOU WORK?

Working at a national park is popularly presented as *the* career path for those entering the parks and recreation field. This overlooks many career opportunities. The National Park Service, with 13,000 full-time employees, most in the maintenance area, employs a relatively small percentage of professionals in this field. With 337 sites covering 76 million acres, the national park system can be broken down into two broad categories: historical parks, which are found primarily in the Eastern United States, and large Western parks, which exhibit those characteristics and hire the types of professionals (rangers) most commonly portrayed.

Although the national parks come to mind first, the public heads for many other federal lands to recreate: national forests, wilderness areas, wildlife refuges, and scenic rivers, to name a few. These lands are managed by numerous federal agencies often overlooked by job seekers. The Forest Service, for example, with over 30,000 employees, manages 200 million acres of land in 44 states with 100 million visitors each year. The Bureau of Land Management, with 9,000 employees, manages 300 million acres, to which public access is mandated. The U.S. Fish and Wildlife Service also manages and provides public access and recreation at its wildlife refuges and other landholdings.

All these federal agencies combined, however, provide far fewer opportunities for parks and recreation professionals than do the 50 state parks and recreation agencies and numerous state forests, scenic rivers, and wildlife refuges. Employment in state park systems is growing relative to federal positions despite hiring freezes in many state governments. Local and regional park systems not given much publicity, although their aggregate employment is significant and growing; even small towns have parks, and in large cities the park system is often run by a major department.

Metropolitan District Commission, Boston, Massachusetts. Vicky Gobetz put her artistic talent to work for the environment by painting interpretive signs for the Boston regional park district.

There are also numerous regional and county park systems. Finally, parks and recreation personnel are employed by private nature centers and other organizations and agencies not easily categorized.

The private sector is a large and growing component of the recreation field. While this sector should not be overlooked, it is not covered extensively here because the overwhelming majority of these facilities tend to be artificial, such as golf courses, marinas, health clubs, and resorts, rather than parks and natural areas.

The composition of the work force differs depending on the sector: The Detroit park system has a different mix of personnel from that of Yellowstone National Park. Still, there are many constants. All agencies hire rangers and law enforcement staff, interpreters, maintenance and recreation program personnel, and administrative staff.

Although a job with Yellowstone may, at first glance, appear more exciting than one with an urban park system, each sector has its own challenges and satisfactions. An interpreter in Detroit would have an endless variety of audiences to work with and a whole city of resources to tap into. On the other hand, with the steady stream of visitors going through our national parks on their annual two-week vacation, an interpreter at Yellowstone might find herself giving the same presentation every night for a month. This is no value judgment, just encouragement to look carefully at all sectors of the outdoor recreation field.

WHAT WOULD YOU DO?

Park rangers and interpreters are the most visible staff in a park system. However, it takes all kinds to maintain and operate a park or natural area. The Indiana Department of Natural Resources, for example, lists 90 different types of positions with the department, including pilot, outdoor recreation planner, streams and trails specialist, and surveyor. The Bureau of Land Management lists the following areas in which its employees work: energy and mineral resources, land and renewable resources, land and real estate, wildlife and fisheries biology, recreation, resource management planning, cultural resource management, soil, water, and air management, forest management, range management, technical support, engineering services, fire management, cadastral surveying, and administration.

The following is a breakdown of some of the major categories of professionals involved in parks and outdoor recreation. Many positions held by park personnel have been discussed in previous chapters: natural resource managers and specialists (chapter 11), environmental educators and interpreters (chapter 6), and planners (chapter 5).

ADMINISTRATION

Parks and outdoor areas are physical and organizational entities that must be managed like any other agency or company. This includes budgeting and finance, public affairs, procurement and contracting, personnel management, management analysis, and related support services. Informational resources management is an administrative area experiencing growth in these agencies; this presents opportunities for computer specialists and analysts, telecommunications specialists, and records management analysts.

PROGRAM PLANNING

These are the park personnel whom the public is most likely to see. First off, there is the ranger. This is a generic term for professionals holding a variety of responsibilities. Rangers are involved in law enforcement and providing for the safety of park visitors, in education, maintenance, and natural resource management activities, and in planning and carrying out recreational programs for visitors. In small park systems, a ranger might handle all of the functions just listed. Elsewhere, it is more likely that specialized positions exist for these various functions. Thus, there are park police, interpreters, recreation planners and programmers, maintenance staff, and natural resource managers (of which there are numerous specialties). The current trend is to separate the roles of interpretation and law enforcement into different jobs and career tracks.

NATURAL RESOURCE MANAGEMENT

This chapter tends to emphasize that component of parks and outdoor recreation which is involved with making resources accessible to the public. The other side are those professionals who must actually manage the outdoors, the natural resource managers. These include foresters, range managers, fisheries and wildlife biologists, ecologists, soil scientists, and various natural resource specialists and planners. These professionals are covered more extensively in chapters 11, 12, and 14.

RESEARCH

Closely related to natural resource managers are personnel involved in research on federal and state lands. Public lands are repositories of biological information, gene pools, and species diversity and are ideal research facilities. Research professionals include those listed under natural resource management as well as virtually every type of scientist imaginable. An area that is receiving increased study is the impact of contaminants— airborne and waterborne toxins and pollutants—on ecosystems and individual plant and animal species. Currently, the effect of acid rain on park ecosystems is undergoing considerable study.

SITE OPERATIONS AND MAINTENANCE

Whether parks and outdoor recreational facilities are maintained in a roughly natural state or are intensively managed facilities, their maintenance and upkeep is a formidable and often chronically underfunded task. Besides providing maintenance and facilities for visitors and staff, personnel in this area must keep up and manage large amounts of land. This work involves landscape architects, engineers, property managers, and administrative staff, as well as laborers, technicians, and seasonal help. Because of technological advancement, park maintenance is an ever more complicated task and professionals need more extensive training and technological skills than in previous years.

ISSUES AND TRENDS

Parks and outdoor recreational areas are moving closer to where people live. Whether it is the work of the Open Lands Project in Chicago to turn vacant lots into small parks, a grass roots effort by the Boston GreenSpace Alliance, Inc., to increase funding for urban parks, or the establishment of the Cuyahoga Valley National Recreation Area outside of Cleveland, we are seeing more parkland near population centers. State, regional, and local park systems are expanding and hiring more year-round staff.

Some say this shift is occurring because the national parks have reached their capacity; others cite the energy crisis of the seventies. Demographics and life-style present the most convincing reason for this change: In one generation there has been a phenomenal increase in the proportion of people who live in or near major metropolitan areas. Moreover, the annual two-week vacation by the two-parent family, while not a thing of the past, is being overshadowed by changes in work patterns and life-style—long weekends, shorter workdays, single-parent families, an older population, and more single people—all of which calls for more and better recreation closer to home. Businesses are the newest supporters of local park systems, viewing outdoor recreation as one of those intangibles that contribute to quality of life and protect their investment.

"The urban setting is the last place to be reached by the environmental movement," says Mark Primack, executive director of the Boston Green-

Space Alliance. "For the first time, urban parks are being taken seriously as a social issue and an environmental issue. Wealthy people can jump in their car and go to the White Mountains or Cape Cod. Poor people don't even have backyards. The parks, the public realm, are their source of rest and relaxation, physical challenge, and contact with the earth. At the same time, a focus on our urban environment offers tremendous educational opportunity, the chance to create the future of our environment by educating the youth of our cities, those who are often cut off from the environment. Our organization, a three-year-old alliance of 100 organizations in Boston, has played a role in increasing the parks budget from $5.7 million to $13 million in two years." If urban youths' desire for outdoor recreation is neglected, we might find that support for environmental and natural resource protection will decrease in the years to come.

In addition to an emphasis on city parks, groups are focusing on open space on an even smaller scale. Kathy Dickhut of the Open Lands Project says, "We are working on establishing permanent community gardens and parks in neighborhoods because people want open space *where* they live. Again and again I hear, 'We want a place where we can watch our kids play while we are cooking dinner.' This is day-to-day open space."

At the other end of the urban recreation movement is an emphasis on outdoor recreational opportunities, sometimes bordering on wilderness, near urban centers. Wetlands, rivers, seacoasts and meadowland, and old farmland are being used and often reclaimed for such purposes. The Boston Harbor Islands State Park and the White River State Park in Indianapolis are just two examples of the federal, state, and regional outdoor areas in and around urban areas. The rails-to-trails movement, which calls for converting abandoned railways to biking, skiing, and hiking paths, is another example of this trend. Finally the President's Commission on Americans Outdoors in 1985 called for the creation of greenways, or corridors of private and public recreational lands and waters that provide access to open spaces (and habitat for wildlife) close to where people live (see Resources).

Tied into the "localization" of outdoor recreation is a change in the way people are using parks. In many areas parks used to close down for half of the year and be vacant during working hours. People now use parks for a wider variety of activities and at all times of day, so that year-round staffing and varied programming are much more important. Part of this shift can be attributed to the aging of our population and the popularity of flexible work schedules, which have increased off-hours use of parks. People come to parks for weekend picnics, but they also return to exercise, play, and further their education and awareness of the environment, culture, and history.

As parks move closer to people and the use of outdoor areas increases, multiple-use issues—the sometimes conflicting goals of access and preservation—become an increasing challenge. This is true for urban parks as well as national recreation areas. Professionals must work to accommodate large crowds, including hikers, users of off-road vehicles, researchers, hunters, and anglers. As Jim Peterson of the National Recreation and Park Association observes, "There is more demand for what is called consumptive uses of public lands: cutting of timber, mining, hunting, fishing, and overuse of facilities. These invariably conflict with nonconsumptive uses of these lands or preservation forces." At the local level, these conflicts often surface in such issues as paving for bicycle access, off-road vehicle use, marina construction, concessions, and festival activity, as well as general development of park lands. As one professional says, "With increased use and expanded constituencies, we don't have the slack we used to have; decisions must be better thought out and more professional, and then implemented efficiently."

Outside threats to the health of parkland, such as development on park borders, acid rain, water pollution, and the introduction of foreign species, also command the attention of outdoor recreation professionals. Mark Primack of the Boston GreenSpace Alliance: "Park professionals are realizing that they cannot limit their activity to within park boundaries, because actions and decisions made outside the park will directly affect them." Park personnel are becoming more active in working with local community organizations and political bodies and are engaging in public relations and media strategies. Interpretive staff who used to be concerned only with helping people enjoy their visits to the park are now working to make visitors aware of the interaction between these issues and the health of the park. "We talk a lot about air pollution and hazardous waste," says Cleveland Metroparks naturalist Barb Post.

Access for all people to parks, a democratization of outdoor recreation, is an issue in many areas. Harriet Saperstein, recreation facilities coordinator with the city of Detroit, emphasizes that "we spend a lot of time worrying about those who are left out. I am thinking in particular about the poor, the elderly, and the disabled. Now, the reality is that the long-term goal of improved quality of life through improved recreation access involves some short-term compromise. Whether this goal can be realized on tight budgets remains to be seen."

The question of access to outdoor recreational areas brings up another topic: the increasing incidence of private as opposed to public ownership of such areas. Professionals are quick to point out that all privatization should not be assumed to impair equal access. Privatization of concessions at the national parks, for example, can raise money for the park system and free up staff for other responsibilities. There is, however, marked concern that a move toward privatization could create a class-based system of recreational opportunities. Waterfront access is mentioned as a prime example. "Unfortunately," observes Saperstein, "people talk a lot about public access, but when push comes to shove, policy makers often opt for the private control or feudal approach to recreation. This concerns me. As development pressures continue throughout the country, the privatization of the outdoors is going to become an issue we must confront."

The scarcity of funding for outdoor recreation at the federal, state, and local levels is a persistent, significant issue for professionals in this field. Rich Heaton of the city of Cleveland reflects, "Despite the public's desire for recreation, in terms of funding priority we are usually at the bottom of the heap—our funding is the first to be cut. I don't think our work will ever be properly funded." Bernard Conn of the New York State Office of Parks, Recreation, and Historic Preservation adds, "This ongoing scarcity of resources means park professionals must be inventive and creative since the resources don't exist to do everything you need to do. So, I spend a lot of time working with volunteers and writing grants. This requires flexibility."

Finally, the parks and outdoor recreation field has become increasingly professionalized. There is less patronage hiring of employees, fewer old-boy networks, and more national job listings; more people enter the field with specialized training. Increased professionalization also means that the employees who do well are those who have developed skills outside of natural resource management or recreation programming: written and oral communication, management, and budgeting.

GETTING STARTED

Dave Buchanan of the Student Conservation Association provides the most concise and practical bit of advice on starting a parks and recreation career: "Job seekers in this field experience the classic Catch-22: We won't hire you without experience; you can't get experience until we hire you. The way around this is simply to be resourceful enough to get the experience, and lots of it. The best way to do this is to attend schools that have cooperative programs with the agency you ultimately want to work for: You work during school, and when you graduate you have a full-time job. The next best thing is seasonal work or volunteering. Seasonal jobs are fairly easy to get if you have some practical skills: try to get your emergency medical technician certification and your law enforcement commission while still in school. I obtained these and found that my liberal arts degree was no hindrance at all. As for volunteering: Don't jump at a parks job just because there is a paycheck; a volunteer fieldwork position is going to get you skills, experience, and, most important, professional references, which will take you a lot further than a paid job handing out parking stickers."

Mark Primack, a former park employee and now executive director of the Boston GreenSpace Alliance, adds, "People come out of school thinking park management is all about managing natural resources. Not so. Today's open space manager needs people skills to interact with subordinates, seasonal employees, the public, businesspeople, and the local community. Those who have the technical skills without the skills in communications and politics do a disservice to us all. We used to speculate that the perfect park employee worked at a five-and-dime retail job: high pressure, low budget. Something else we looked for was combined backgrounds: combinations that included such skills as public relations, planning, computers and graphics, education, and horticulture."

This advice drives home an important point: You need specific skills and a careful strategy to get your first job in parks and outdoor recreation. However, you also need a broad arsenal of skills and education to have a successful career in the field.

There are so many different careers in parks and recreation that it is impossible to note one particular way to prepare for a career in the field. Further, professionals observe that it is difficult to specialize until you get a job, and they recommend against attempting to specialize as part of undergraduate training.

Most professionals advocate a broad undergraduate education, possibly leaning toward the sciences, but with a heavy emphasis on the liberal arts. There are, however, distinct career paths that you can begin to work toward as an undergraduate if you are fairly certain what it is you want to do. If your major interest is in the areas of natural resource management or research, a hard science background with a strong ecological base is recommended; a master's degree is probably needed (see chapters 11, 12, and 14). If park management and administration is your ultimate goal, a degree in recreation and parks management, possibly combined with some hard sciences, is a good path. These are not the only ways to get started in these subfields, but they are among the most common.

No matter the educational background, just about all professionals in this field start at the bottom and work their way up, specializing as they go along. To advance your career, it is important to have held some of the entry-level jobs, especially those that entail contact with park visitors; administrators were once rangers, interpreters, or foresters. This speaks for a broad-based education designed to develop a variety of skills, both technical (natural resource management, computers, and so on) and inter-personal (communications and management).

With the exception of some specialized positions, this is generally not a field where a master's degree is absolutely necessary. Many indicate that rushing into a master's program right away might not have the payback it would in other fields. Instead, they view a graduate degree as a way to specialize later in a career or as a way to broaden oneself, as a complement to an undergraduate degree. So, for example, if you have a B.A. in a hard science you might consider a master's emphasizing management.

"In addition, always be looking to add to your skill base," advises Harriet Saperstein of the Detroit Recreation Department. "This can happen while in school, but most skills are developed outside of the classroom." These skills, of course, are communications, writing, fund-raising, negotiation, computers. Knowledge of a foreign language, especially Spanish, is often named as a skill that can be very valuable to your parks and recreation career. The seasonal park ranger application, besides focusing on law enforcement and medical and safety experience, asks about outdoor skills (hiking, rock climbing, canoeing), leadership and ability as a tour guide, experience in the theater and dramatic arts, operation and repair of equipment (chain saws, firefighting equipment) and vehicles (farm equipment, boats), knowledge of archeological and historic preservation, and ability to work with persons of varying ages, abilities, and backgrounds.

These experiences must be obtained in the field, as a volunteer or as a seasonal employee. The entry-level job in the parks and recreation field is the seasonal position. Few people are hired for a full-time position without previous seasonal experience. Seasonal positions include work in all areas of park operations, including as interpreters, law enforcement workers, general park rangers, laborers, researchers, and recreation programmers. If your seasonal work is part of a cooperative education program, you are on a career track with an agency; if you do a good job, you will probably be hired full time on completion of your degree. Not all schools have cooperative agreements, but some have programs with many state and federal employers. Because of the challenge of getting that first job in the field, some professionals suggest students might make this an important part of their evaluation of schools.

If such a program is not available to you, then you need to obtain seasonal employment on your own and use your initiative to turn it into a job. You do not have to be a college graduate to be eligible for seasonal employment, but to qualify for a job at the federal level you must be 18 and have a driver's license. Summer employment application deadlines are mid-January for summer positions, mid-July for fall and winter jobs. Since you can apply for positions at only two locations with the National Park Service, you might want to consider applying at lesser-known parks, which receive fewer applications. Check with state and local park systems for their seasonal application requirements.

So, you are a seasonal employee. Now what? "You can be a seasonal employee for 50 years and not get a permanent position," says Dave Buchanan. "First off, you have to complete the federal application (Standard Form 171), which is a lot of paperwork. It is, however, part of the procedure allowing you to apply for openings in the federal government. Your work experience is a factor in the grading and evaluation of your application. Second, use these seasonal positions to get to know people and build up professional references. Go that extra mile. Finally, don't spend all your efforts at one agency, unless you simply *must* work there. Seriously consider starting your career at the state or local level, as competition is not as harsh and there are more openings. Another option is to look at obtaining federal employment with an agency that is less competitive than the Park Service, such as the Bureau of Land Management, and transferring later in your career."

One thing working in favor of most people reading this book is a decline in patronage, the hiring of relatives and political friends. This is especially relevant to those considering careers in municipal or regional park systems. This does not mean it doesn't help to know your council member or local elected official, only that such a connection probably isn't going to carry the weight it once did.

One final piece of advice. Look closely at the philosophy of an agency before you decide to devote a lot of time and energy to getting a position there. Are you comfortable with their priorities, both mandated and informal? Their traditional career paths? Their programs and special projects? Spend some time on these types of questions; it will pay off later.

SALARY

Traditional entry-level positions in parks and outdoor recreation are fairly uniform in salary. Interpretive, ranger, and recreational positions offer starting pay in the range of $16,000 to $22,000, usually near the low end of that range. See chapters 11, 12, and 14 for additional salary information on careers in forestry, interpretation, natural resource management, and fisheries and wildlife. Entry-level federal park ranger positions are usually graded GS-5 ($15,118 to $19,654, as of January 1988) and occasionally GS-7 ($18,726 to $24,342). Seasonal employment in entry-level positions is likely to pay in the neighborhood of $250 to $300 per week. Seasonal federal positions in interpretation are graded between GS-2 and GS-7, in law enforcement between GS-3 and GS-7, depending on education, skills, and experience; this means these positions may pay as little as $11,000 per year or as much as $16,000. Seasonal employees who have been working for some time can make up to $450 per week, with few if any benefits. Entry-level salaries in most state parks are slightly lower than those in federal positions; pay for local park positions varies widely but is usually at the lower end of the scale.

CASE STUDY

Hibernia County Park

The field of parks and outdoor recreation must be seen in the context of changing life-styles in the United States. Americans are moving to urban areas and need year-round recreation, a place to take their kids on weekends, to exercise, to learn. In this sense, it might be more instructive to look at professionals involved in responding to these particular demands: not at the employees of grand parks like Yellowstone and Yosemite (where professionals are dealing with their own set of demands), but at the staff of Hibernia County Park, on the outskirts of Philadelphia. It could just as easily be one of the thousands of parks, just down the street or right off the interstate, near where you live.

Hibernia County Park, run under the auspices of the Chester County Parks and Recreation Department, is called a regional park. Regional parks, distinct from community or city parks, have attractions that draw people from a broad geographical area who pack up the family and take a day off. The 800 acres of the park, three-fourths wooded, encompass hiking and biking trails, the Ironmaster's Mansion (listed on the National Register of Historic Places), six picnic pavilions, 46 campsites, baseball and volleyball fields, picnic areas, a creek stocked with trout, a recreation hall, and the Springton Manor Farm interpretive center.

The superintendent's position in a park this size is a far cry from the image it usually conjures up. Chuck Pella, the superintendent, is involved in every day-to-day function in the management of a park facility: scheduling maintenance, taking pavilion and campsite reservations, yearly evaluations of staff, acting as purchasing agent, programming, patrolling the park, managing all of the equipment (trucks, tractors, trailers, hand tools), administering first aid, and assisting in maintenance work. As Pella puts it, "You have to have more of a business, management, and public relations sense about you than most people realize. There is a lot more to maintaining a park than just mowing the grass and keeping track of every piece of equipment from the playgrounds to the barbecue grills and the Ironmaster's Mansion. In handling this aspect of the park, I meet routinely at the beginning of every week with the park foreman, giving him a list of about 18 to 20 things to do. When patrolling the park, I may notice that visitors tend to picnic in a particular area where there presently are no picnic tables or grills, so the next time we are installing new equipment, I'll have the crew position them at the site. Or perhaps there was a thunderstorm the night before and we'll walk the park and trails to check for any downed limbs, power lines, or washed-out bridges and trails. It is very important to me that the park is a safe and clean place."

A key figure in Pella's role as maintenance manager is Sam Cantrell, the park foreman, who supervises the maintenance and natural resource management crew. Cantrell explains how he assists Pella in keeping the park running smoothly: "I coordinate the day-to-day maintenance of the park by setting priorities and coordinating the work crews and equipment. I also help the crews, supervise projects, purchase necessary materials, and process paperwork.

"Being a part of county government, we have responsibilities outside of the park. In the winter we are responsible for plowing the county seat's facilities as well as the park, so we're up and on the road by 3:00 A.M. to get the snow cleared by 8:00 A.M. Another ongoing project during the winter is woodcutting. We use wood to heat some of our facilities or to make picnic tables and signs or build bridges."

Job seekers should consider the park superintendent's responsibility to deal with bureaucracies. Pella recounts his attempt to repair a broken tractor: "Last May the transmission and brakes went out on one of our tractors. I first had to obtain three quotes for the repair work, along with the purchase order I submitted to the county for review. The county rejected the first proposal so the process began anew. I obtained three more estimates and submitted another purchase order, which was accepted. Finally, I was able to send the tractor to a shop to be repaired. By the time we actually had a working tractor back on the premises of the park, three months had passed during the height of the growing season. This is part of the bureaucracy of working for local government—you get used to it and learn to work within the system."

For Pella, it was the positive experience of constant interaction with the public while working as a seasonal park ranger for Cook Forest State Park in Clarion, Pennsylvania, which first inspired him to pursue a career in parks and recreation. "Although I had a B.S. in environmental resource management, the very positive experience of interacting with the public in a recreational setting propelled me to go on and get an M.S. in park planning. Some of the most enjoyable days are when we have up to 10,000 visitors at the park for one of our special events. These include the Fiddler's Picnic, the Country Fair at Nottingham, a maple sugar festival, candlelight tours of the mansion at Christmas, and Darken the Park and haunted trails during Halloween."

Perhaps the figure most visible to the public at a regional park is the park ranger. Karen Hesser, the chief park ranger at Hibernia, says that one of her most important duties is as host to the public, whoever that public may be. "While on patrol one day, I received a call from the front gate alerting me to a van full of drunken men who had driven onto the premises and were causing a disturbance among the visitors. When I arrived at the scene and approached the van, most of them were already out and running for the woods, but two rather large and drunk men remained behind to confront me. They closed in and began jabbing me in the shoulder and saying, 'You can't tell us what to do, we're taxpaying citizens.' Under park regulations, I wasn't carrying a firearm because it was still daylight. I talked my way out of that situation and in the end the guys had their arms around me and were saying, 'That's OK, honey. We'll round up the guys and won't cause you any more trouble.' You have to like working with people and be able to handle all kinds.

"As chief park ranger, I live on the premises and am basically on call 24 hours a day. When I started in the position at the age of 22, as the first woman chief park ranger in the county, I was paranoid about leaving the park and never wanted to make plans with friends. It's a lot of responsibility to take on, but as I got to know my staff better I gained a lot of confidence in their abilities. The kick for me on this job is getting out to meet the people and exchanging information on, say, the best places to camp.

"In general, my days are split between paperwork and patrolling. Today I updated the personnel files of four new rangers, filled out purchase orders for new equipment, and did the daily shift reports, which tell how many incidents occurred and how they were handled. Then I received a report of a rabid raccoon, which I tried to find, and I did my routine patrol. While on patrol a ranger is either in a vehicle or on foot and is on the lookout for any disturbances, people suffering from heat exhaustion, maintenance work to be done, and so on. During the drought, we are very concerned about open fires. I also conduct nature walks for Boy Scouts and other community groups and coordinate security for major events. Perhaps my biggest learning experience has been opening myself up to training in law enforcement. I realized its value after being shot at for target practice while boating on the lake. My friend knew exactly how to handle the situation, but I was unsure I could've done the same. The following year I used a month of my vacation time to pursue additional training in law enforcement."

When asked about trends that affect employment in parks and recreation, Chuck Pella replies, "The parks and recreation profession is grasping for an identity; I definitely believe we are in a time of transition. There are few schools left in the country that offer programs in traditional park management. Pennsylvania State, North Carolina at Chapel Hill, and Indiana University, and the Universities of Illinois and Michigan are a few, but otherwise universities are gearing themselves toward commercial, entertainment, and amusement park management. Another influential factor in the quality of parks and recreational facilities has been the shift from funding with tax dollars to funding through user fees, which has lead to a decline in the national park system and an increase in subregional, community parks. People are more apt to pull together their resources for a facility that will be used by their own children on a regular basis than to support a national park thousands of miles away from their home which they might visit once in their lifetime.

"I might also note that therapeutic recreation for the physically and

PROFILES

Dave Jansen, Harbor Region Supervisor, Boston Harbor Islands State Park

"Boston Harbor Islands State Park is comanaged by the Metropolitan District Commission (MDC) and the Massachusetts Department of Environmental Management. The MDC park system includes islands, reservations, beaches, pools, golf courses, bird sanctuaries, salt marshes, hiking and biking trails, picnic areas, and other recreational facilities in or close to Boston.

"As chief administrator for the Harbor Region, I coordinate and direct all aspects of planning, resource management, and visitor services for the MDC-owned harbor islands (Georges, Lovells Island and Peddocks islands), Castle Island, Wollaston Beach Reservation, Belle Isle Marsh, and the Nantucket Lightship. I am responsible for a year-round staff of 30 with a seasonal complement of 105. Four of the staff members are supervisors who assist me in managing the region and completing projects at the various properties. Just about everything runs through my hand at one time or another, but my primary activities involve determining the regional agenda and directing the capital planning and the allocation of operating resources.

"Yesterday, for example, I inspected some park properties, revised and signed off on permits, reviewed some planning documents, coordinated a meeting with a superintendent at Castle Island, set up a meeting with a supervisor of the state Department of Transportation and Con-

mentally disabled is a highly specialized field requiring certification and a college degree. Such professionals are in increasing demand and earn substantial salaries.

"To best prepare yourself for some of these demands, be careful in choosing a school, making sure its particular program will suit your needs; take the time to visit schools and talk to students enrolled in the program. Couple this education with part-time or summer work experience in some aspect of parks management; it will give you a frame of reference for your studies. Finally, join professional associations and try to make contacts in the field."

Chuck Pella concludes, "Driving in to work on a crisp, clear fall morning, I am apt to ask myself with a little wonderment, I work here? I think ultimately it is an unwillingness to settle behind our desks for the majority of our careers that sets park personnel apart from the rest of the public."

---

struction, attended a meeting with my supervisor, arranged a job interview for a position here, and attended two more meetings, one with a museum regarding their water exhibits, and another with a group of Japanese dignitaries who toured the Charlestown Navy Yard. My work cuts across a lot of bureaucratic lines, which can be a challenge at times. However, because of the interrelatedness of state government and the limited resources, jurisdiction coordination and communication is essential.

"To give you some sense of the diversity of our work, some of the projects I am currently involved with include the formation of a master plan for Georges Island, including a restoration of Fort Warren, drafting of an environmental monitoring program for Belle Isle Marsh, coordination with the National Park Service of pier renovations at the Charlestown Navy Yard, and going over the program for the Nantucket Lightship. I received my B.S. in natural resources from the School of Resource Development at the University of Rhode Island in 1980 and began my career as a seasonal ranger on Georges Island in 1984 and was promoted to island supervisor to establish year-round operations. I managed staff including visitor services and maintenance personnel and volunteers, scheduled daily ecological and historical interpretive programming, and implemented standard operating and maintenance procedures. During this time I was also given a grant by the Lloyd Center to plan, develop, and implement a comprehensive salt marsh inventory designed to be used by municipalities, developers, and state offices.

"My advice to those wishing to enter this field is to take as many general science and liberal arts courses as possible to get a good general background. Park work is multidimensional and issues oriented, yet also based on the natural, cultural, and constructed features that are its components. It is more important in park work to know how pollution affects creatures in a broad sense than it is to know the exact biological function of an oil-blocked pore in a frog.

"Park work is working with people and generally low budgets. Concise communication is essential to stretch limited resources to meet unlimited demand. Those wishing to enter this field must be willing to work in seasonal capacities for about one or two years before being hired as full-time staff. Most people we hire have two to four years' experience in part-time seasonal work. Nobody likes to hire only seasonal help, but budgets often demand it. Besides, most people also need seasoning before they are working up to grade. The pay is not as high as in other fields, but I find the rewards unique and fulfilling."

Teresa DeMuri, Assistant Ranger for Other Resources, Iron River Ranger District, Ottawa National Forest, Michigan

Teresa DeMuri is involved in outdoor recreation work in one of the many agencies you may not associate with this field: the U.S. Forest Service. However, as you will see, making these lands accessible to the people is an important part of this agency's mission, as is the case with the U.S. Fish and Wildlife Service and the Bureau of Land Management.

"Whereas national parks are lands set aside mainly for recreational use, national forests provide that service as well as serve many other functions. Working for the U.S. Forest Service consists of managing for multiple, sometimes conflicting uses. Managing a national forest encompasses timber sales, wildlife projects, recreation, fire prevention, mineral rights, and other special uses. An additional variable that makes our job interesting is that within national forest boundaries there are often large tracts of privately owned land.

"The Ottawa National Forest is divided into six districts. I work in the Iron River District. Each has a district ranger who oversees all operations and two assistant rangers who administer the divisions of Timber Resources and 'Other Resources.' I am the assistant ranger for other resources, which encompasses all areas except timber. As for recreational resources, within the 225,000 acres of the Iron River District, we have four campgrounds, ten boat landings, two picnic areas, two beaches, and nine miles of hiking and cross-country trails that are managed by me, one other permanent staff member, one summer seasonal worker who covers night and weekend shifts, and three senior community service employees. There are a total of 13 permanent staff who work in all functions of the Iron River District.

"We separate the recreation program into two areas: the developed recreation program, designed for those who use the campgrounds, boat landings, hiking trails, and other facilities, and the dispersed recreation program, for people who recreate in the forest at large, such as hunters, photographers, and those who drive on our scenic routes. The developed recreation program requires more maintenance, but we actually have more people recreating in the dispersed manner. It was this type of variety that first attracted me to the field. Not only do we run a variety of programs, but they also vary according to the time of year.

"In the summer the emphasis of my job is on recreation. Contrary to the popular concept of this being an isolated job, it is very much a people-oriented job. You have to be willing and able to work with the people who visit the forest as well as those within the organization. In the fall I do more timber-oriented work such as inventorying forest stands. These types of activities overlap a bit with the Timber Resources Division, but we limit my function to assistance rather than administration. We try to save all of our writing for the winter as well as opportunity area analysis, which is a review of how we are going to implement the National Forest Plan. The spring is the busiest time of year in that we are finishing up projects carried over from the winter, preparing the recreational sites for the upcoming season, and conducting our annual fire prevention seminars. The latter is a cooperative effort with the Michigan Department of Natural Resources to educate children in kindergarten through fifth grade on the forests and fire prevention.

"On any given day I meet with a wide range of people on a whole spectrum of projects. Today I visited the owner of a small lumber company who submitted an application for a permit to sell his extra slab wood as firewood to campers. I also met with another permit applicant who wanted access to his private land via one of our roads. Yesterday I was out at the campsites talking to the visitors and helping the cleanup crew, and earlier in the week I and a fisheries biologist walked a stream to determine where to put bank structures to provide shelter for trout. Another area that occasionally takes up a lot of my time is reviewing mineral speculation permits for exploration companies. This is highly technical work requiring detailed research on regulations. The work is very diverse and I never stop learning.

"I'm one of the lucky few in this field who doesn't have a bundle of horror stories of how I got my first job. This is probably because I was in a cooperative education program with the U.S. Forest Service and was hired full time straight out of school. I received my B.A. in forestry from Southern Illinois University at Carbondale through a five-year cooperative program in which I took time off from my studies to work as a trainee forester. When I graduated I entered directly into the Forest Service without having to go through the normal federal hiring process. I would encourage potential foresters to take advantage of this program or similar programs."

Rich Heaton, Manager of Research and Planning, Department of Parks, Recreation, and Property, City of Cleveland

Parks and recreation professionals in the Cleveland area are employed by the city park system (discussed in this Profile), the Metroparks System (with over 400 employees), the Cuyahoga Valley National Recreation Area, numerous suburban park systems, and several private nature centers and state parks within 50 miles of the city. Clearly, one does not have to look to the Rocky Mountains for the jobs in this field.

"The Division of Research, Planning, and Development is one of the smallest divisions in the Department of Parks, Recreation, and Property. In addition to the commissioner, we have a manager of site development, a manager of research and planning, four landscape architects, two surveyors, a parks and recreation planner, and a contract administrator. Our mission here is to do the planning, research, and design for the city's parks and recreational centers. This includes everything from developing master plans of the entire system to making drawings of a particular playground. As manager of research and planning, I'm in charge of planning capital improvements, developing both short- and long-term master plans, system-wide inventory and assessment of parks and playgrounds, and assessment of the delivery system, that is, determining if our programs and parks suit the needs of the public.

"We have 16 recreational centers (each with an indoor pool), outdoor swimming pools, various ball diamonds and tennis courts, and 110 playgrounds—altogether 180 sites throughout Cleveland. Many of these sites were established in the 1950s to accommodate the rapidly growing population, which approached one million at one point. Since that time we have lost a good proportion of that population and consequently tax revenue. As a result, we are trying to streamline our parks and recreation system into community district centers, which will be programmed, controlled, and maintained by particular areas of the city, a decentralization of sorts. As part of our master plan, we are looking at the location and programming of our facilities in the context of limited resources.

"One of our most recent recreational centers was constructed in 1986 and is the best-equipped indoor facility in the system. I am currently working on the plan for the surrounding park. Although I was not involved in obtaining the original funding to build the center, I did help obtain the funding for the outdoor improvements. The city purchased the land from the Ohio Department of Transportation; we then applied for and received a grant from the federal Land and Water Conservation Fund to complete financing.

"The outdoor improvement of the center is intended to meet many of the recreational needs of area residents. A

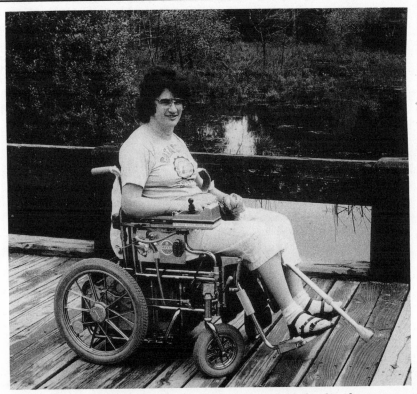

Blue Hills Reservation, Milton, MA. Ceil Blumenstock developed recommendations for redesigning the facilities at Houghtons Pond, Massachusetts, to make the public park fully accessible to the handicapped.

major goal is for it to be accessible to the disabled, a population that park departments have not always served adequately in the past. There are a lot of details to be worked out. For example, the edge treatment for play areas with gravel or wood chip bases is usually a curb, which presents a barrier to the disabled. I've been doing research on products that will make play areas accessible to the disabled; one such product is a rubberized surface similar to that used on all-weather tracks. Planning a playground also requires research into playground safety and how to maintain play areas on a low budget, so I've been talking to a lot of other communities on what has worked for them as well as other design experts and playground equipment manufacturers.

"I decided to enter the field in a rather straightforward manner. I was reading a career guidance book and thought the section on landscape architecture sounded interesting, so I sent away for more information and applied at various schools across the country. I ended up obtaining my B.A. in landscape architecture from Louisiana State University at Baton Rouge. After graduation I moved to Houston, where I worked for a design and construction firm that handled commercial, retail, and residential planning. I then moved back to Cleveland and worked as a landscape architect with the city for a couple of years until a managerial position opened up.

"There is no one way to prepare for a career in a municipal park system. I would suggest that you spend some time thinking about where you might want to end up. For example, to go anywhere in this division you simply must be a registered, licensed architect. This is true of many if not most planning positions here. In general, however, there are a range of degrees you can pursue; in fact, it is pretty hard to specialize as an undergraduate. I chose the landscape architect approach, and there were many ways to go with that course of study. Recreational planning would have been another good route. Degrees that have a strong interdisciplinary element are also useful. Training as a landscape architect incorporates social issues, city planning, soil study, geography, plant study, engineering, and a host of other disciplines. Recreation planning requires a knowledge of statistics and of the standards and day-to-day activities of recreational systems. The latter can be obtained only through hands-on experience. Combining this with a master's degree in public administration would put you on an administrative track in a park system."

RESOURCES

Contact individual government agencies for information on the application process for full-time and seasonal employment, or contact the nearest Federal Job Information Center. Information on cooperative education programs can be obtained from agencies and schools. Each agency can provide materials that acquaint you with the agency's objectives, the range of full-time and seasonal jobs available, and the application process.

For other information on careers in parks and recreation, see the Resources sections in chapters 6, 11, 12, and 14.

The Report of the President's Commission on Americans Outdoors: The Legacy, The Challenge (1987). This report represents the federal government's first attempt in 25 years to document Americans' need for expanded recreational facilities and opportunities. Includes recommendations, case studies, market research, and testimony. The *Washington Post* predicted this report, with its surprising findings and controversial conclusions, wouldn't "see the light of day." Island Press.

National Parks and Conservation Association. A private citizens' organization dedicated to promoting and improving national parks. Provides extensive membership services, publishes *National Parks* (bimonthly), and organizes local groups near national parks (National Park Action Program). 1015 31st St., N.W., Washington, D.C. 20007.

National Recreation and Park Association. Association of parks and recreation professionals and citizens' advocates. Holds annual meetings, conducts professional development activities, provides technical and general information in publications and periodicals, including *Parks & Recreation* (monthly); *Employ* (nine times a year), which is designed to assist individuals in preparing for the job search; and *Parks and Recreation Opportunities Job Bulletin* (22 times a year). Job Mart is held at annual conference. 3101 Park Center Dr., 12th Floor, Alexandria, Va. 22302.

Student Conservation Association, Inc. See Resources, chapter 3, for more information.

14 Forestry

Jim Stone, a silviculturist with the U.S. Forest Service in Silver Lake, Oregon, is responsible for timber sale planning in the district. Working with an interdisciplinary team of engineers, wildlife specialists, and soil scientists, he puts together and oversees contractual plans for timber harvesting.

James Skiera, the city arborist for the city of Urbana, Illinois, administers the tree planting and maintenance program as well as designs and implements urban greening programs.

Lynn Bakker is a forest technician with the Michigan Department of Natural Resources. She handles the surveying, sales, planting, and overall administration of 100,000 acres of Michigan forest.

Gary Schluter is a private forestry consultant in Park Falls, Wisconsin. With a 13-year background in industrial forestry, he now works primarily on overseeing timber sales and forest management for small private landowners.

Karin Van Dyke is an area forester for Mead Corporation in Escanaba, Michigan. She supervises logging crews, reforestation projects, and timber sales, working with private individuals, state government, and the U.S. Forest Service.

THERE IS no longer a standard forestry career. The field, once typified by the jack-of-all-trades forester, the timber cruiser, and the firefighter, has become a diverse, specialized profession. Greg Smith, associate director for educational and professional standards at the Society of

American Foresters, remarks, "The range of opportunities has tremendously expanded from just 15 years ago. You might say we have finally turned the corner on the Smokey the Bear/sitting in the fire tower image."

Foresters are moving into the cities, helping to stem the loss of urban forests and protect watersheds; they specialize in such areas as entomology, forest genetics, forest hydrology, soils, planning, and forest economics; foresters work in Third World countries on tropical reforestation projects, as well as clear-cutting; they are involved in providing recreational opportunities and wildlife habitats. Today's foresters cannot get by with just a technical background: They are learning and using management skills, computers, economics, and communications skills. Finally, even in an age of specialization, there is a call for foresters to obtain a broader ecological base in their training.

Some elements of the profession have remained relatively unchanged or are changing slowly. There has been no dramatic shift in the structure of the industry: the federal government has not sold off its landholdings; despite some centralization, there are still many small timber companies and sawmills; and the small landowner still owns close to 50 percent of the nation's forests.

Still, there will likely be significant changes in the forestry profession over the course of this generation's working life. Today's young forester must learn to interpret larger shifts and developments in the industry; the one point of consensus among foresters is that change keeps happening more quickly. There are, however, two kinds of change in forestry: the cyclical ebbs and flows and the longer shifts. It takes a discerning eye to tell which is which.

WHERE WOULD YOU WORK?

About 30 percent of the United States is forested. Of this land, 58 percent is owned by private individuals, 14 percent by corporations, and the rest by federal, state, and local governments. There are approximately 40,000 foresters employed in the United States and 13,000 forestry technicians (many more likely perform the work of forestry technicians without having the formal designation). According to the Society of American Foresters, about 30 percent of the undergraduate students presently in forestry programs are female.

According to Greg Smith of the Society of American Foresters, slightly under one third of all foresters work for the federal government, and that proportion is shrinking. Federal employers include the U.S. Forest Service, which manages 191 million acres in 156 national forests, the Soil

Conservation Service, the Bureau of Land Management, the National Park Service, and the Army Corps of Engineers. Another third work for state and local government—primarily the former, though local government is probably the fastest-growing category of forestry employers. In local government, however, foresters are often called on to do other work as well, such as managing watersheds or parks.

The remaining third work in the private sector. Foresters work for companies that manage forests for lumber, pulpwood, and other products; paper mills; suppliers of forestry equipment and materials; and urban tree care companies. Consulting firms, although not as prominent in forestry as in the environmental protection fields, are a growing presence. Consulting foresters manage timber sales for private landowners and even public agencies. They supervise planting and spraying, survey forests, and perform other tasks for companies that find it more cost-effective to use consultants than to employ in-house specialists. Most consultants have previous experience in the public and private sector.

WHAT WOULD YOU DO?

The Society of American Foresters lists over 700 job categories in the forestry field. Nevertheless, there are many common work objectives and tasks. Hence, entry-level jobs have many common elements. Entry-level foresters are usually given responsibility for a particular piece of forest, ranging from several thousand to 100,000 acres. Working with a supervisor, they maintain boundary lines, conduct surveys, determine what needs to be cut, manage timber sales and logging, and oversee regeneration activities. This work is usually done with the assistance of a number of forestry technicians.

In the private sector a variation of this job might entail working with private landowners to acquire standing timber, making volume estimates, and authorizing purchases. Ermine Venuto, vice president for woodlands and solid wood products for Mead Corporation in Columbus, Georgia, says, "Entry-level foresters are putting their names on agreements involving hundreds of thousands of dollars. They also must oversee the work of three or four hardened logging contractors who were probably working before they were born. This *is* responsibility; many thrive on it."

Entry-level jobs in state or federal agencies often involve foresters in recreation, wildlife, and watershed management. This might mean talking to the public—hikers, campers, and hunters—trail maintenance, wildlife surveys, and multipurpose management of your piece of the forest.

After a stint in an entry-level position there are a number of tracks to follow. One path involves managing larger parcels of land and supervising the foresters assigned to these parcels. You might move to the corporate office or develop a specialty. Just some of the specialties you might choose include data base development, forest entomology and pathology, forest economics, forest hydrology, forest recreation, silviculture, planning, fuels management and fire suppression, bioengineering, forest ecology, contract administration, public relations, and soil science. Many of these specialties require an advanced degree; given the large amount of basic forestry that must be learned in college, it is difficult to do much specialization as an undergraduate.

Three categories of occupations in forestry deserve special mention: urban foresters, international foresters, and forestry technicians.

URBAN FORESTERS

Urban forestry is mentioned separately because it is becoming distinguished from rural forestry, even though each discipline has much to learn from the other. Donald Willeke, director of the American Forestry Association, recently predicted, "In the not too distant future, urban foresters will probably outnumber their rural colleagues. The need for urban foresters in cities and towns is growing rapidly. The demand for traditional forestry skills is certainly not growing at such a rate."

Clyde Hunt, an urban forester with the U.S. Forest Service in Pennsylvania, says, "The primary difference between urban and rural foresters is that the urban forester is more oriented toward individual trees, not whole forests." Urban foresters work on such issues as replanting, planning, and using trees as a means of preserving urban water supplies. They often work for municipal governments and parks, where they plan and supervise tree maintenance programs or work on watershed management. Urban foresters are also employed by tree maintenance services, and many have their own consulting operations.

You can prepare for a career in urban forestry by completing a traditional undergraduate forestry program. However, you may want to attend one of the growing number of schools that have special programs for urban forestry or find a school that offers a minor in urban forest management. The urban forester must be able to identify and know the characteristics and requirements of literally hundreds of types of trees. Urban foresters must also be well versed in entomology, pathology, and herbicide and pesticide applications. Since planning and design are key functions, so design and landscape architecture would be useful courses. Urban foresters also work closely with people in an education and public relations capacity.

Much of the work on urban trees is performed by arborists and horticulturists. Most prepare for these professions by combining a two-year technical degree and on-the-job training or by completing a four-year program.

INTERNATIONAL FORESTERS

Forestry is an area of much concern internationally, especially given forestry practices in many less-developed countries. Because of population escalation, poverty, and the practices of some timber companies and other corporations, deforestation is occurring around the globe at an alarming rate. Professionals are needed who will help shape renewable forestry management practices, working for both governments and private organizations.

Many timber companies have international operations, and some international positions are available through the U.S. Forest Service. The Peace Corps places much emphasis on reforestation projects in Third World countries. (Remember that returning Peace Corps volunteers have one year of noncompetitive eligibility for federal jobs.) Any overseas experience that gives you a working knowledge of a foreign language will set you apart from the pack.

FORESTRY TECHNICIANS

Those considering entering natural resource management often aspire to do work that is actually performed by technicians and not generally by those with bachelor's or graduate degrees: the hands-on fieldwork. Forestry technicians, who usually have two-year degrees and sometimes bachelor's degrees in forestry, serve as timber cruisers, recreational area custodians, fire dispatchers, tree nursery workers, tree maintenance staff, research aides, and log scalers. In short, they spend most of their time in the field. Technicians are in steady demand.

ISSUES AND TRENDS

Carl Stoltenberg, president of the Society of American Foresters, observes, "By nature, foresters are always dealing with the future by planting tomorrow's tree." Here is a glimpse of the present and future in the field of forestry.

Greg Smith, also with the society, comments on one major trend: the importance of a forest supporting multiple uses. "From a management standpoint there are five primary uses of the forest: timber, water, wildlife, recreation, and grazing. In the past, the timber aspect received most of the attention. There has been a significant shift toward considering multiple uses of the forest and attention is now given to the other aspects of forest management. This necessitates curriculum changes at the forestry schools to produce a forester who has a broader base of skills instead of such a heavy fiber-production or timber emphasis."

Some in the profession aren't convinced this is a reality and see it as more of a goal. A couple of factors, however, point to movement toward the multiple-use orientation. First, there is more and more demand on less forest. Demand for forest products has grown 70 percent in the past 30 years, and that rate is expected to accelerate between now and the turn of the century. At the same time, demand for recreation and other consumptive and nonconsumptive uses of the forest has steadily increased.

This is reflected in a flurry of forestry planning efforts that garner the attention of many different interests. Jim Stone, the silviculturist with the U.S. Forest Service in Oregon, observes, "I see a steady rise in the concern of people for forests, both public and private. These citizens are demanding more participation in the planning of forest management; the days of managing forests without public scrutiny are over." Citizens' vehicles, at least for federally owned lands, are various congressionally mandated periodic planning processes; the predominant legislation in this area is the National Forest Management Act of 1976. Andy Stahl, a forester with the Sierra Club Legal Defense Fund, Inc., in Seattle, observes, "A small cottage industry has been created whose mission is to appeal forest management plans proposed for the 156 national forests by the U.S. Forest Service."

The legislation behind these regulations mandates that the U.S. Forest Service manage for multiple use of forests, a requirement that advocates charge the Forest Service has not always lived up to. The concerns of those appealing these plans vary by region and include below-cost timber sales, construction of roads in roadless areas, clear-cutting as opposed to selective harvesting, logging of old-growth timber, monoculture plantings in areas that previously had a variety of trees, and, finally, lack of wildlife protection and enhancement (see Profile of Gustav Bekker, chapter 12).

There is some evidence that this movement is carrying over to the management of privately owned forests. Timber companies that own land are becoming sensitized to public opinion and a mobilized constituency of people concerned with forests and wildlife. These companies have responded in a limited manner with a variety of wildlife enhancement and recreation projects. A number of states, including New York, Massachusetts, and New Jersey, are providing incentives in the form of tax abatements for small landowners who develop and adhere to forest management plans (this is creating a new market for consultants who help landowners develop and implement these plans). The efforts to ensure coherent forest management are often frustrated by the checkerboard pattern of ownership, which may include federal, state, and local governments, small landowners, and large timber companies within several square miles of land. A trend toward subdividing land parcels, especially on the East and West coasts, has exacerbated this situation.

Because of technological advances, today's forester is moving out of the forest and into the office. Much of the work of foresters has become less labor intensive or has been farmed out to forestry technicians. Where maps and surveys were once used, computers and aerial photography or computerized geographical information systems now do a quicker and more accurate job. Consequently, today's forester must have a high degree of skill with computers, statistics, and accounting, along with good interpersonal skills. The latter are necessary because not only are foresters communicating more with a variety of colleagues and coworkers—specialists, consultants, and the like—but they are more in the public eye than ever before. Consequently, part of their job increasingly entails public relations and public education; this is true whether one works in the public or private sector.

Forest health is an issue of growing concern. The same pollutants that affect the rest of the United States impinge on that third of the country which is forested. Howard Burnett, special projects forester with the American Forestry Association, says, "Our position is that whatever affects the ecosystem eventually affects the forest, whether it is acid rain destroying lakes or toxic pollution of groundwater." Smog, commonly associated with urban areas, is now thought to harm forests. While the source or identity of particular pollutants or the manner in which they damage trees is not clearly understood, few can argue with the results; one prime example is the decline in sugar maples on the eastern seaboard. Clearly, there is much to be learned about the effects of pollutants on forest ecosystems. This is one reason many inside and outside the profession are calling for a broader ecological component to undergraduate education.

One of the more pronounced trends in the forestry profession is the increasing emphasis on urban areas. While this might be surprising at first, consider that the mixed-use forests in urban areas encompass more acreage than all the land managed by the U.S. Forest Service. Further, this naturally follows a larger trend toward concern for environmental and natural resource issues closer to home, where people live. Trees play an important role in urban areas. In addition to its aesthetic benefits, the urban forest helps purify the air, provides shade, moderates temperatures, improves water quality, and reduces flooding.

Although municipalities are increasingly hiring urban foresters and arborists, there is unfortunately a steady decline in urban forestland.

Nationwide, one tree is planted in an urban area for every four removed; in one third of urban areas, one tree is planted for every eight removed. This can be attributed to tight budgets and unpredictable funding for overall urban forest planning and management. Some foresters have been slow to acknowledge urban forestry as a legitimate field, but many are enthusiastic about the opportunity to educate and interest the 80 percent of voters who live in or near the urban forest. These foresters hope rallying around the decline of urban forests will bolster public support for the profession as a whole.

Global deforestation is one of the most pressing international environmental issues. Between 1950 and 1980 tropical forests decreased from 5.6 billion hectares to 2.6 billion. Little has been done to stem this decline. Commercial logging and conversion to farms, pastures, and cities contribute to this decrease. The end result includes increased flooding, loss of soils, downstream siltation, and the reduction of genetic diversity, especially in those species that are important sources of food and medicinal materials. As forestry continues to become an international business and concern increases, international forestry will become increasingly relevant to foresters in the United States, many of whom have worked abroad on forestry projects with the federal government, commercial logging operations, or the Peace Corps.

Finally, keep in mind that the forestry industry is a combination of many smaller, regionally based industries. Although there are trends that affect all regions, such as demand for forest products, there is considerable variety in issues and in the structure and health of the industry.

GETTING STARTED

> *There has been a broadening of the training and background necessary to enter the field of forestry. To be successful, today's forester should have a good technical background in the basics of forestry as well as an understanding of mathematics, statistics, computers, and the basic sciences. In addition, foresters must have a grasp of and appreciation for associated natural resource fields and, in particular, ecology and economics. These are necessary for effective total management of forest resources. We are no longer just cruising timber and cutting trees, but telling our story to the public and providing for their recreation. Don't let a summer pass without a forestry job. Get a different job each summer, in the field and in an office.*

> Charles H. Driver, Professor Emeritus,
> College of Forest Resources, University
> of Washington

Foresters have a tall order to fill. As one forester acknowledges, "We are trying to pack into four years of school what, realistically, should take seven." This is where experience and graduate school are increasingly coming into the picture.

Most foresters obtain a B.A. or B.S. from one of the 50 or so forestry schools accredited by the American Society of Foresters. Most schools require students to hold at least one field position, but don't limit your fieldwork to the bare requirements—obtain as much experience as you can.

Keep in mind that all schools, even those that are accredited, are not created equal; it is quite legitimate to ask professionals about a school's reputation. Many schools have a tendency to specialize, either on a particular application of forestry (forestry management, recreation, economics, forestry engineering, ecology) or on the type of forests in the region in which the school is located. Decide whether you are interested in a particular focus or want a more general background. Finally, spend some time comparing the courses offered and required by the various schools.

Barely meeting the basic undergraduate requirements in the liberal arts to get to the forestry course work is a strategy forestry students will later regret. All professionals stress the value of a strong liberal arts background for a forester; some go so far as to put the liberal arts courses above forestry course work. Consultant Gary Schluter of Park Falls, Wisconsin, says, "Sure you have to be literate in forestry, but I really believe a lot of employers view the degree as merely evidence that you are trainable. Ultimately, what separates the technicians from the foresters is not the forestry expertise as much as the liberal arts skills: written and oral communications, management, political science, accounting, and economics. These are the skills that will make or break your forestry career."

To specialize or generalize as an undergraduate? Forestry professionals offer various perspectives on this question. Employers are looking for broadly educated graduates, but there is a pull toward specialization once you start working, and some employers want to see an inclination toward a specialty before they hire. Some foresters felt undergraduates could hurt themselves by being a mile wide and an inch deep; others felt specializing early in a career can limit your options before you have a chance to learn about the field and make career decisions based on experience. The latter camp advises that specialization be left to graduate school.

There are several ways to walk this fine line. Perhaps the most widely recommended is to get a minor or possibly a second major in addition to your forestry degree. This could be in a technical area—soil science, wildlife, or surveying—or might be more liberal arts oriented—business, economics, political science, or computer science. A similar route is to pursue one of the forestry tracks offered by many schools, such as forest economics, management, hydrology, or economics. These might be formal options or might merely consist of the student taking a block of courses in a particular specialty.

You can realistically expect to acquire only limited specialized knowledge during your undergraduate education and college work experience, and that is probably a good thing. Specialization, if it is the route you choose, can be developed in graduate school and the early years of your career. You may find that you don't want to specialize in your forestry career.

Another crucial component of preparation is experience. As is the case with all natural resource professions, work experience is necessary to obtain a full-time job; seasonal work *is* your entry-level job. Finding seasonal work is possible if one uses the same resourcefulness and diligence that went into locating and getting into school—it certainly is of equal importance. Some of these positions will have tolerable paychecks; your first experience may be as a volunteer. Use this as an opportunity to test out various types of forestry work, build up skills, make contacts in the profession, and collect letters of recommendation.

There are a variety of volunteer and seasonal work programs; some are arranged through agencies, others through institutions and universities. You may want to consider broadening your work experience with a stint in a nontraditional setting such as policy work with a nonprofit organization, research with a botanical garden, or interpretation with a park system. Assuming you also obtain some of the more traditional forestry experience, this will considerably strengthen your résumé. Formal cooperative education programs with state and federal agencies offer the best odds of getting full-time entry-level employment upon graduation. The trick is getting into a school with a co-op.

In both course work and job experience, as an undergraduate you should be on the lookout for opportunities to develop some of the skills specific to forestry, such as inventorying and timber cruising, grading lumber, identifying species, using aerial photographs and maps, administering contracts, and controlling pests. Demonstrating your knowledge of these hands-on skills is your best assurance of obtaining an entry-level job.

Next comes the question of whether to go on and obtain a graduate degree after earning a bachelor's in forestry. This decision should be based largely on what you wish to do in the field. Certainly, you can have a successful career in forestry without going to graduate school. On the other hand, given the increasingly technical nature of the field, a graduate degree is much more useful now than it was ten years ago. Many forestry specializations require graduate study. A graduate degree is also an opportunity to broaden your skill base. For example, foresters may go back to school to obtain M.B.A.s, master's degrees in public administration, and even law degrees.

A master's degree will probably be useful later in your career. Whether it helps early on depends somewhat on the demand for foresters. One employer in industrial forestry points out, "There is currently an abundant supply of foresters. In these circumstances we tend to let the applicants sort themselves out. One way to choose is to see whether they have a master's degree. In the last few years two of every three persons we have hired have had graduate degrees. This doesn't mean the job is necessarily any better or pays more than what used to go to those with a B.S."

This same forester feels it is ideal to get a master's degree after working in the field for a while, but says that his company, at least, cannot always guarantee ex-employees jobs after they return from graduate school. Don't go to graduate school unless you have a pretty good idea what you want out of it and are aware of the type of work environment that this degree will lead to.

JOB PROSPECTS

Here is another area where there is very little agreement, except to say that prospects in the late 1980s have been mediocre, although markedly better than in the early eighties, and that the market is expected to open up in the 1990s. In general, employment prospects for foresters have been rather cyclical and are tied closely to the economy as well as to the demand for forest products. There are three factors that speak to a fairly healthy hiring pattern. First, demand for forest products continues to grow. Second, many foresters, at least in the public sector, are nearing retirement age. This is particularly true for the U.S. Forest Service. Third, the number of students entering forestry programs has dropped dramatically. According to Greg Smith there has been a 50 percent decline in students entering undergraduate programs in forestry or forestry-related programs. One reason for this has been dismal reports, not all accurate, about job prospects. Another reason is articulated by Dr. Richard Parker, a professor in the University of New Hampshire's Department of Forest Resources: "Many of the newer natural resource programs, such as water resource management and environmental conservation, are drawing students who ten years ago would have otherwise gone into forestry. For this reason I think the availability of jobs will improve even if the industry contracts."

Not all agree with the projection of healthy long-term hiring prospects for forestry graduates. But there will always be a steady supply of positions for the best and most persistent.

SALARY

Entry-level positions in private sector forestry generally pay in the $17,000 to $20,000 range, with increases of $2,000 per year considered normal. Larger companies tend to pay higher starting salaries than smaller companies. Consulting firms pay entry-level foresters less because they generally don't have the resources to train. A typical arrangement might be a base salary of $12,000 to $15,000 with a draw-plus arrangement, which is a financial incentive to bring in customers. In the private sector, someone with an M.S. will command a slightly higher starting salary.

In federal jobs, new employees with B.S.s and no experience start at GS-5 to GS-7; with M.S.s, GS-7 to GS-9; and with Ph.D.s, GS-11 to GS-12. January 1988 pay scales for these grade classifications were as follows: GS-5, $15,118–$19,654; GS-7, $18,726–$24,342; GS-9, $22,907–$29,783; GS-11, $27,716–$36,032; and GS-12, $33,218–$43,181.

CASE STUDY

Hiawatha National Forest

The Forest Service is charged with managing all resources of the nation's national forests, including water, fish, wildlife, minerals, and trees. The Hiawatha National Forest, located on Michigan's Upper Peninsula, has 77 miles of shoreline bordering three of the Great Lakes, four lighthouses, an inland water system of 413 lakes, and 770 miles of streams.

The management of these resources requires an equally diverse team of natural resource experts and other professionals, including biologists, hydrologists, archeologists, foresters, landscape architects, soil scientists, land appraisers, and engineers. As part of a newly developing integrated resource management program, the Forest Service has been moving toward a system of technology sharing among its various divisions.

Mary Mumford, an information specialist and forester for Hiawatha National Forest, explains how the program has been implemented at Hiawatha. "Hiawatha has been a little ahead of the game for a while as far as integrated resource management is concerned. We found long ago that it is more practical and more stimulating to employees to allow professionals with diverse backgrounds to cross over into other areas of expertise rather than to hire extra people to fulfill specific job requirements. For example, we have four forest staff officers with administrative responsibilities defined by issue rather than by territory. One of these staff officers supervises a group known as LAFFMIT, which stands for its seven functions: lands (ownership, exchange, and acquisition), aviation (managing our regularly scheduled fire detection flights and aerial surveys of loon, eagle, and osprey nesting sites), fire management, fisheries, minerals (gas, oil, gravel), information, and telecommunications.

"There is also a recreation staff officer who is responsible for a combined group including the forest archeologist, landscape architect, soil scientist, hydrologist, and recreation program and budget directors. The timber and wildlife supervisor is responsible for timber management and sales, monitoring growth, insect and disease control, replanting, wildlife management, and habitat manipulation. The engineering staff officer is responsible for land management planning. Engineering traditionally handles everything from designing proper rest area facilities to building bridges, other structures, and roads; combined with this staff function is long-range forest management planning for all resources within the Hiawatha National Forest.

"As you can see, each of these supervisors handles a wide variety of responsibility, but the real integration comes when, for example, a request for a new roadway is submitted. Under the old system each supervisor may have submitted a request for construction of an access road to each respective resource project; this resulted in a jumble of roadways often paralleling or crossing over one another. Now, with an integrated system, when such a proposal is made, all supervisors collaborate in developing one properly designed road to serve many purposes. This not only saves construction materials but helps preserve forestlands. Two construction and maintenance units serve the entire forest with road maintenance, reforestation, gravel pit, and other related work."

These supervisors are responsible for certain resource activities within the forest. There are also five districts within the forest, each managed by a district ranger with one or two assistants, two or three professional foresters, six or seven technicians, and seasonal workers. Roger Jewell, one such district ranger, manages the 240,000 acres of forest in the Sault Ste. Marie District. "This job," he says, "is a lot like running a cookie company, only instead of having bakers, flour, sugar, and cookies to sell, you have foresters, timber, wildlife, recreation, and forests to market. My administrative functions as a district ranger are a lot like those of a business manager. Today, for example, I attended a meeting in order to project the next 75 days of legal commitment in our budget. It is our responsibility to make sure that any funds or grants received for specific projects are allocated to those projects and that the work is completed in a timely manner. I'd estimate that I spend 20 percent of my time in meetings, 30 percent in a management capacity, 20 percent in supervision, and the other 30 percent in decision making, quality control, and research. I have three assistants who share in the responsibility of managing the forestlands; a timber management assistant who handles the sale of over 12 million board feet of timber annually and oversees a forester and technicians who work on reforestation, genetic programs, timber inventory, and insect and disease control; an administrative assistant responsible for payroll, personnel, office management, registration, park maintenance, purchasing, budget, mail, communications, and paperwork; and an 'other resource' manager who handles just about everything else— fire protection, recreation, wildlife, fisheries, law enforcement, minerals, lands, and planning.

"Unfortunately, much of our time is spent in enforcement; this is really why we are here. If we didn't make sure the land was protected, it would be stolen blind, diseased, ravaged by fire, or developed. We recently painted five very nice signs providing a historical description of the forest; within a week two were shot up and one was stolen. It is these types of costly repairs that we are constantly trying to avoid."

Jewell hasn't always been on the administrative side of the Forest Service. "I first became interested in the Forest Service because of my uncle, who worked in a state department of natural resources. I went to the University of Minnesota, where I received a professional forest management degree and got started as a forester on an inventory crew out of

Hiawatha National Forest, Michigan. Roger Jewell photographs a recently constructed swinging bridge on the North Country Trail, which runs along the shore of Lake Superior. Photo courtesy of the U.S. Forest Service.

college. I moved along in the ranks during the Kennedy-Johnson era, a time of great environmental expansion. Federal employment opportunities have gone downhill ever since, but a big turnaround is expected in the next five years. I believe the Forest Service is one of the few places a forester can actually work in the forest performing multipurpose management. Otherwise you would be in private industry, which for the most part buys and sells timber rather than manages lands themselves."

Jewell advises those looking to get in on this upswing to contact the Society of American Foresters and obtain a list of colleges offering programs that train professional forest managers. "Enter one of these programs and graduate in the top 30 percent of your class. Also, try to work in the field during the summers because it is very important to find out if you enjoy the work before you are too committed. You move around a lot in the Forest Service and live in small, remote towns. Expect to be on the low end of the yuppie life-style. The rewards in this field are not monetary. You should also have a good degree of commitment to government work—this is still where the majority of the forest management jobs are located. If you are serious about becoming a forester, you also must assess your philosophical alignment in order to place yourself within the right sector. The Forest Service role is in both protection and production; if you believe in pure protection, parks and recreation would be a better area for you; if you believe in pure production, private industry would better suit you."

Barb Jones is one of the assistant district rangers working with Roger Jewell at the Sault Ste. Marie District of the Hiawatha National Forest. "Roger Jewell is ultimately responsible for all of the activities within the district, but as his assistant I am directly responsible for timber-related activities such as reforestation, site preparation, timber inventory and sales, budgeting, and work planning. I supervise three forestry technicians and a forester. The 'timber shop' also includes another forestry technician and four or five summer forestry technicians. With timber sale activities being an important aspect of the job, I frequently deal with timber loggers. All the duties include administrative paperwork and I spend about two thirds of my time in the office and one third in the field.

"I received my B.S. in forest management from the University of Wisconsin, Stevens Point, under the co-op program. I really enjoyed my co-op experience. At first I had no concept of what it was like to work on a timber crew and it gave me a real sense that I was helping to manage the land, doing something good, and making an impact. After graduation, the Sault Ste. Marie District offered me a full-time position as a trainee forester. Since that time I've earned an M.S. in forestry from Michigan State University and have been promoted to my present position. It is somewhat unusual to have received a promotion within the same park—transfers are fairly common."

These are some typical roles of foresters. Assisting foresters with day-to-day hands-on activities are forest technicians, whose minimum educational training is generally a two-year associate's degree and significant field experience. Joe Carrick is a fcrestry technician specializing in fish and wildlife for the Forest Service.

"I think if I had to pick one reason for being a forest technician, it would be the fact that I am out in the field and forest every day, and the type of work I do is very hands on. Some of my projects include building brook trout shelters, removing beaver dams and barriers, making artificial spawning beds, stabilizing eroding stream banks, and removing boulders. On the wildlife side, I do openings maintenance, which means monitoring deer and other wildlife that use open areas in the forest and making sure enough area is cleared for them. I am working on a study for the Fish and Wildlife Service of the sandhill crane nesting areas in the forest, which includes live trapping and monitoring their activities via a radio collar. Finally, I am collecting bear scat, which is sent to North Central Forest Experiment Station for analysis to determine their diet.

"I really couldn't imagine doing anything else. I grew up on a nearby reservation and have always hunted, fished, and hiked. It's great to have a job doing what I enjoy most. To prepare for this job I obtained a one-year natural resources technician's degree from Nicolet College."

PROFILES

Karin Van Dyke, Area Forester, Publishing Paper Division, Mead Corporation, Escanaba, Michigan

Compared with forestry jobs in the state or federal government, private sector positions tend to be more bottom line oriented and there is often more flexibility with regard to promotions. Public sector foresters also focus more on multiple-use management of forests.

"The Woodlands Department of Mead Corporation in the Upper Peninsula of Michigan is divided into western, central, and eastern regions. Each region has eight foresters working in teams of two. I share respon- sibility for an area of 45,000 acres with my partner. Our work is divided into two areas, land management and procurement. The land management section relies on its own data base on the age and condition of every stand of trees within our district. From this data we determine which stands need to be harvested or replanted. We contract this work out to independent logging companies.

"A typical day begins at 7:00 A.M. I do my paperwork for about one or one and a half hours, then I drive to a job site for inspection. While inspecting the site, I make sure the contractors are logging within the boundaries, scale or measure any miscellaneous by-products such as pulpwood and firewood, calculate the volume of pulpwood cut to make sure they are within the quota, record the volume of wood for invoicing and collection purposes, and then spray paint the piles of wood to indicate they have been accounted for and to prevent theft. I enjoy the contact with loggers and have learned much from them.

"All of this takes anywhere from one to two hours, and I usually make inspections two or three times a week. Other days I may be out supervising preparation of a site for reforestation or the actual replanting, or on a reconnaissance mission to investigate land or timber for sale by private individuals, the state, or the Forest Service.

"Seeking a balance between the bottom line and the aesthetic, moral, and ethical value of maintaining forests is the challenge that I find exciting in private industry. I also enjoy the flexibility in this type of work. We are responsible to our district manager but essentially work independently. I coordinate with my partner when the need arises; otherwise we work on our own.

"I graduated from Michigan Technological University with a B.S. in forestry, pursuing the school's forest management option. Before joining Mead, I worked for two years for Louisiana Pacific in Wisconsin as a procurement specialist, buying logs for the company. The travel got to be too much; after moving five times within 18 months, I decided being a vagabond wasn't for me. Fortunately, a friend from college knew of the opening at Mead, and I started here within three months of leaving Louisiana Pacific.

"I feel my college education prepared me for the technical aspects of my work, but there is a shortfall in formal forestry education as far as real-world situations are concerned. For example, I wish I had more communication and people skills before starting my career. However, I've developed in that area by becoming active in outside groups and professional associations.

"My advice for those who want to start a career in forestry would be to make sure you complement your formal education with real-world skills. You can also benefit from cooperative educational experiences, internships, and volunteer work. The current tight job market means that many students may go on to obtain master's degrees. This makes for overqualified foresters, who may make things even tougher for those with B.S.s or two- to four-year technician's degrees. A master's degree is usually not needed for an entry-level position. Although this field is traditionally very tight, there has been a demand for women, and the general hiring trend in the next five years may improve as some current foresters reach retirement age. Those just starting out have a bright-looking future, so hang in there."

James Skiera, City Arborist, City of Urbana, Illinois

"As city arborist for the city of Urbana, I am responsible for the management of the city's tree planting and maintenance program, the urban landscape beautification and maintenance program, and our encephalitis prevention program. My division is composed of two branches. The Forestry Branch is responsible for the care of approximately 11,000 street trees in Urbana. The Landscape Branch is responsible for maintaining the appearance of the community's public landscapes.

"An important duty of our landscape team is landscape design. My degree in landscape architecture and field experience in landscape construction have made me aware of the importance of design. I look at design not only as a visual expression but also as an important problem-solving tool.

"I am responsible for maintaining effective relations with other government officials, community leaders, citizens, and the news media. I coordinate division functions such as Arbor Day, community educational seminars, and Tree Commission meetings.

"I like the variety of my work. If this were a larger city my duties would have a much narrower focus. For example, I started the morning doing a hazardous tree evaluation. Following that, I returned to the office to discuss an alley maintenance program with the supervisor of street maintenance. I then discussed some personnel issues with the forestry supervisor and visited a sidewalk construction site with him to determine what precautionary measures need to be taken to protect the trees on the site. Later, I returned a few phone calls and met with a local businessman to discuss how the city's plan for a river walkway will affect the development of his new restaurant adjacent to the project.

"One ongoing project is an enhancement of the city's corridor, which starts at the interstate and continues for three miles into the downtown area. We are focusing on improving the impression one gets while entering the city at three different speeds: 55 miles per hour, 35 miles per hour, and from 25 miles per hour down to pedestrian speed. Our diversified greening strategy includes tree plantings, perennial and annual beds, construction of medians, and irrigation. Developing a project like this encompasses obtaining maps, site visits, project design, graphics, developing management plans, financing the project, and presenting it to the City Council.

"There are more possibilities for urban foresters than there have been at any time in the recent past. Some of this is due to an increased need for expert consultants to assist in litigation over the environmental impact of development on communities. Most educational programs in the United States, however, are still forestry oriented, providing little design background or concept of the varieties of vegetation and problems specific to plant care in an urban setting. Urban forestry is unique in the sense that almost all of the vegetation managed by the urban forester is not native to the region. Another perspective unique to urban forestry is that in the city, vegetation forms a sharp contrast to the miles of cement and asphalt; people care about each individual tree. What this means for the urban forester is a greater concern for vandalism, drought, exposure, and pests—anything that affects a single tree, shrub, or flower.

"I have found that my B.S. in landscape architecture and secondary major in ornamental horticulture from the University of Wisconsin, coupled with work experience in landscape architecture, has been excellent preparation for this field. I advise students of urban forestry to take as many electives in design, horticulture, and public administration as possible. Join professional organizations such as the International Society of Arboriculture or the National Arborist Association and begin networking early on."

Russ Stallings, Deputy Forester, Los Angeles County Department of Forester and Fire Warden

"The Los Angeles County Department of Forester and Fire Warden has two major natural resource functions: fire protection and erosion control. Fires and floods have done extensive damage to Southern California. Some of our major activities include urban forestry, conservation education, homeowner protection, working with contractors and developers, research and development of infrared mapping, analysis of weather systems, prescribed burning, propagation, planting, and distributing of trees to the public.

"Being a forester for this area means taking on a multifaceted role: On the one hand, you are an urban forester in charge of an urban forest where trees do not grow naturally; on the other hand, you are a forester managing natural resources for aesthetics and for fire and flood protection. Urban forestry often has this dual element.

"My daily activities are varied. Today, I took some representatives of the state up in the helicopter and flew over a couple of prescribed burn areas. We periodically burn brush cover areas surrounding the city so that if a wildfire does approach there will be little brush left to catch on fire.

"As part of our fire prevention program we also work with homeowners to selectively remove brush from

RESOURCES

Society of American Foresters. National organization representing various segments of the forestry profession, including public and private practitioners, researchers, administrators, educators, and students. Publishes *Journal of Forestry* (monthly) and *Forest Science* (quarterly) as well as other publica-

around structures while preserving the sense of living amid natural vegetation. The policy in Los Angeles County is that any resident can have a free home inspection for fire protection. This requires that I visit homes and discuss fire prevention methods with owners. In some areas, the brush may be removed with a brushcrusher or prescribed fire. This is not a relaxing task when working next to a multimillion-dollar home in Bel Air or the Malibu area. I also work with developers, planners, and city councils to make sure future developments are fire resistant.

"A related aspect of my work is erosion control and reseeding. And periodically, I inspect roadsides to determine whether the existing vegetation is adequate to prevent erosion. I also visit burned sites to determine whether reseeding is necessary. If we need to reseed, I locate the site on aerial maps, compute the number of pounds of seed needed per acre, schedule a crew and helicopter, arrange for transportation of the seed, and then do the actual seeding by helicopter. After seeding I periodically spot-check the areas and make sure the plants are growing.

"Perhaps my most exciting project has been cooperative research and development with NASA on fire prevention methods using infrared photography. In the spring of 1985 we took some routine aerial photographs of Los Angeles County and noticed four unusually shaded areas. In July of that year a forest fire followed exactly the outlined pattern of two of the shaded areas on the infrared image. The following October another forest fire followed the pattern of the remaining shaded areas on the photo. We are working now with scientists to find the correlation among stressed vegetation, its susceptibility to forest fires, and the infrared image it projects.

"I received my B.S. in forestry from Oklahoma State University in 1955 and my M.S. in environmental management from the University of Southern California in 1972, and I am currently completing an undergraduate degree in finance at the University of California at Los Angeles.

"To meet tomorrow's forestry goals, we'll need philosophy, for gaining an overall view of a project or program; economics, for seeing the purpose of or need for a program; science, for reality's sake; logic, for orderly implementation; math, to give a project concreteness and definition; and communication, for passing on the wisdom of your decision so others may follow or improve on it.

"There has been a lot of talk about the field being extremely competitive, with little room for entry. No field is overcrowded if you're good enough— the L.A. Lakers have a full bench but are always looking for new talent!"

tions. Accredits undergraduate and graduate forestry programs (write for list). 5400 Grosvenor Lane, Bethesda, Md. 20814.

American Forestry Association. A national citizens' organization devoted to trees, forests, and forestry. Publishes educational materials on forests as well as *American Forests Magazine* (monthly). Other publications include *So You*

Want to Be in Forestry (single copies free) and *Directory of Urban Forestry Professionals.* P.O. Box 2000, Washington, D.C. 20013.

Association of Consulting Foresters. Publishes *The Consultant* (quarterly). 5410 Grosvenor Lane, Suite 250, Bethesda, Md. 20814.

Municipal Arborists and Urban Foresters Society. Publishes newsletter (bimonthly). P.O. Box 1255, Freehold, N.J. 07728.

International Society of Arboriculture. Publishes *Journal of Arboriculture* (monthly). P.O. Box 71, 5 Lincoln Sq., Urbana, Ill. 61801.

National Arborist Association. Publishes *The Reporter* (monthly). Meeting Place Mall, Route 101, P.O. Box 1094, Amherst, N.H. 03031.

Peace Corps. Peace Corps volunteers are needed in at least 38 countries in Asia, Africa, the Pacific, South and Central America, and the Caribbean to help restore and maintain forest resources. There is at least one former Peace Corps volunteer working in most national forests. Recruitment Office, 806 Connecticut Ave., N.W., Washington, D.C. 20526.

Directory of the Forest Products Industry. Updated biannually, a comprehensive listing of forest product industries, by state and province. Includes addresses, products and volume, key personnel and telephone numbers. Miller Freeman Publications, 500 Howard St., San Francisco, Calif. 94105.

Conservation Directory (annual). See National Wildlife Federation listing, Resources, chapter 12.

Timber Harvesting (monthly). January issue contains listing of personnel employed by the wood supply and forestry departments of all major pulp and paper companies and industrial timber firms in the United States. Hatton-Brown Publishers, P.O. Box 2268, Montgomery, Ala. 36197.

Index

Stringos, Darlene, 190–191
Student Conservation Association, Inc., 59, 281
  internships and, 61, 63
Sullivan, Carl, 251
Superfund Amendments and Reauthorization Act (SARA), 4, 15–16, 94, 120, 152, 154, 156, 158, 164–166
Survey of Compensation in the Fields of Fish and Wildlife Management, A, 251
Swann, Don, 111, 116, 118

Tahoe, Lake, 237–243
Tahoe Regional Planning Agency (TRPA), 238
Taylor, Richard L., 216–217
Taylor, Sylvia, 6, 38, 252, 254, 257, 259–260
teaching, 28–29, 112, 114–115, 250
technical schools, 40–41, 182
technicians, 28, 40, 64–66, 69–70, 180, 187, 188, 209, 259–260, 278
  in forestry, 297, 298, 300, 311
Tennessee Valley Authority, 93, 232
Tholin, Kathy, 144
Tice, Dean, 274
timber firms, 19, 250, 254, 297, 300, 301, 303
Tinianow, Jerry, 54–55
Title III, Emergency Planning and Community Right-to-Know Act, 164
tourist attractions, 116, 118
toxicologists, 82, 182, 198, 206, 207, 209
trade associations, 21, 44, 119, 155, 208
training of personnel, 113–114
Transportation Department, U.S., 94
Triphan, Sandy, 239–240
Trust for Public Land, 229, 245–247
Tsuji, Joyce, 167, 169
Turner, Beth, 197

undergraduate programs, 35–36
United Nations Environment Program, 47
urban forestry, 297, 299–300, 302–303, 313–315
urban planning, 93, 94, 100, 108
  megalopolis in, 95–96
utilities, 95, 194–195, 250, 256, 268

Van Dyke, Karin, 296, 311–312
Venuto, Ermine, 298
Vermont, 138, 146–147, 226, 234
volunteering, 43–44, 47–58, 281, 282, 305

volunteering (*continued*)
  career-oriented, 52–53
  checklist for, 53–55
  getting started in, 50–51
  job search and, 79
  profiles of, 54–58
  reasons for, 49–50
  resources for, 71–73
  selecting programs for, 50
Vopelak, Patricia, 194–195
Vrdolyak, Edward, 143

Walters, Bill, 30
Washington, 48, 91, 227, 269–271
  Olympic National Forest in, 232, 242–244
  Puget Sound and, 204, 210–213
Washington, Harold, 143
waste management, *see* hazardous waste management; solid waste management
waste reduction, 116, 136, 138, 159, 160
waste-to-energy facilities, 136, 140, 183
wastewater management, 40, 69–70, 153, 199, 201, 202, 204–207, 209
water conservation, *see* conservation, land and water
waterfront planning, 3, 91, 106–107, 281
water quality management, 16–17, 96, 197–219, 226–227, 230, 233, 256, 258
  academia in, 208
  case study of, 210–213
  Clean Water Act in, 4, 13, 16–17, 94, 153, 197, 198, 199, 201, 203, 205, 206, 207
  consulting firms in, 198, 204, 207–208
  corporations in, 207, 216–217
  education for, 209
  federal government in, 201–203
  getting started in, 208–209
  issues in, 197, 199–201
  job opportunities in, 201–208
  local government in, 198, 204–207, 215–216
  nonprofit organizations in, 17, 208, 213–215
  private sector in, 17, 198, 204, 207–208, 213–215, 216–217
  profiles of, 213–217
  resources for, 218–219
  salaries in, 210
  specialists in, 198–199, 206–207, 209, 227
  state government in, 198, 203–204, 210–213
  trends in, 199–201
watershed management, 93, 97, 230, 233, 253, 297, 298, 299

ALSO AVAILABLE FROM ISLAND PRESS

Americans Outdoors: The Report of the President's Commission
The Legacy, The Challenge, with case studies
Foreword by William K. Reilly
1987, 426 pp., appendixes, case studies, charts
Paper: $24.95 ISBN 0-933280-36-X

The Challenge of Global Warming
Edited by Dean Edwin Abrahamson
Foreword by Senator Timothy E. Wirth
1989, 350 pp., tables, graphs, index, bibliography
Cloth: $34.95 ISBN: 0-933280-87-4
Paper: $19.95 ISBN: 0-933280-86-6

Crossroads: Environmental Priorities for the Future
Edited by Peter Borrelli
1988, 352 pp., index
Cloth: $29.95 ISBN: 0-933280-68-8
Paper: $17.95 ISBN: 0-933280-67-X

Environmental Agenda for the Future
By Leaders of America's Foremost Environmental Organizations
Edited by Robert Cahn
1985, 155 pp., bibliography
Paper: $9.95 ISBN: 0-933280-29-7

Forest and the Trees: A Guide to Excellent Forestry
By Gordon Robinson, Introduction by Michael McCloskey
1988, 272 pp., indexes, appendixes, glossary, tables, figures
Cloth: $34.95 ISBN: 0-933280-41-6
Paper: $19.95 ISBN: 0-933280-40-8

Hazardous Waste Management: Reducing the Risk
By Benjamin A. Goldman, James A. Hulme, and Cameron Johnson for
Council on Economic Priorities
1985, 336 pp., tables, glossary, index
Cloth: $64.95 ISBN: 0-933280-30-0
Paper: $34.95 ISBN: 0-933280-31-9

Our Common Lands: Defending the National Parks
Edited by David J. Simon
In cooperation with the NPCA
1988, 575 pp., index, bibliography, appendixes
Cloth: $45.00 ISBN: 0-933280-58-2
Paper: $24.95 ISBN: 0-933280-57-2

The Poisoned Well: New Strategies for Groundwater Protection
Sierra Club Legal Defense Fund
1989, 225 pp., index, glossary, charts, appendixes, bibliography
Cloth: $31.95 ISBN: 0-933280-56-4
Paper: $19.95 ISBN: 0-933280-55-6

Public Opinion Polling: A Handbook for Public Interest and Citizen Advocacy Groups
By Celinda C. Lake with Pat Callbeck Harper for Montana Alliance for Progressive Policy
1987, 166 pp., bibliography, appendixes, index
Paper: $19.95 ISBN: 0-933280-32-7

Reforming the Forest Service
By Randal O'Toole
1988, 250 pp., graphs, tables, notes
Cloth: $34.95 ISBN: 0-933280-49-1
Paper: $19.95 ISBN: 0-933280-45-9

Rush to Burn: Solving America's Garbage Crisis?
From **Newsday**
1989, 225 pp., photographs, graphs, tables, index
Cloth: $22.95 ISBN: 1-55963-001-9
Paper: $14.95 ISBN: 1-55963-000-0

Saving the Tropical Forests
By Judith Gradwohl and Russell Greenberg
Preface by Michael H. Robinson
Smithsonian Institution
1988, 207 pp., index, tables, illustrations, notes, bibliography
Cloth: $24.95 ISBN: 0-933280-81-5

Sierra Nevada: A Mountain Journey
By Tim Palmer
1988, 352 pp., illustrations, appendixes, index
Cloth: $31.95 ISBN: 0-933280-54-8
Paper: $14.95 ISBN: 0-933280-53-X

Wildlife of the Florida Keys: A Natural History
By James D. Lazell, Jr.
1989, 225 pp., photographs, illustrations, index
Cloth: $31.95 ISBN: 0-933280-98-X
Paper: $19.95 ISBN: 0-933280-97-1

For additional information about Island Press publishing services and a catalog of current and forthcoming titles, contact Island Press, P.O. Box 7, Covelo, California 95428.